Advance praise for
THE OTHER SIDE
OF MERCY

"Headlines fade fast, regardless of even the most horrific content, and journalism is too often in the business of headlines. Ken Armstrong and Jonathan Martin went far beyond the headlines in *The Other Side of Mercy*, far beyond, out into deep water, where there are no easy answers. What emerges from their research is not just a snapshot of a remorseless killer, but a portrait of a man careening towards destruction and how he was helped along the way by a cast of unwitting accomplices: a racially-biased justice system, a do-gooder politician with an agenda, and an incarceration industry that is overworked and underfunded. Solidly researched and brilliantly written, the book is a real heartbreaker, a compelling story that will leave the reader sadder but wiser. This is what journalism should be."

Robert Ferrigno, *New York Times* best-selling author
of *Prayers for the Assassin*

**THE OTHER SIDE
OF MERCY**

THE OTHER SIDE OF MERCY

A KILLER'S JOURNEY ACROSS THE AMERICAN DIVIDE

KEN ARMSTRONG AND JONATHAN MARTIN
WITH THE STAFF OF THE SEATTLE TIMES

First published by Dog Ear Publishing
4010 W. 86th Street, Ste H
Indianapolis, IN 46268
www.dogearpublishing.net

dog ear
PUBLISHING

ISBN: 978-160844-734-3

TABLE OF CONTENTS

Photo inserts start on pages 55 and 146.

FOREWORD

ON AN OVERCAST SUNDAY MORNING after Thanksgiving 2009, a madman walked into a strip-mall coffee shop outside Tacoma, Washington, intent on fulfilling a vision. What he did there, violating the most fundamental tenet of civilized society, threw the Puget Sound region into a state of anxious shock. On that morning and in the days and weeks after, the staff of *The Seattle Times* worked furiously to address the public's need for information and for comfort. Employing virtually every modern reporting tool available—Flip cameras, smartphones, relational databases, Twitter, Google Wave, Dipity mapping—the newspaper engaged in investigative reporting on the run. Our reporters compiled a breathtaking mountain of information on the man and the path he had traveled from boyhood in Arkansas cotton country to that morning of madness in the nation's upper left corner.

What that reporting revealed was ugly and alarming. It laid bare failures of the criminal-justice system, a system that had helped turn a small-time thief into a dangerous and delusional powder keg, then repeatedly unleashed him onto the people it was charged with protecting.

Our work in those early days earned plaudits—indeed, we received the 2010 Pulitzer Prize for Breaking News Reporting—but a newspaper's format, even in its Internet iteration, comes with limitations. We had accumulated thousands of pages of documents, from employment records to property transactions to criminal histories. We had mined those records—along with scores of interviews in Washington and Arkansas—for a flurry of stories and Web postings, but the wealth of information compelled us to do more.

We wanted to take advantage of the one format best suited for drawing upon and further developing all that work and delivering a definitive account, one layered with history, context, detail and nuance. We wanted to offer our community, and other communities, not only information, but understanding. At one end of the spectrum is Twitter, with its 140-character bursts. At the other end is the book.

A few months later, here it is. Two of our finest reporters and writers—Ken Armstrong and Jonathan Martin—corralled their colleagues' work and built upon it with more interviews, more documents, more research and some one hundred hours of their subject's tape-recorded telephone conversations.

Although a book is the most traditional of forms, this one offers an untraditional twist. By using a respected print-on-demand publisher, we were able to make a book available quickly, while it might best serve the processes of both healing and reform. *The Other Side of Mercy* is a new manifestation of the journalistic public service to which *The Seattle Times* has long been committed.

David Boardman, Executive Editor, The Seattle Times

PROLOGUE

THE TROUBLE I'VE SEEN

October 2009

You have a VAC collect call from ... Maurice ... an inmate at the Pierce County Jail. This call will be recorded and monitored. To accept this call, press 5 now.

NICOLE WOULD HEAR THOSE WORDS—a woman's voice, recorded—and she would press 5, and she and Maurice would have twenty minutes to talk, Maurice on the inside, Nicole on the outside, their marriage reduced to telephone calls that came with unbending deadlines and which cost $2.67 apiece, a profit center for the jailers and a financial suck for the inmates, forever scrounging another ten, twenty-five or fifty dollars to put on their books and to keep their lines to the outside world open. When he was worked up, when his brain was on fire, Maurice Clemmons would make as many as seventeen calls a day, careening from Nicole to the Reverend Reggie to his buddy Boo Man to his lawyer in Arkansas, a lawyer Clemmons couldn't praise enough, calling him "a good dude," "a righteous guy," "a heavyweight." "That's one white man there that we can trust," Clemmons would say, and for Clemmons that was saying something.

Most calls went to Nicole. Twenty minutes doesn't sound like much time, but for Maurice and Nicole it seemed plenty. By the fall of 2009 he'd been in jail long enough to drain any sense of urgency from these calls, the two having said whatever needed saying. There were days when they could be mistaken for two people reading magazines, murmuring, sighing, lost in their heads, instead of two people holding a conversation. There were days when their exchanges sounded like a replay of the day before. He'd ask her to look up the Powerball numbers, and she'd say, "12, 24, 48, 50, 57, 22," and he'd say, "Well, not us," and she'd say, "Nope." The numbers were never them. But every day he'd ask, and every day she'd say nope. There were days he'd get on the phone and hum and hum and hum. She'd brush her teeth. Or eat chips. Or sit on the pot and piss.

"All right?" she asked him on October 19.

"Um hmm. I just get this over with and do what I gotta do."

"Hmm."

Add his recent jail stints up—he'd been arrested in May, and again in July, and again in August—and he'd been in the county lockup for three months now. But Maurice Clemmons knew how to do time. That's what he told his wife and anyone else who'd listen. He knew how to do time. This was nothing—this was "a picnic," this was "a light scrimmage"—compared to the time he'd served before.

Clemmons began to sing.

"Nobody knows the trouble I've seen …"

His voice traversed the middle registers—nothing as deep as Louis Armstrong's, not a bass that scooped up gravel—and he remained faithful to the spiritual's lyrics, until the final word.

"… nobody knows but me."

Jesus became *me*. Stretching the word out, Clemmons took the note higher, not lower.

Seconds passed, filled with silence. One second became five became ten became eighteen.

Clemmons was thirty-seven years old. To him, the Pierce County Jail held nothing to fear. It was crowded, yes. They're all crowded. The jail—in the port city of Tacoma, thirty minutes from Seattle, sixty miles from Mount Rainier, hard on the Puget Sound—housed fourteen hundred inmates, so many inmates and so few guards that some guards worked unbelievable OT and an inmate might wait ten days to have a dentist look at a cracked molar and exposed root. For Clemmons, this mass of inmates was not an issue. The jail had squirreled him away in the hole, leaving him with no company but his thoughts for twenty-three hours a day. *The hole.* When Clemmons said the words, they came out flat, a trifle. What was the hole compared to Cummins, the Arkansas prison farm where Clemmons had seen his youth go to dust, where he'd spent year after year swinging a hoe? People wrote songs about Cummins. They made movies about Cummins.

He started to sing again.

"This going down. Down … down … down."

"Yeah, man," he said.

"Never should have been let out of the penitentiary," he said.

When Clemmons talked like this—"never should have been let out"—a threat lurked behind his words. But there were other days when he abandoned all allusion.

"There gonna be bullets and gunsmoke," he'd tell Nicole. Or he'd tell his half brother: "Woe to the one that sees me first."

The jail staff recorded these conversations. But Clemmons—a man awaiting trial on eight felony charges, a man for whom caution would have seemed a more obvious choice—could not have cared less. He talked bold and sometimes taunted, throwing vulgar insults at whoever might be listening.

You have sixty seconds remaining. It was the woman's voice again, recorded.

"Yup, yup, yup, yup. All right, baby," Clemmons told his wife. "It don't mean a thing. Bye."

So often, this is what happens. Someone does something shocking, and people want to know: What was he thinking? What was Timothy McVeigh thinking? What were those kids at Columbine thinking? What about that student who killed thirty-two people at Virginia Tech?

In the fall of 2009, Maurice Clemmons planned to do something shocking. And he left no doubt what he was thinking. In the weeks and months before he hoped to execute his plan—"I've always been a man of action," he said—Clemmons left one of the most detailed manifestos possible, produced not on paper but in one-hundred-plus hours of telephone calls placed from the Pierce County Jail.

The record he left was contemporaneous. The record he left was candid. It was not embroidery after the fact; he wasn't rationalizing to a reporter or a psychiatrist or a sentencing judge. Clemmons told the people close to him what he planned to do. And he told them why. "Sometimes it burns me in my chest, man, I have so much hatred toward the police ... The strategy is gonna go, kill as many of them devils as I can, until I can't kill no more ... A dude ain't no man if you don't make no stand ... I ain't no more catch the cuffs ... I'm going to war ... Maurice against the world."

Maurice against the world. That's how he saw it. That's how he always saw it. And if his story was nothing more than that—a story of delusion and self-pity—then maybe a long telling would serve minimal purpose. But Clemmons left behind more than all of those telephone recordings. He left behind a document trail stunning in its detail and a life's history that merged exodus with odyssey. He exposed myths that surround the challenges of posting bail. He exposed fault lines in how states deal with one another in handling violent felons. He illustrated the allure and attendant dangers of easy money, the only kind there seemed to be in the years before this recession. A suggestible man who forever seemed to be both predator and prey, Clemmons believed in prophets named Ralph and Yasmin and Crystal. He believed Donald Trump could make him rich. He believed he could game the Bank of America, play it like a slot machine. Clemmons also renewed our nation's fevered debate about the merits of mercy—and, in the process, may have doomed the presidential aspirations of Mike Huckabee, the former Arkansas governor who, in the fall of 2009, while Clemmons was making all those calls from a county jail, had emerged as a Republican front-runner in the next race for the White House.

Clemmons planned to hunt down and assassinate police officers. He wanted to kill as many as possible—"until I can't kill no more." In the United States, the premeditated killing of law-enforcement officers is a rare crime, one with remarkable power to unnerve. But in October of 2009, in the country's northwest corner, Clemmons wasn't the only person plotting to target police. Another man—one who had left so shallow an imprint on this world that a police investigator would later call him a "ghost"—was nursing grievances rooted in the academic study of racial disparities and news reports of police abuse. The ways in which Clemmons and this second man pursued their sense of injustice rocked a community and reverberated nationally. The politics of crime kicked in, sweeping up everyone from judges in Tacoma to state lawmakers in Olympia to prosecutors in Little Rock to candidates for president of the United States. Like shards of metal blasting from a pipe bomb, blame flew every which way. Governors sparred. Bureaucrats scrambled. Fox's Bill O'Reilly called names.

The events that rattled the Puget Sound showed how ripples can extend beyond state lines and across the decades. They exposed lingering resentments borne of our country's racial divide, and building resentments generated by our prison population, which grows so fast we've been dubbed Incarceration Nation. But at the same time, the eruption of violence managed to remind us of the bond between community and police. By enforcing our laws, police become our surrogate. When madness or resentment or obsession turns to violence, police can become the target. It isn't right. It isn't fair. But police officers know, their spouses know, their parents and friends and brothers and sisters know, that pinning on a shield doesn't make you safe. More often it places you in danger.

1

A PLACE TO ESCAPE

WHEN MAURICE CLEMMONS WAS BORN—"sweet as gold," his Aunt Mamie says—in Marianna, Arkansas, the smell of smoke hung in the air, the vestige of seven storefronts that had gone up in flames, including the office of the Concerned Citizens Committee, a group of young black leaders who had organized a boycott of white-owned businesses. "Firemen do not rule out arson," the newspaper said. The date was February 6, 1972, a Sunday. At the time, the town, the county, the whole Delta region, was on edge, put there by the threat of racial violence. A white schoolteacher in Marianna carried an automatic pistol in her car while driving to school. The deputy administrator of a medical clinic that served the poor kept a gun in her office; her clinic, run by blacks, had become a target of white hostility. "The idea was to blow them away before they got to you," she said.

These measures were understandable—reasonable, even—given the town and the times. Marianna's police chief called the place a "powder keg." Three weeks before Clemmons' birth, black students held a sit-in at the high school, demanding an assembly to commemorate the birthday of Martin Luther King Jr. The sheriff ordered the students doused with a fire hose; 117 were arrested on misdemeanor charges of disrupting school. Later that night, the home of a white sheriff's deputy was firebombed. The same deputy had been targeted days before by a sniper, the .38-caliber slug missing by two feet. Four days after Clemmons' birth, the president of the Marianna School Board, a white man, was nearly hit with a shot from a high-powered rifle while walking through his home's front door.

When Clemmons was born, the violence had been pitched for seven months. The previous summer, a white policeman in nearby Forrest City had shot and killed a black man during a traffic stop. In Marianna, a white judge, Hack Adams, had nearly run down two black organizers with his pickup truck. When the two men went to the courthouse to complain, the judge rushed in, drew a gun, and ordered them out. (Adams so despised the medical clinic run by African Americans that he wrote the state's governor: "They remind me of a bunch of children playing 'hospital' with real medicine, which in my opinion is endangering the health of our citizens.") Threats flew back and forth. Olly Neal, the director of the medical clinic, was a leader in the black community. Harold Meins, owner of the Holiday Sands motel and restaurant, was president of the White Citizens Council. If an ominous call came into Meins' business, he directed the person answering the phone to say: "If you kill Harold, Olly Neal's a dead nigger." National newspapers took note of the turmoil. "A notion is going around, mostly in the North, that the race issue is fading away in the South," the *New York Times* wrote. "The people of eastern Arkansas know better." Of course, the most telling line in this story may be its description of Olly Neal: "He is open-faced and straight-forward. He does not lower his eyes when he talks to white men." Folk singer Joan Baez came to Marianna the week after Clemmons' birth.

The boycott's roots could be traced to all kinds of causes. The desegregation battles of Little Rock in the late 1950s may as well have happened on the moon, as far as Marianna was concerned. In Marianna, nothing changed. But now, African Americans in this small town were fighting back against the degrading treatment from police and the schools and local businesses; they were sick of spending their money in stores that wouldn't consider hiring them. The boycott leaders issued twenty-three demands. Some went to employment, naming places where black residents must be hired. *2. Black in all Drug Stores. 3. Black in Court house.* Some went to education. *13. Students to receive fair treatment and graded fairly. 15. Black teachers not to be demoted.* Some went to policing. *16. No more police brutality and insults.* The boycott lasted thirteen months. At least eleven businesses closed, devastating Marianna's economy—what little there was of it.

Maurice Clemmons grew up in one of the poorest counties in one of the country's poorest states. The 1980 census of Lee County, Arkansas, taken when Clemmons was eight years old, tells the story in numbers. The county's per capita income was fifty-nine hundred dollars. Forty-four percent of its residents lived below the poverty line. Only 17 percent of the adults had graduated from high school. Optimists in the Delta region had once predicted a boom for Marianna, the county seat. But the boom never came. Gripped by poverty, Marianna's population dwindled to nearly five thousand.

Clemmons' mother, Dorthy Mae, had six children. Her mother had twenty-one, although six died young. Maurice had four half brothers and a half sister. One of his closest friends was his Uncle Ray, who was only two years older than Maurice. "We were poor, but back then, there wasn't the crime," Ray Clemmons says. "We spent our days running through the woods, swinging on vines. Doing what kids do." They played hide-and-seek and rode bikes—and if they had only one bike, they took turns. "It was a small town," Ray says. "Everybody knew you." Maurice's dad worked in a factory that made frames for automobile seats, but the factory closed amid all the racial violence and Maurice's father moved away. Maurice's mom worked two jobs, one as a nursing aide. Maurice lived in a mobile home with his mother and siblings. Many aunts, uncles and cousins lived in tarpaper shacks or tiny clapboard houses.

Clemmons would later say of his childhood: "I felt like I didn't belong." He'd say he was "amazed" by the "crooked, wicked things people would do." "I used to be slow to anger. I used to be real gentle with everybody." Clemmons attached a mystical quality to his youth, saying he had already tapped into a belief that would consume him in later years, a certitude that his life was an endless loop, that he had already passed this way and had the same conversations and performed the same acts many times before. "When I was young, I would always say to God, 'What is my purpose here?'"

For the people growing up there, Lee County had little to offer—few jobs, limited prospects, poor schools. What Lee County had was lots of history—most of it ugly, if you happened to be black. Lee County borders Mississippi; Marianna is closer to Oxford than to Little Rock. Crops and furrows dominate the landscape; in places, cotton fluff forms a haze that stretches almost to the horizon. In 1891, cotton-field workers in Lee County went on strike, demanding more than fifty cents per hundred pounds of cotton picked. A white mob settled the matter by lynching nine strike leaders on the way to the Marianna jail.

Lee County, like so much of the South, continues to celebrate its Confederate past. Marianna spreads out in a spider web of one- and two-lane roads—most paved, some not—from a square dominated by a statue of Robert E. Lee, the county's namesake. Dedicated "in loving memory to Lee County's Confederate soldiers," the statue is inscribed: "No Braver Bled for a Brighter Land; No Brighter Land Had a Cause So Grand." Forrest City, sixteen miles away in St. Francis County, is named for Nathan Bedford Forrest, a founder of the Ku Klux Klan.

For the people growing up there, Lee County was a place to escape. And that's what many members of the Clemmons family did, putting down roots in St. Louis, Chicago, Detroit. Marianna never recovered from the racial violence in the early '70s. The town couldn't shake its past, distant or recent. One of its biggest employers, a Coca-Cola bottling plant, moved away, taking jobs with it. Other places simply closed.

In the late 1970s, one of Maurice's uncles, Joe Lewis Clemmons, moved to the Pacific Northwest; he started a business for transporting disabled people to their appointments and eventually had a fleet of more than a dozen vans. He beckoned other family members to follow his lead and settle in Seattle, Tacoma, Everett. "Joe started the string of us coming out here," says Carol Henderson, one of Joe's nieces. "The whole reason for him trying to get his family to venture out here was for better opportunities and to do something different." Chrisceda Clemmons—one of Joe's sisters, and another of those twenty-one kids—took Joe up and moved to Seattle. "He was a saint," she says. "He brought us up here one by one."

The best-known exodus from Marianna involved not the Clemmons family, but the Chambers family. In the 1980s, Billy Joe Chambers and three of his brothers dominated the crack trade in Detroit, a fifteen-hour drive north of their hometown. They recruited other young men from Marianna to join their empire—and empire is the right word, considering the operation grossed maybe $55 million a year. In the book *Land of Opportunity*, William Adler provided a remarkable account of the Chambers brothers, detailing their background and placing their choices into context:

> Pushed away from the South and pulled into the economic underground of the North and driven by the same aspirations for material gain as most everyone else, the Chambers brothers recognized crack as a lucrative business opportunity—their best chance at upward mobility. Shut out of the American Dream and given the choice of a lifetime of minimum-wage drudgery in the city or, worse yet, the stifling farm life back home, it is little wonder that such smart, brash, ambitious young men took the only road open to wealth and power and respect. What is surprising is that so few policy makers and drug warriors fail to make the connection between crack-dealing as a rational career choice and the lack of any other economic opportunity.

Adler's book didn't forgive the Chambers brothers their crimes. It accounted for the damage they did; it accounted for other black men who, in similar circumstances, abided by the law. But it explained the allure. It painted the contrast between what had been and what could be. The book opens with a striking scene: Billy Joe, in 1986, returning home to Marianna, inspiring awe, inspiring cheers, parading through town in a caravan of five white stretch limousines, throwing money out the windows.

For Maurice's mother and her children, the exodus came in the mid-1980s. "Their house was clean, they had food on the table, but they still were poor, and you're going to want more," Maurice's Uncle Ray says. Marianna had no more to give. When Maurice was a teenager, his family drove eighty-five miles west, moving into Little Rock's East End Housing Project. Uncle Ray and his family moved there, too. Their arrival coincided with the first waves of the crack epidemic. "That was when all the friends started killing each other over money," Ray says. But Ray stayed out of trouble: "I was into sports and school." He went to his classes. He went to the recreation center. Then he went home—every night. Ray, like many members of the extended Clemmons family, found his way without turning to crime. These days he lives in Marianna and works as a prison guard—one of the few jobs available to those people still committed to the dying town.

After moving to Little Rock, Maurice's family settled into a house on Welch Street—a block from Confederate Boulevard and a block from a national cemetery where the country seems destined to fight the same war forever, with the Union dead buried on twelve acres and the Confederate dead on eleven acres adjacent. In years to come, three of Maurice's half brothers would have run-ins with the law—Russell, for drugs and theft; Rickey, for burglary; Timothy, for dealing drugs and spraying gunfire. As a teenager, Maurice liked to spend time at the Circle K, playing video games. But he found trouble, too. "He was a normal kid until he was fifteen or sixteen," Ray says. "Like a lot of kids in the projects, he started running with the wrong crowd."

In November of 1988, when Clemmons was sixteen, he approached a seventh-grader from behind and ripped a necklace, worth all of thirty dollars, from the kid's neck. When the seventh-grader turned and grabbed for his jewelry, Clemmons punched him in the face. In January of 1989, a month before his seventeenth birthday, Clemmons and two friends broke into the house of a Little Rock police officer who also lived on Welch Street. They stole two pistols, handcuffs and ammunition. Caught later the same day with the officer's service revolver, Clemmons and his friends confessed.

Between robbing the seventh-grader and burglarizing the cop's home, Clemmons racked up three felony charges. But he was released from custody, pending resolution of the charges. For Clemmons, the threat of prison didn't induce caution or second-guessing. Instead, he doubled down. In April, Clemmons, now seventeen, broke into the home of another cop—this time an Arkansas state trooper who lived in Little Rock. The trooper, Keith Eremea, came home to discover his garage door kicked open and house ransacked, with tables flipped, drawers pulled open, electronics pulled from the walls. The burglars had taken a police scanner, a portable cellular phone, weapons, a holster, and all kinds of jewelry, including Eremea's graduation ring from the police academy. Making Clemmons for the crime proved easy. He left a fingerprint on one of the overturned tables, and the stolen telephone was used to call Clemmons' home—a call that showed up in records. Plus, Clemmons kept some of the stolen property. This was not a case that any prosecutor would lose sleep over.

Clemmons now had five felony charges pending against him. But he kept going, bringing a .25-caliber pistol to his high school in May. An assistant principal caught wind of this and summoned Clemmons to his office. You carrying a gun? the assistant principal asked. "Hold on a minute," Clemmons answered. Then he stepped outside the office—*just* outside the office—and handed the gun to a friend. The assistant principal saw the whole thing. He took the gun away and called police. Clemmons was not only expelled, he became one of the first students in the state charged under a new law aimed at keeping guns off school grounds. *Hold on a minute.* As if that alone would freeze time and allow Clemmons to deep-six the evidence.

Two weeks later, on a late night in June, Clemmons approached a woman named Karen Hodge in the parking lot of a Little Rock nightclub. As Hodge neared her car, keys in hand, Clemmons walked up with a hand in his jacket pocket.

"I've got a gun," he told her. "Give me your purse or I'm going to shoot you." Hodge couldn't believe this was happening.

"Well, goddamn it, why don't you just shoot?" she told Clemmons.

His bluff called—there was no gun—Clemmons took his hand out of his pocket and punched Hodge on the side of her head, a blow that knocked her against the hood of her car. He tore the purse off Hodge's arm and took off, jumping into a big bomb of a car, metallic silver. The robbery netted sixteen dollars and a credit card. Clemmons was arrested soon after. Police found on him the exact amount of money Hodge had reported stolen. Hodge also picked his face out of a photo array.

In all, Clemmons picked up eight felony charges in seven months, a spree that started when he was sixteen and ended when he was seventeen. Prosecutors brought him up first on taking the necklace. With a judge hearing the evidence instead of a jury, Clemmons was found guilty of robbery, a felony. The judge, Floyd Lofton, gave Clemmons five years—a prison sentence that ticketed him for one of the South's most feared destinations.

2

YEARS ON THE HOE SQUAD

ENTERING THE ARKANSAS STATE PRISON SYSTEM—a "dark and evil world," in the words of a federal judge not so many years before—Maurice Clemmons looked more prey than predator. He was only seventeen, a teenager who should have been looking forward to his senior year of high school. His size did not compensate for his youth. He was only five feet nine, 156 pounds. His rap sheet did not intimidate. In the penitentiary, serving time for clocking a seventh-grader doesn't rate.

In the summer of 1989, Clemmons was assigned to serve his five-year sentence at the Tucker Unit, a sprawling prison farm forty miles southeast of Little Rock. A torture device, called the "Tucker Telephone," had been invented at the prison and put to frequent use there. "It was likely used on inmates until the 1970s," says *The Encyclopedia of Arkansas History & Culture*, which includes a rather lengthy listing on the telephone:

> The Tucker Telephone consisted of an old-fashioned crank telephone wired in sequence with two batteries. Electrodes coming from it were attached to a prisoner's big toe and genitals. The electrical components of the phone were modified so that cranking the telephone sent an electric shock through the prisoner's body. The device was reputedly constructed in the 1960s by, depending upon the source, a former trusty in the prison, a prison superintendent, or an inmate doctor; it was administered as a form of punishment, usually in the prison hospital. In prison parlance, a "long-distance call" was a series of electric shocks in a row.

Embarrassing publicity helped remove the device from the Arkansas prison system. But the invention lived on; variations were employed by police in Chicago and, more recently, by U.S. soldiers at the Abu Ghraib prison in Iraq. The Tucker Unit's infamy also lived on, only in different form. In 1984—five years before

Clemmons was assigned to Tucker's No. 20 Barracks and the No. 7 Hoe Squad—the *Washington Post* published an exposé on Tucker's continuing brutality. Former guards described inmates being beaten and prison employees falsifying reports to cover it up. One summer day, with the temperature in the nineties, the warden ordered that six inmates be chained to telephone poles, where they stood for hours in the sun. He said they refused to work. "I don't have anything to hide about that," the warden told *Post* reporter Ted Gup. Another inmate, in an account corroborated by two guards, wrote that he was forced to behave like a dog: "Two officers put a gun and rifle on me. ... I was made to get on my knees and crawl like a dog. I was made to go and pick up sticks like a dog and bring it to these officers. I was made to bark up at a tree like I was treeing a coon. I was even made to get on my knees and sniff horse manure and bark at it." One former guard said this inmate came to be called "Old Blue." "He'd be walking to the building and a field officer would say 'Hit off Old Blue!' and he'd holler like a bloodhound."

Checking in new inmates like Clemmons, prison officials took an inventory of sorts—a personal history that would allow for a before-and-after snapshot, a profile that could be compared to the man who emerged on the other side of an inmate's sentence. They charted Clemmons' scars—a half-inch scar above his left eye, a half-inch scar below his right eye, a two-inch scar on his right forearm, a two-inch scar above his left buttock. They recorded Clemmons' family history, writing down three half brothers who had previously served time in the Arkansas prison system. In the box marked "Enemy Alert," they listed three inmates who should be kept separate from Clemmons. They typed up an official version of the crime for which he had been sentenced, then asked Clemmons for his version: "Subject denies the crime and states he knows nothing about the crime." They filled out a basic plan for his time in custody, including goals. Educational? "If time allows." Vocational? "If time allows."

They also tried to figure out what was inside Clemmons' head. After jotting down a first impression—"shouldn't be a management problem"—corrections officials ordered up a variety of psychological tests. They had Clemmons do drawings of human figures, a silly exercise from which they drew sweeping conclusions: "Drawings indicate a tense and anxious individual who compensates for feelings of inadequacy by stressing masculine attributes." They had Clemmons take the MMPI, or Minnesota Multiphasic Personality Inventory, requiring him to answer some 550 true-or-false questions. "My daily life is full of things that keep me interested ... I am easily awakened by noise ... My hands and feet are usually warm enough ... I think I would like the work of a librarian." They thought the answers would yield insight into his moods, outlook and ways of thinking.

The Arkansas Department of Correction wrote up its mental evaluation of Clemmons on August 22, 1989. The two-page report is loaded with qualifiers—

"may be," "tends to be," "appears to be"—and offers up I-told-you-so language for almost any contingency, no matter how Clemmons turned out. Some results indicated Clemmons was a "well-adjusted" individual "whose offenses do not stem from serious problems in personality, interpersonal relations, or psychological adjustments." His spirits? "Relatively good." Attitude? "Seems to be good." The report says: "These offenders are usually not dangerous" and require no special precautions in how they are managed.

But other results—described elsewhere in the same report—indicated Clemmons was "sullen ... overly sensitive and argumentative, seeing threats and insults where there are none." He fit a profile of people who "may feel at the mercy of circumstances rather than in control ... They see themselves as having little responsibility for having produced their problems, and they may put little effort into solving them. ... Failures and problems may be blamed on others." The report says: "Anger tends to be acted out through fights or assaultive behavior. ... Abrasive behavior or poor anger controls indicated in test results. ... Test results indicate possible personality disorder."

So take your pick. Clemmons was safe or dangerous, sound or disturbed. He attended orientation and received a copy of the Inmate Handbook. He signed a form saying he had been afforded the opportunity to ask questions. Corrections officials assigned Clemmons a number, 92616, and took his picture, front and side. In those pictures, Clemmons does not look scared. His eyes are hard, his jaw firm. If anything, he looks like business.

Clemmons received his bed assignment at Tucker on September 7, 1989. Six days later, he got into a fight with another inmate. Prison officials attributed the fight to a gambling debt, but Clemmons said it started when the other inmate began putting Clemmons' personal items—deodorant, comb, mirror—into a pillowcase. "I had to confirm to him about giving back my property," is how Clemmons put it. The other inmate grabbed a broken razor and slashed Clemmons across the face. Clemmons responded with such ferocity that a prison lieutenant had to beat him on the neck to get him off the other inmate. Clemmons received a trip to the infirmary and disciplinary charges. But his point had been made. And in case anyone missed it, Clemmons reinforced the message one week later, joining four other inmates in beating and kicking another prisoner.

In July of 1990, a fellow inmate named Glover approached Clemmons and asked about getting some cakes. In prison, commerce takes all kinds of forms. Just about anything can become the subject of barter, negotiation or force: food, shampoo, legal advice, drugs. For Clemmons, one item with considerable market value was Little Debbie cakes, those snacks that picture a curly red-haired girl in a blue gingham shirt, hawking devil crème, frosted fudge or—the favorite of the band Southern Culture on the Skids—oatmeal. *All I want is just one more oatmeal pie / Little Debbie, Little Debbie!*

Clemmons agreed to provide a single box of Little Debbies, on condition: Glover would have to pay two boxes back. It was two for one, simple as that. Glover took the deal. But when Glover returned, the two boxes in hand, he learned the terms had changed. Clemmons said the price had gone up. Now Glover owed six boxes of Little Debbies. Glover was ordered to deliver them to Clemmons' "pick-up man"—an inmate named Wells—or else he'd be in for a beating. Like someone in deep to a loan shark, Glover incurred new debts to pay off old ones. He borrowed two boxes of cakes from other inmates, bringing his total offering up to four boxes. That's not good enough, Clemmons said. He told Glover that if he didn't have the other two boxes by midnight, the price would go up again—this time, to twelve boxes of cakes. Glover didn't know what to do or where to turn. No option held much appeal. In the end, he opted to tell prison officials about Clemmons' threats—a decision that risked his being tagged a snitch, a label no inmate wants to wear. But Glover apparently saw no good alternative. Prison officials ordered Clemmons into isolation for thirty days. They also stripped him of 184 days of good-time credit.

By the time of this shakedown, Clemmons had been in prison for less than a year. He was still young, just eighteen. But already a pattern had emerged. In prison, Clemmons was no patsy—and certainly no punk, the label attached to any inmate who became the object of rape. Clemmons was an enterprising, manipulative thug, as comfortable with extortion as he was with dealing drugs.

In his two-and-a-half years at Tucker, Clemmons got into more than a half-dozen fights with other inmates. Once, he grabbed another inmate's lock and took off. When the other inmate tracked him down, Clemmons said: You want the lock back, pay me. "Quit the bullshit," the other inmate said, and the fight was on.

When another inmate refused to pay Clemmons for items that had been stolen, Clemmons removed the lock from his locker box and placed it in a sock. With this makeshift weapon—the equivalent of a medieval mace, a weight that could be whirled and whipped—he laced into the other inmate, a spectacle that drew a crowd of other prisoners. Before the guards closed in, Clemmons pulled the lock from the sock and dropped it on the floor. Another inmate picked it up and disappeared into the crowd, preventing the guards from seeing what he was holding. This inmate handed the lock to another inmate, who, in turn, put the lock back on Clemmons' locker box. Clemmons got caught. But this effort to discard the evidence was at least more enterprising than the *hold-on-a-minute* tack he'd taken with that assistant principal.

In those same two-and-a-half years, Clemmons made countless threats. When he suspected two other inmates of snitching about his dope dealing, Clemmons walked up to the pair and said: "You better watch ya'll's back on hoe squad today, because I've paid a hit man to fuck ya'll off." He lied to guards and, at times, told them off. Ordered to pick up a can of Mountain Dew he'd thrown to the ground, Clemmons told a guard: "You motherfuckers can't make me pick up no can. What will you charge me with? Littering?" He got popped repeatedly for contraband. Guards found a marijuana joint taped to the bottom of his locker box and a shank—a piece of glass, eight inches long, cut into a V—at the bottom of his envelope for legal mail. Clemmons denied everything: "I am a victim of circumstances … I don't know why I'm being charged … How is it that I can be found guilty?" He might have been innocent of something, but there's no way he was innocent of everything. He'd veer from one excuse to another, no matter how inconsistent. Take the piece of cut glass. Clemmons initially said he used it to shave. Then, on appeal, he claimed it wasn't his, that it belonged to his roommate. Clemmons responded to various disciplinary charges by insisting he'd been set up (by other inmates or by some guard with a vendetta), or that he was the victim of mistaken identity, or that he had an alibi, or that he acted in self-defense. In 1991 Clemmons was disciplined for having sex with another inmate—and for being a lookout while other inmates took a turn with the same man. Again, Clemmons denied everything, claiming he'd been in the prison chapel, a sanctuary called the Island of Hope.

A prisoner who keeps a clean institutional record can cut his time in half. But Clemmons racked up major disciplinary charges at least thirteen times while at Tucker. At least nine times he was ordered into isolation, typically for thirty-day stretches. Because he was considered such a threat, prison officials dropped Clemmons' status from Class II to Class IV, meaning maximum security. They also sliced into whatever good time he had accumulated, making him forfeit 25 days, 66 days, 145 days. Only later would Clemmons appreciate how his hoodlum behavior had extended his time behind bars.

To compound matters, Clemmons' sentence was no longer a mere five years. At the same time he was forfeiting all that good time, Clemmons was being escorted from prison to court for resolution of the other criminal charges stemming from his seven-month crime spree. Two weeks after Clemmons began his stint at Tucker, he was convicted of two other felonies, burglary and theft, for breaking into the home of the Little Rock police officer. His sentence stretched from five years to thirteen.

With five other felony charges pending against him, prosecutors offered Clemmons a deal—plead guilty, and get an additional twenty-five years for the whole bundle. Had Clemmons accepted, the deal would have extended his total sentence to thirty-eight years. That sounds like a lot, but in Arkansas, inmates serve a fraction of their sentence. Clemmons probably would have served about seven of those thirty-eight years, allowing him to leave prison in his mid-twenties. But Clemmons rejected the offer. He elected to go to trial.

In November 1989, Karen Hodge took the stand and testified about Clemmons stealing her purse while pretending to have a gun. The jury deliberated for an hour and fifteen minutes before convicting Clemmons of aggravated robbery and theft. Jurors gave him twenty-five years for the former, ten for the latter. The judge ordered the sentences to run back-to-back, rather than concurrently. Clemmons' total sentence stretched from thirteen years to forty-eight.

The judge at this trial was Floyd Lofton, of Pulaski County Circuit Court. Lofton had also been the judge when Clemmons was convicted of his first felony. He'd been the judge when Clemmons was convicted of his second and third felonies. Now he'd watched Clemmons rack up felony convictions Nos. 4 and 5.

Too poor to hire a lawyer, Clemmons was represented in each case by a public defender—or a "public pretender," as Clemmons liked to say.

To the lawyers in Little Rock, Judge Lofton amounted to a mixed blessing. He was pointed, direct and consistent to a fault. If a sixteen-year-old was accused of a violent crime, Lofton would order him tried as an adult. If a jury sentenced a defendant to multiple prison terms, Lofton would order those terms to run back-to-back, believing that reflected the jurors' judgment in each case. In deciding the value of property stolen—an important distinction that can affect both the crime and the time—Lofton favored the wholesale price, not the retail one. Lofton's approach made him utterly predictable—which meant lawyers knew what he would do (which can be good), but stood little chance of persuading him to do something else (which can be bad).

Before the trial involving the robbery of Hodge, Lofton had urged plea negotiations, saying of Clemmons: "He's got a hard row to hoe. ... This is just going to get worse." After the trial, Lofton, knowing Clemmons had yet more charges pending against him, again advised Clemmons to cut a deal. He didn't want to see this seventeen-year-old take his chances with yet another trial. As a young thief—as a burglar, as a robber—Clemmons was not what anyone would call clever. He consistently left a trail of evidence; yet he just as consistently insisted upon trial, where he would claim mistaken identity or some other defense easily dispensed with by the prosecution. Going to trial carried serious risk. Lose, and the sentence almost always eclipsed the pre-trial offer.

"You've got forty-eight years, Maurice," Lofton told Clemmons. "I would seriously want you to consider the exposure that you're going to have and to minimize the damages as it were. I don't know what the prosecutor has offered or can offer or will offer. I just know that there comes a point." But Clemmons refused to listen. He opted for trial again—and again, the case would be tried before Judge Lofton.

The next set of charges stemmed from the burglary of the home of Keith Eremea, the Arkansas state trooper. Because Clemmons had stashed some of the stolen property at home, his family became entangled. Clemmons' stepfather, knowing he had to testify against his stepson, broke down and cried in the office of Clemmons' lawyer. Before and at trial, Clemmons became a menace. He reached for a guard's pistol while being transported to court. He extracted a lock from a holding cell and threw it at a guard—and missed, instead hitting Clemmons' mother, who had arrived with street clothes for Clemmons to wear in court. When Eremea testified about his home being ransacked, Clemmons greeted him with an obscene gesture. Before a pretrial hearing, Clemmons dismantled a restroom's pneumatic doorstop and hid a piece of metal—maybe ten inches long, with the weight of a wrench—in his sock. A guard discovered the makeshift weapon before Clemmons reached the courtroom. When the metal was confiscated, Clemmons vowed that the next time he went before Lofton he would punch him in the mouth—and maybe that way he'd get a new judge.

Lofton, exasperated, told Clemmons' lawyer before trial: "It's getting too complicated for me. Just get the subpoenas out. ... Let's get the motions filed and have hearings. But these are a waste of time because I can't even understand this man's problems. There are just too many of them. ... Let's just tee it up and try it—and everybody do the best job they can to represent this man and help him out the best we can. If we can, fine. If we can't, fine."

Because of the threat Clemmons posed, Lofton ordered that he be shackled with leg irons during the trial. The judge also placed a uniformed sheriff's deputy directly behind Clemmons, for added security. The jurors saw all this, of course. Their perceptions of Clemmons could hardly have been unaffected. But to the judge's mind, he had little choice. He needed to minimize the risk of Clemmons attacking someone in court.

The trial was held on February 23, 1990. The jurors took all of sixteen minutes to convict Clemmons of burglary and theft. Because he was a habitual offender—in all, Clemmons now had seven felony convictions—the sentencing parameters shifted, allowing for a tougher punishment. The jurors took twenty minutes to decide Clemmons' sentence—thirty years for each charge. The prosecutor asked for the thirty-year terms to be served back-to-back rather than at the same time. Lofton agreed. That meant another sixty years was being tacked onto the forty-eight that Clemmons had already received.

"You have broken your mother's heart," Lofton told Clemmons.

"I have broken my own heart," Clemmons answered.

The numbers, put together, were stunning. Clemmons had just been sentenced to a total of 108 years—all for a string of crimes in which the worst injury anyone suffered was a punch to the face. The punishment seemed almost unthinkable. But what it showed was the cumulative power of the system's assumptions, incentives and misunderstandings. Clemmons was entitled to a jury trial, yes, but if he exercised that right, rather than copping a plea, he would be punished. The court system, laboring under so many cases, hungers for and rewards pleas. It imposes a trial tax, payable in extra years. Clemmons exercised his right to trial four times. He was punished four times.

In Arkansas, juries determine sentences. But many jurors know the numbers aren't real. They read it in the newspapers. (Headline in the *Arkansas Democrat-Gazette*: "It's the law: Criminals only serve bit of time.") In Arkansas, offenders typically become eligible for parole after serving one-sixth of their sentence, a fraction that can turn a long sentence into the court system's equivalent of Monopoly money. A thirty-year sentence equals five years. Sixty equals ten. Apply that fraction to Clemmons, and those 108 years become eighteen. He would enter prison at seventeen and leave at thirty-five.

But not every case fits the formula. For Clemmons, several factors combined to push back the date he would become eligible for parole. His conviction for aggravated robbery—for taking the purse while pretending to have a gun—was a Class Y felony, a particularly serious count to which the fraction of one-sixth did not apply. He had been sentenced as a habitual offender. And he was a disciplinary problem in prison, reducing his good-time credits. In prison he landed in trouble from the outset—as do lots of young inmates, determined to send a message that they're not to be messed with.

The Pulaski County prosecutor's office crunched the numbers and determined that Clemmons would become eligible for parole in 2021, at the age of forty-nine. But when the state's Department of Correction forecasted his release date—taking into account the way he was bleeding good-time credits—the numbers shifted. One forecast showed Clemmons becoming eligible for parole in 2027—at the age of fifty-five.

For a seventeen-year-old inmate, any of these numbers would have been unnerving. Freedom at thirty-five would have meant half a life spent in prison. And getting released at fifty-five? How does someone start a life at fifty-five?

Mark Fraiser prosecuted two of the cases that netted ninety-five years: "For us to prosecute a seventeen-year-old, and for him to get a ninety-five-year sentence without a homicide, you've got to be a bad little dude to draw that kind of a sentence." And Clemmons still wasn't through. He was convicted of one more felony before the year was out. That conviction, his eighth, was for bringing the gun to school (*hold on a minute*). But for once, Clemmons relented and cut a deal. He pleaded guilty and received a six-year sentence—to run concurrently with the time he'd already accumulated, meaning his total would not climb higher.

But 108 years looked like forever. He seemed destined to grow old in prison or even die there.

By the summer of 1992, the officials at Tucker had seen enough. The kid who had arrived as a teen with a five-year sentence was now a twenty-year-old man staring at 108 years. To make matters worse, he had proved to be a dangerous inmate. In a letter to the Tucker Unit's warden, one corrections officer said Clemmons "immediately became a discipline problem and has been a problem since." Two inmates had recently requested protective custody in order to be separated from Clemmons, the officer wrote, adding: "Both seem to feel that inmate Clemmons means what he says about hurting them." After a hearing before a transfer committee, the Arkansas Department of Correction decided to move Clemmons "based on disciplinary problems, assaultive behavior, suspected drug dealing, length of sentence, and threats made toward inmates." Clemmons would be shipped to the Cummins Unit—a prison farm even older than Tucker, and even more notorious.

Some prisons with ignominious histories have grabbed hold of the popular imagination: Louisiana's Angola, Mississippi's Parchman, New York's Sing Sing. But to many penologists and historians, the most infamous may be Cummins prison: sixteen thousand acres in southeastern Arkansas, vast, flat and fertile, ringed by cypress swamps, where long-line riders—armed guards on horseback—keep watch over inmates swinging hoes, and where mules bring water and bloodhounds stay at the ready, in case of escape.

Cummins has been in operation since 1902. Its name may not resonate in the way of San Quentin or Folsom, but Cummins is the heart of the Arkansas prison system, and the Arkansas prison system has long been one of America's worst. In the 1960s, media accounts didn't bother to attach qualifiers. "The worst in the country," UPI wrote. "The most medieval," wrote *Newsweek*. "Hell in Arkansas," was the headline in *Time* magazine. In 1967, the state's newly elected governor, Winthrop Rockefeller, did not contest the point. He called Cummins "probably the most barbaric prison system in the United States." Rockefeller hired a young prison reformer, Thomas Murton, to clean the system up. Murton's brief stint in Arkansas—he quickly went sideways with both Rockefeller and the state legislature—became the basis for the movie *Brubaker*, with Robert Redford playing the quixotic role of the new warden in town. In 1968, Bobby Darin released a song about Cummins called "Long Line Rider." *This kind of thing can't happen here, especially not in election year.* In 1969, Johnny Cash performed at Cummins and donated $5,000 toward a prison chapel.

But it was in 1970 that Cummins changed the national landscape, forcing a reevaluation of the way prisoners are treated. That year a U.S. District Court judge, J. Smith Henley, ruled that conditions in the Arkansas prison system were so abysmal they amounted to cruel and unusual punishment. The case, *Holt v. Sarver*, marked the first time an entire state's prison system had been declared unconstitutional. But rulings soon followed in other states, with judges demanding reforms that lawmakers had dismissed. What *Brown v. Board of Education* was to America's schools, *Holt v. Sarver* became to its prisons.

At the time, Arkansas paid nothing for its prisons. The two prison farms, Tucker and Cummins, even turned a profit for the state. The system managed this by having as few paid employees as possible. Inmates were guarded mostly by other inmates—and the ones given the weapons and power, the trusties, were often the most sadistic. When describing how one inmate was beaten by a trusty named James Pike, Henley couldn't help noting: "Pike, an illiterate, is a convicted murderer serving a sentence for beating to death a warden at the Mississippi County Penal Farm where Pike was formerly confined on a misdemeanor charge." Trusties could murder other inmates "with practical impunity," Henley wrote, adding: "Very recently a gate guard killed another inmate 'carelessly.' One wonders." When it came to brutality, the paid employees could be worse than the trusties. Tales of torture seeped out of the prisons and into investigative reports. There was the Tucker Telephone, of course. And blackjacks. And the "teeter board" (descriptions can be hard to come by; one says inmates, in bare feet, would be forced to balance on carpenter nails driven through a small, see-sawing plank of wood). And hypodermic needles driven under inmates' fingernails. The whip was not only tolerated, it was officially sanctioned. "That punishment consists of blows with a leather strap five feet in length, four inches wide, and about one-fourth inch thick," Henley wrote. "A prisoner who is to be whipped is required to lie down on the ground fully clothed, and the blows are inflicted on his buttocks." The strap was called "Oh Capt'n," because that's what inmates were required to say when whipped.

The prisons' open barracks encouraged stabbings and rape. Henley's ruling provided a vocabulary lesson, describing how, at night, inmates called "creepers" or "crawlers" would prey upon other inmates, and how the weak would, in vain, seek safety by sleeping at the front of the barracks ("punk row") or by clinging to the bars all night ("grabbing the bars"). And the problems didn't end there. At Cummins, the barracks were still segregated. The food was awful. So were sanitary conditions and medical care.

In *Holt v. Sarver*, Henley wrote one line that has been recited many times since: "For the ordinary convict a sentence to the Arkansas Penitentiary today amounts to a banishment from civilized society to a dark and evil world completely alien to the free world, a world that is administered by criminals under unwritten rules and customs completely foreign to free world culture." But other language is even more striking—confronting the historical divide over the goals of prison, the push-pull between retribution and rehabilitation, and the public's refusal to see or care. Henley, a Republican placed on the federal bench by President Eisenhower, disdained the way people took comfort in believing "convicts who were whipped deserved to be whipped," and that convicts who behaved themselves would be treated fairly. A "myth," Henley called it. "This Court has no patience with those who still say, even when they ought to know better, that to change those conditions will convert the prison into a country club; the Court has not heard any of those people volunteer to spend a few days and nights at either Tucker or Cummins incognito."

Henley described Cummins as by far the worst prison. Used predominantly for black inmates, Cummins had no rehabilitation program whatsoever. To Henley, inmates who received neither an education nor useful skills were more likely to wind up back in the penitentiary. He wrote of the Arkansas prison system:

> As a generality it may be stated that few individuals come out of it better men for their experience; most come out as bad as they went in, or worse. Living as he must under the conditions that have been described, with no legitimate rewards or incentives, in fear and apprehension, in degrading surroundings, and with no help from the State, an Arkansas convict will hardly be able to reform himself, and his experience in the Penitentiary is apt to do nothing but instill in him a deep or deeper hatred for and alienation from the society that put him there.

The same themes popped up elsewhere. Murton, the reformer hired by Governor Rockefeller, supported rehabilitation and opposed life sentences: "When you sentence a man to life in prison, with no chance of getting out, he's going to die one day at a time because he knows he's doomed to walk the halls of purgatory for as long as he's alive." Just like Henley, a *Newsweek* reporter was struck by the public's embrace of brutal prison conditions. He wrote in 1967: "Many Arkansans are the sort of fundamentalists who believe fleshly sin deserves fleshly punishment. Many state officials have remained unmoved by the appalling disclosures. At a recent State Penitentiary Board meeting, the beating of prisoners was discussed, and a majority argued for continued use of the strap. At the same meeting, however, the board vetoed a proposal for branding Tucker Farm cattle. Such treatment, they felt, would be 'inhumane.'"

After the federal judiciary intervened, Arkansas made dramatic improvements to its prison system. Still, troubles remained. When Maurice Clemmons came to

Cummins in 1992, the prison still had not been accredited by the American Correctional Association, which sets standards for prison systems nationwide. Cummins didn't receive the association's stamp until 1996—the last prison in the state to achieve such status. Cummins continued to find itself embroiled in corruption and controversy. In an international scandal linked to shoddy screening and profiteering, tainted blood from Cummins prisoners infected Canadians and Europeans with hepatitis and HIV. Arkansas didn't stop selling prison plasma until 1994—long after the risks were known and only after every other state had ended the practice.

Torture also continued to make headlines. A federal grand jury returned indictments against six Cummins guards, accusing them of torturing inmates in 1998 and covering up the abuse with falsified reports. The ringleader admitted that the guards used stun guns and a six-foot-long "shock stick," resembling a cattle prod, to deliver high-voltage currents to inmates' genitals. All six guards were convicted and sentenced to federal prison.

Embarrassing disclosures also extended to the Tucker Unit, the prison where Clemmons entered the system. In June 2009, nearly forty years after *Holt v. Sarver*, the Associated Press wrote a story with a lead that would make any prison administrator cringe: "An Arkansas prisoner nearly died after guards left him lying naked in his own feces for a weekend, and while investigating the incident corrections officials found that guards received lap dances while on the job. ..."

Maurice Clemmons arrived at the Cummins Unit on June 19, 1992. He was four months past his twentieth birthday.

In the Arkansas prison system, inmates work. Clemmons worked mostly in the fields, on one of the hoe squads. In summer, when heat baked the earth, the hard ground was called buckshot. When rain turned the dirt to mud, the soil was called gumbo. He'd be shifted from 7 Hoe to 8 Hoe due to "squad alignment," and from 8 Hoe to 3 Hoe "to increase work force on the high line." Over the years he worked on hoe squads 2, 3, 4, 5, 6, 7, 8 and 21, planting and cultivating cotton, beans, rice, cabbage, broccoli, squash, onions, cantaloupe, sweet potatoes, tomatoes, peas. At other times Clemmons worked as a barracks porter. Or on the fence crew. Or in the vinyl bindery, the garment factory, the laundry, the furniture plant, the kitchen. He served most of his time at Cummins. But he also had a return stretch at Tucker in addition to stints at the Wrightsville Unit in Pulaski County, the Varner Unit in Lincoln County, and the Delta Unit in Chicot County, down in the southeast corner of the state. His itinerary sounds like someone barking out military code: *Cummins, Delta, Cummins, Varner, Cummins, Varner, Wrightsville, Delta, Tucker, Cummins.*

He made little headway in terms of classroom education. He enrolled in a GED program in April 1994 but was removed a few weeks later by request of the program's principal. Meanwhile, his disciplinary file kept getting thicker, reaching hundreds of pages. "Fuck you," he told one guard. "Punk ass motherfucker," he called another. During a strip search, guards at Cummins found a pouch filled with money attached to Clemmons' testicles. Clemmons made like he was going to hand the money over, folding the bills up. But then he jammed the money into his mouth. A guard grabbed at Clemmons but was too slow. When Clemmons raised his tongue, the bills were gone. Another guard, also at Cummins, monitored a telephone conversation in which Clemmons, brazen as can be, asked a relative to bring him drugs—"a quarter, soft." Clemmons told his relative that what cost eighty dollars outside could be sold for two hundred dollars inside. Hide the drugs under the tongue of your shoe, Clemmons said. And bring me a gold chain, too.

The disciplinary penalties kept piling up: thirty days in isolation, restricted commissary privileges for two weeks, the loss of good time. By the spring of 1995—nearly six years after he entered the state's prison system—Clemmons had managed to forfeit six times more good-day credits (1,196) than he had earned (186). He continued to prey ("You have been identified repeatedly by various inmates for robbing locker boxes to victimize weaker inmates," an assistant warden wrote); to plot ("Clemmons has been plotting to break into the 12 barracks penitentiary store and has already made several unsuccessful attempts," a captain wrote); and to threaten ("Inmate Clemmons stated that he was not going to stay at this Unit and when he went to the barracks he was going to stick 8 or 9 people so that we would ship him away," a major wrote). Clemmons' prison file would eventually stack up eight inches high, an eighteen-hundred-page compendium of violence, threats, recrimination, manipulation and fear, and a testament to bureaucracy's compulsion to document.

"I did my time like a champ, brother," Clemmons would say.

Clemmons also continued to stew, taking note of all the inmates around him who had done more harm but received less time. Clemmons became friends with Darcus Allen, a barracks mate at both Cummins and Tucker. But Clemmons compared their punishments, and the disparity rubbed on him for years. Allen had been convicted of first-degree murder and been sentenced to twenty-five years, not even a quarter of Clemmons' sentence. "They did me bad," Clemmons would say years later. "It ain't never been fair for me, it ain't never been right, I ain't never really saw no justice. You feel me?"

Clemmons' enemy-alert list got longer and longer, as he continued to find trouble with other inmates. One inmate stabbed Clemmons in the side while they were in the chow hall. Prison officials rushed Clemmons to the infirmary, where his wound was cleaned and dressed. But Clemmons gave as good as he got, bloodying mouths and cracking heads. In one fight over a gambling debt, Clemmons apparently broke the arm of a gang member, triggering threats of reprisal. Clemmons warned prison officials: "If I'm approached by any inmate who has a problem about what took place, it will be a blood bath. I've seen a lot of people die because they took things lightly. I will not."

For Clemmons, some disputes originated inside prison. He was watching TV. Another inmate changed the channel. Change the channel back, Clemmons said. The other inmate said, "Fuck you ho ass nigga" and walked away. Fifteen minutes later this inmate returned—and doused Clemmons with a bucket of scalding water. Clemmons answered with so many punches that guards had to blast him with pepper spray to make him stop. Clemmons wound up with burns, stinging eyes, another enemy on his list, a ninety-day loss of good-time credits, and a renewed sense of being wronged. Clemmons crossed another inmate by getting $150 worth of drugs on credit—and, when the time came to pay, failing to make good. Sometimes Clemmons blamed tension on gang allegiances. But mundane matters were more typical. He once wrote of two other inmates: "They already think I'm a white folks nigger, cause I won't let them use my clippers to cut stars in their head and stuff."

But other disputes rippled in from the outside. Early on at Cummins, Clemmons crossed paths with an inmate whose mother and uncle he had robbed at the age of sixteen. The two inmates tried to kill each other, Clemmons wielding a pipe, the other inmate an ice pick. Wanting to avoid Round Two, Clemmons wrote a letter urging prison officials to keep the two separated. Clemmons confessed to the early robbery—"I hit his mother several times with my fist and I hit his uncle with a gun a number of times to the head!"—and said he had beat the charges when the victims failed to show up in court.

Clemmons' predations created all kinds of problems for prison officials, who worried that he might be killed in some kind of group assault. Their fears seemed justified when a number of inmates chased Clemmons across the yard, carrying broken broom handles. Clemmons' constant shuttling from one prison to another was prompted, in part, by the desire to keep him away from specific inmates. He would also be moved about within the prisons—from 1 Barracks to 2 Barracks, from 11 to 10, from 15 to 13—all, to avoid enemies. Clemmons often asked for protection, sometimes sensing threats from inmates he knew only by nickname— T. Ray, Disco Joe, Boo-Boo. "I have too much time to serve to be looking over my shoulder every time I turn a corner or when I go to chow."

Clemmons wrote one letter after another to prison officials, fuming, protesting, claiming some denial of his rights. Sometimes he bristled when he was transferred to another unit. Sometimes he bristled when he wasn't. He contested disciplinary charges, either on the facts or on procedural grounds. "An inmate must be served written notice of charges within 72 working hours!" Confined to segregation, he insisted on a daily break from "this 8 foot 8 inch x 12 foot 3 inch cell." In 1994, Clemmons was accused of stealing a gold cross and a ring from another inmate who was found unconscious, the victim of a "sleeper hold." When Clemmons was placed in segregation, he became so incensed that he sued several prison administrators. His lawsuit even made it to trial, before a judge in federal court. Clemmons, representing himself, lost.

Clemmons' letters became a storm of exclamation points. "I'm not taking no more!" "The whole thing was a conspiracy against me!" "I'm tired of being held down!" He accused guards of telling lies and nursing vendettas. And who knows? Maybe he was right a time or two. Maybe he suffered the fate of the boy who cried wolf, his credibility shot by all the alarms he sounded. Cummins' institutional record during Clemmons' time there certainly did not inspire confidence in the place.

In January 1994 Clemmons wrote to the warden of the Delta Unit. Clemmons had been transferred there a few weeks before and wanted to return to Cummins. Clemmons first tried lying, making up a story about having two enemies at the Delta Unit. Then he came clean, saying he was desperate to remain housed with a Cummins inmate he had hired to handle his legal appeals. Clemmons implored the warden to help put the transfer through.

What must I do to plead my case to you ... must I get on my Hands and Knees and Beg or say yes sir Boss every time I see you! ... I know I shouldn't be concerning you with my personal problems. But we're all Human Beings. I eat, smell, walk, talk, and have feelings too! The only person I expect not to have feelings for me is the white man! They have proven to me that they are some cold hearted people when they gave me all this time!

Sir!

Help!

Me!

Please!

Clemmons' line about "the white man" reflected a theme that coursed through his letters. He repeatedly accused the prison system of treating black inmates worse than white ones. Refused his request to return to the general population, he wrote: "If I were white would this here took place Hell No!" Refused protective custody, he wrote that it was "because I was not a white homosexual." He said one prison administrator "ain't shit but an old senile prejudiced white man who is hindering me from being transferred!" And he described Arkansas—the place of his birth—as "this Great White State."

As his youth faded in prison, as year after year passed, Clemmons had ample time and opportunity to mount legal challenges. Public defenders handled his early appeals; later petitions fell mostly to a fellow inmate, whom Clemmons paid. "I do not know enough criminal law," Clemmons wrote to one warden. "I'm not smart enough to respond to my legal documents."

Even with eight felony convictions to contest, his appellate arguments did not fare well. He claimed there wasn't enough evidence to convict him of robbing that seventh-grader. The state court of appeals said yes there was. In grabbing Karen Hodge's purse, Clemmons argued, he should have been convicted only of robbery, not aggravated robbery, since he didn't really have a gun. The Arkansas Supreme Court said pretending to be armed was good enough. In the burglary case with the state trooper, Clemmons argued that having a uniformed deputy sit directly behind him had been so prejudicial that he'd been deprived of a fair trial. The Arkansas Supreme Court agreed, to a point. Was the deputy's presence prejudicial? Of course it was, the court wrote, "inherently" so. "Common sense immediately told each juror that, in the judge's mind at least, this defendant was an unusually dangerous man." But the court's next sentence was: "Only in the rarest circumstances will the State's interest in security and order justify such action, and this is one of those rare circumstances." The court summarized Clemmons' conduct—the metal in his sock, the thrown lock, the threats directed at the judge—and concluded that he posed "a real danger" and that "extreme measures were justified."

His direct appeals all turned away, Clemmons turned to post-conviction proceedings, in which he could raise a new set of arguments—for example, ineffective assistance of counsel. This round of appeals wound up before Marion Humphrey, a Pulaski County circuit judge with a distinguished résumé. Bachelor's degree from Princeton. Divinity degree from Harvard. Law degree from the University of Arkansas. Humphrey, an African American, was not only a judge; he was also a Presbyterian minister.

Clemmons filed his legal pleadings in the summer of 1997. A few months later, in a letter dated October 13, Clemmons sent a personal appeal to Humphrey.

"Honorable Sir,

"It is my sincerest prayer that this correspondence finds you in your very best of health, and your spirit is bound with that of our Lord and Savior. I further extend this prayer to your Honorable family. As for myself, I am thankful to our Lord for another day of living and for the will and desire to seek forgiveness and understanding from both our Lord and the people of this great State."

Clemmons asked Humphrey to consider how he had been only sixteen when these crimes started but was now twenty-five.

"In short sir, I have outgrown the impulsiveness and ignorance of a child. I have grown to be a responsible young man, I've developed an entirely new set of values, I've learned the value of responsibility, respect for others, as well as their property and I've learned the purpose and importance of having laws as well as why we all must abide by them. Sir, I humbly pray you to allow me another opportunity to be free in my youth, and not grow old in confinement. ..."

Clemmons asked Humphrey to "give this lost and searching soul an opportunity to show our society that this young man of 25 years has corrected that 16-year-old child, and wishes to make right the wrongs he committed against our society."

"In closing, I declare under the watchful eyes of our Lord that I will do all in my power as a man to live a drug-free, crime-free life to the end of my existence."

For Clemmons, this letter marked a dramatic shift in approach. Scan his other writings from prison—the rants, the beseechings, the threats—and, to this point, there's hardly any mention of prayer, religion, remorse, or desire to right wrongs. In this letter to Humphrey, "this Great White State," a reference filled with history and anger, becomes simply "this great State." Of course, it's possible there was some sincerity to Clemmons' letter; but if there was, the prison records don't bear it out. The month before he wrote this letter, Clemmons assaulted another inmate and was ordered into isolation for thirty days. Two months after writing the letter, Clemmons was again disciplined for assault; he received another thirty days in isolation, forfeited 180 days of good-time credit, and saw his custody level dropped back to class IV, maximum security. Within this timeline, Clemmons' letter to Humphrey suggests not so much sincerity as manipulation.

In the summer and fall of 1997, Humphrey reviewed the pleadings and heard witnesses testify. On December 12, he issued his ruling. In a two-page order, Humphrey denied the first, second and third arguments in Clemmons' appeal. But on issue No. 4, Humphrey sided with Clemmons. He ruled that in the case with the trooper—the case where Clemmons had been convicted of burglary and theft—Clemmons' trial lawyer should have asked Judge Lofton to recuse himself, given that Lofton believed Clemmons had threatened him. The failure to do so constituted ineffective assistance of counsel, violating the Sixth Amendment. "Even though the jury would decide issues of guilt or innocence, and further would decide on the length of punishment, because the judge had sole discretion on whether a sentence would be run concurrently or consecutively, and because a judge would make evidentiary rulings throughout the trial and decide on jury instructions, the importance of an unbiased judge is axiomatic," Humphrey wrote. Humphrey vacated those two convictions and ordered a new trial. The ruling left six of Clemmons' eight felony convictions in place. But the two convictions that were thrown out accounted for sixty years of Clemmons' 108-year sentence. The potential effect of Humphrey's ruling was a dramatic resetting of Clemmons' punishment.

For Clemmons, any celebration was short-lived. Prosecutors appealed the ruling—and, in October 1998, the Arkansas Supreme Court reversed Humphrey. Assessing a trial lawyer's performance, the court wrote, "requires that every effort be made to eliminate the distorting effects of hindsight." Clemmons' trial lawyer, public defender Llewellyn Marczuk, had testified on appeal that he didn't seek recusal because he believed Lofton would treat Clemmons fairly, that Lofton was consistent and treated everyone the same. Marczuk's trial tactics "proved ineffective," the court wrote, but that doesn't mean his work fell below constitutional standards given what he knew at the time. The Supreme Court reinstated Clemmons' convictions—along with his 108-year sentence.

Despite the setback, Clemmons may have learned something from all this. For once, he had found some semblance of give in the system, the possibility of sympathy or relief. Starting in 1998, he stopped getting into trouble in prison. The tone of his letters began to soften. Clemmons' mother, Dorthy, died from diabetes in the spring of 1999. Clemmons said he learned this news from God. "I just knew that she had died, before anybody else told me, because He told me." Clemmons' mother was only forty-nine. She had visited Maurice in prison, although the way he moved about, she sometimes couldn't make it. Clemmons received a six-hour furlough from prison so he could go to the funeral home—Hightower & Sons, on Liberty Street in Marianna—and see his mother's body. Lee County sheriff's deputies accompanied him. His mother's funeral was the next day; the program listed Maurice as an honorary pallbearer.

Clemmons began asking for vocational training that would be of use on the outside. "I don't want to deteriorate in this cell," he wrote one prison administrator. "Even the Lord Jesus wasn't accepted by everybody. But on the other hand, nobody is rejected by everybody. Give me an opportunity to prove that my change is real. Take a chance on me." He wrote to the warden at Varner: "During these ten years of my incarceration I have done nothing with my life that I consider productive and that will help me in my adjustment to society. I am 27 years old and it is time for me to do something with my life!"

With his legal appeals at a dead end, Clemmons also began preparing paperwork for the one option he had left, the one option that could set him free while still a young man: Appeal to the governor for mercy.

3

AN ACT OF GRACE

IN THE FIRST WEEKS OF 2000, Maurice Clemmons' application for executive clemency made its way to Little Rock, landing on the desk of Arkansas Governor Mike Huckabee. Clemmons' application would not have occasioned special notice. His crimes were not notorious, his name was not well known. Huckabee received about twelve hundred clemency applications a year, including dozens from killers and rapists, some on Death Row.

The state's Post-Prison Transfer Board, known less formally as the parole board, had already reviewed Clemmons' application. By a 5-0 vote, the board recommended that Huckabee say yes, that he commute Clemmons' sentence so Clemmons could be eligible for parole. From the date of that recommendation—January 13, 2000—Huckabee had 120 days to decide whether to grant or deny.

Huckabee, a Baptist minister from the small town of Hope, had been governor now for three-and-a-half years. He worked in the Arkansas Capitol Building, his office in the northeast corner of the second floor. Like every state capitol, Arkansas' is a living museum, with history and stories everywhere. The capitol building—neo-classical, dome, cupola, gold leaf, stained glass—was finished in 1915, after considerable delay and a whiff of scandal. Six state lawmakers were indicted on bribery charges connected to its construction, although only Senator Frank Butt was convicted. The land the capitol sits on used to be home to a penitentiary. But owing to the acreage's value, the state moved the inmates to prison farms. Two hundred prisoners stayed behind to help build the capitol, replacing metal bars with Ionic columns. Convict labor is cheap.

History also graces the capitol grounds, alongside the purpleleaf plums, the crape myrtles, the sweetbay magnolias. There are monuments to Confederate soldiers and Confederate women, and memorials to the hundreds of Arkansans killed in Vietnam and to the dozens of Congressional Medal of Honor recipients. Sculpture honors the Little Rock Nine, those African-American students who enrolled at Central High School in 1957, a defining stand of the Civil Rights Era. Another memorial, a graceful bend of rock, lists more than two hundred law-enforcement officers killed in the line of duty. They include officers from Hot Springs, Fort Smith, Bentonville, DeQueen and Texarkana; deputies from the counties of Craighead, Jackson, Clay, Miller and Woodruff. Each May a service is held at this memorial, with the names of any officers killed during the preceding year added to the roll.

For years Clemmons had nurtured the belief that he had been wronged, that forces had conspired against him—race, history, poverty, place—and that he would never catch a break. In one respect that psychological evaluation had nailed him: "may feel at the mercy of circumstances … they see themselves as having little responsibility for having produced their problems … failures may be blamed on others." But whether Clemmons realized it or not, he had caught a break now.

In some ways, Huckabee was just another in a long line of governors, part of the political cycle that churns away—out with the old, in with the new, even if the new happens to resemble nothing quite so much as the long ago. The governor's work space served as symbol. When Huckabee moved in, he complained of how awful the offices looked. He put in carpet. Applied baby-blue paint. Glued wallpaper on the ceiling—a star pattern, gold and brown. When Huckabee moved out, his successor moved in—and complained of how awful the place looked. He pulled out the carpet. (Look: Hardwood floors!) Stripped the paint. And he didn't much care for that wallpaper. "Get rid of that and just paint the ceiling white or something," he said.

But in other ways Huckabee departed dramatically from the course adopted by his state and country. Take his views toward criminal justice. In one of his books, *From Hope to Higher Ground*, Huckabee wrote: "Being tough on crime is certainly more popular than being soft, but America needs to be careful that in our attempt to stoutly enforce our laws and protect our citizens, we do not end up with a system that is based more on revenge than restoration."

For inmates, clemency is typically a long shot. Let's say Clemmons had filed his application ten years before—when the governor wasn't Mike Huckabee but another man from Hope, Bill Clinton. Yes, Clinton connected with the black community. He exuded empathy. He spoke of social justice. But if Clemmons' application had landed on Governor Clinton's desk in 1990, his plea would have been dead on arrival.

Clinton was a man who did the political calculus—particularly the Clinton of 1990, the more seasoned executive on his second tour through the governor's mansion. The year before, a legislator-lawyer named Cliff Hoofman asked Clinton to grant clemency to Robert Baggett, a convicted murderer. Hoofman, a fellow Democrat who once served as Clinton's floor leader in the state Senate, summarized their meeting in a memo: "Was advised by him that he would pardon Robert either upon 1) an announcement that he does not intend to seek political office or 2) after the November election in 1990 if he does seek political office." Clinton never issued that pardon. He had learned that clemency equals risk.

Huckabee and Clinton may have come from the same town, but they took different paths out. Clinton was a lawyer, Huckabee a preacher. Clinton was a Democrat, Huckabee a Republican—and not some moderate Republican, but a Republican who opposed abortion, no exception for rape or incest; a Republican who opposed civil unions for gays; a Republican who wanted creationism taught in the public schools. But for all of Huckabee's conservative credentials, Clemmons could not have picked a better governor to review his application—more likely to sympathize with his background, to hear the notes he played, to brave clemency's perils. Huckabee called himself a "grace" Christian, not a "law" Christian, and what was clemency but an act of grace?

Clemency fell outside the strictures of the legal system—an act of mercy that, in the words of one law professor, could be granted "for a good reason, a bad reason, or no reason at all." By the turn of the century, many legal experts in the United States fretted about clemency's decline. In a country with an exploding prison population—where states embraced one rigid sentencing mechanism after another: three strikes, mandatory minimums, truth in sentencing—they believed clemency, with its allowance for exceptions, was needed more than ever. To these experts, Huckabee stood as a potential champion for a cause in urgent need of one. He was "a tiny glimmer of hope."

February passed without any decision on Clemmons' application. So did the first weeks of March.

For governors, few powers produce such immediate, unalterable consequence as clemency. Clemency can determine life or death, or set someone free, or eradicate a person's criminal history. Yet when it comes to the power's exercise, governors remain on their own. Clemency, more often than not, is whatever they want to make it.

In Texas, George W. Bush took a pinched view, with no accounting for mercy. He approached clemency like an appellate court, insisting upon evidence of innocence or violations of due process. If he saw neither, his answer was no. That was his answer to Karla Faye Tucker, condemned for hacking a man and woman to death. The sincerity of Tucker's remorse—along with her conversion to Christianity and exemplary prison record—attracted supporters from Newt Gingrich to Pat Robertson. When Tucker was executed in 1998, Robertson called it "an act of barbarism." The next year, Darrell Mease came up for execution in Missouri. A triple murderer whose victims included a paraplegic, Mease was no one's idea of a sympathetic figure. But Pope John Paul II happened to be passing through St. Louis—and happened to stop and talk to Missouri Governor Mel Carnahan after services at St. Louis Cathedral—and the governor, when asked by the pope to show mercy to Mease, happened to believe his answer should be yes. When Carnahan spared Mease's life, Mease's lawyer exclaimed: "It's a miracle!"

Clemency, defined broadly, refers to an executive action that relieves the consequences of a criminal conviction. Its forms include commutation and pardon. A commutation reduces a sentence while preserving the conviction; a pardon strikes the conviction altogether. Because pardons often get granted after a sentence has been served, they tend to be more common—and less contentious—than commutations. A pardon need not derive from a belief in innocence. A governor might pardon someone simply to lift restrictions that accompany a conviction—for example, the inability to secure a commercial driver's license.

Clemency "is a sort of living fossil that has really changed very little over the course of thousands of years," writes law professor Daniel Kobil of Capital University Law School in Columbus, Ohio. In ancient Babylon, the Code of Hammurabi declared that a wife "surprised with another man"—that is, caught cheating—"shall be tied and thrown into the water." But if she was a slave, the king could pardon her. The Greeks had clemency. So did the Roman Empire (Caesar was said to be generous) and the British Crown. The United States cast off royalty but retained clemency. Without it, Alexander Hamilton wrote, "justice would wear a countenance too sanguinary and cruel."

The motives behind clemency have varied throughout history. A grant could be political—say, to quell an uprising. It could be profitable; some kings sold pardons. It could acquire shades of Faust. As governor of California, Pat Brown denied one Death Row inmate's plea in order to secure a legislator's vote on a farm bill. But in the classical sense, the purpose of clemency is captured in one word—*mercy*, however defined by the emperor, king, president or governor. Clemency accounts for intangibles outside the judicial system. When Governor Bush removed mercy from clemency's sweep, he was an exception to history.

In the United States, clemency used to be an integral feature of the political landscape. Now it's threatening to fade away. Legal commentators apply adjectives like "atrophied" and bemoan the timing: As the prison population explodes, courtesy of rigid sentencing laws, the system's safety valve, its way of making exceptions, has "shut tight." "The contemporary insistence on combining harsh punishment and little mercy is not sustainable," one commentator wrote. Several years ago, U.S. Supreme Court Justice Anthony Kennedy told the American Bar Association: "Our resources are misspent, our punishments too severe, our sentences too long. ... The pardon process, of late, seems to have been drained of its moral force."

Although clemency's decline eludes exact measure—there's no repository of numbers for all states for all years—examples abound. Take Arkansas in the 1960s. In his last six years as governor, Orval Faubus commuted 533 sentences. In Winthrop Rockefeller's four years as governor, he commuted 331. Now move forward three decades. From 1995 to 2003, thirty-four states commuted 20 or fewer sentences—for the entire stretch. Faubus and Rockefeller commuted 80 to 90 sentences a year. These days a governor might commute 2.

By 1995, every governor knew the story of Willie Horton—the convicted murderer, serving life in Massachusetts, who received a weekend furlough; who never returned; who raped a woman in Maryland; and whose image destroyed Massachusetts Governor Michael Dukakis when he ran for president in 1988. A furlough isn't clemency, but it is mercy, and mercy in all its forms suffered a devastating setback. As Massachusetts' governor from 2003 to 2007, Mitt Romney didn't grant clemency once. "I get a lot of recommendations. I haven't pardoned a one," he told a radio show. Post-Willie Horton, that was par for the course in Massachusetts. The state's governors went more than ten years without granting a single commutation.

On the opposite coast, Washington state has likewise been in retreat. Chris Gregoire became governor in 2005—a moderate Democrat and former assistant attorney general with a law-and-order bent. In five years she granted clemency twenty-six times, a number Kobil calls "ridiculously low." Only two of those grants were commutations. The others were pardons. In fourteen instances Gregoire denied clemency when her five-member board—which includes two law-enforcement officers and the widow of a slain Seattle police officer—recommended mercy. For Gregoire, clemency correlates with the political calendar. Facing re-election, she granted three pardons in a year and a half. A month after winning re-election, she granted eight on a single day. Her most publicized act of mercy came with ample political cover. She commuted the life sentence of Stevan Dozier, an inmate sentenced under the three-strikes law even though all three convictions were for purse snatching. Dozier's petition had broad, bipartisan support; his backers included King County's Republican prosecutor and the conservative talk-show host who championed the three-strikes law.

In 2006, Barry Massey asked Gregoire for clemency. His case, one that received national attention, epitomized the tough choices a governor can face. At the age of thirteen, Massey was still scared of the dark. A shy sixth-grader, he dreaded being called to the front of class for book reports, his confidence shot ever since he had to repeat first grade. He was in and out of special education with an IQ of about eighty. He spent his allowance—earned sweeping pine needles off the roof—on posters of football and basketball stars. He dreamed of becoming a star himself, but was not a leader on his sports teams. "He was and is a follower," a teacher later wrote. Massey's mother and father split while he was in elementary school. He was close to his grandmother, but a family move took her away. Into the void stepped Michael Harris, an older neighborhood boy who had found trouble with the law several times before leaving middle school. Two years older than Massey, Harris flattered him with attention. A follower found a leader.

In December 1986, Harris asked Massey to help him burglarize the home of an elderly woman on Harris' paper route. After climbing through a window, Massey watched Harris steal a gun and money. When the two discovered the woman was home, they pushed her down and fled. A month later, Massey helped Harris rob a tackle shop in the town of Steilacoom. Massey hoped to use the money to buy candy and Garbage Pail Kids cards. The two walked into the shop on January 10, 1987. What happened inside remains in dispute to this day. The owner, a Taiwanese immigrant named Paul Wang, wound up being killed, shot in the head and stabbed with a fishing knife. Massey, questioned by police afterward, took the blame for the shooting and stabbing; he later recanted, saying Harris was responsible.

Despite their ages at the time of the crime—Massey was thirteen, Harris was fifteen—the two were tried as adults. At separate trials, both were convicted. Massey was sentenced to life without parole—becoming, at the time, the country's youngest person to receive such a sentence. Entering the penitentiary system at fifteen, Massey accumulated thirty-two major infractions in his first eight years. But then he turned it around—going fourteen years without a single write-up. "What I realized was that I needed to start accepting my role in the crime, accepting the fact that I had a hand in the death of a man," Massey wrote. "When you participate in taking something so precious, you've got to give back so much."

Massey earned his GED. Took community-college courses. Developed expertise as a sheet metal fabricator, among other vocational skills. He mentored other inmates and, for years, counseled at-risk teenagers brought into the prison. When Massey asked for clemency, fourteen prison guards and administrators signed letters of support, including Shane Zey, a self-described right-wing Republican, a proponent of the death penalty and the son of a police officer. "If Barry Massey were to be granted clemency and moved in next door to me, I would greet him with open arms and welcome him to the neighborhood and not lose a minute of sleep over it," Zey wrote. "Award him clemency. Give him a chance. He has paid for his crime and he's earned it!"

Massey's petition went before the state's Clemency and Pardons Board in October 2006. His lawyers detailed changes in state law that, if applied to Massey's case, would have led to a sentence of about twenty-five years. The victim's family opposed Massey's request. Jonathan Wang, Paul Wang's son, wrote: "I'm a good person. My sister is a good person. My mother is a good person. My father was a good person. You were a bad person who made several bad choices on my family's behalf and you might or might not be a good person now and might or might not be a good person in the future. You want to walk free after 20 years. For the rest of us, nothing changes."

The board recommended clemency, by a vote of 4-1. But five months later, Gregoire turned down Massey's petition. Her denial provided no explanation.

Mike Huckabee became the forty-fourth governor of Arkansas in July 1996; he left office in January 2007. In his ten-and-a-half years as chief executive of Arkansas, Huckabee emerged as a political force, an ordained minister who could draw voters from across the spectrum, blending fluency with Scripture with such progressive causes as improved health care for poor children. In a state dominated by Democrats, Huckabee won re-election twice. Neither race was close.

In 1999, the year before he received Clemmons' plea for mercy, Huckabee commuted the death sentence of Bobby Ray Fretwell, a murderer who shot an eighty-one-year-old farmer in the head and stole his truck. A juror in Fretwell's case asked Huckabee to intercede, saying he had voted for death out of fear of being ostracized if he didn't because he shared the same hometown as the murder victim. In sparing Fretwell, Huckabee became the first Arkansas governor in nearly thirty years to stop an execution. "I have prayed and sought God's help with this decision," Huckabee told reporters. "I had rather face the anger of the people than the wrath of God."

Huckabee subsequently gave speeches on "restorative justice" in which he returned to these themes. Speaking in Florida, he said Fretwell "had not one advocate save his own attorney. There was no particular public support for him. But I also knew this: If justice didn't work for him, how could I say it worked for anybody? And I was reminded of what Jesus said, 'Inasmuch as you have done it unto the least of these my brethren you have done it unto me.'" Huckabee told a Little Rock audience: "If one acts by pure raw political instinct and a pure Machiavellian approach to public office, you'll never ever, ever, ever, ever grant clemency. … Ultimately, my life will not be judged by voters who can be swayed by 30 seconds of television. The ultimate evaluation of my life will be made by a God who will look at every breath I took from birth to death, and I want him to evaluate my life by the totality of it, not by any one moment."

Huckabee's candid infusion of religion came with a political benefit. Candidates cannot afford to be labeled soft on crime—but neither can they survive being distant from church. Huckabee established competing storylines. Sympathetic to criminals? Huckabee could say he was attuned to the wishes of God.

The governor's faith—and his belief in forgiveness—colored his handling of clemency applications. So did the shame he felt at how blacks had been treated in his state. After tagging along with Huckabee, *Newsweek* reporters wrote: "He speaks emotionally about the legacy of Jim Crow and the dangers of ignoring lingering racism." Before going into politics, Huckabee integrated his church congregation in Pine Bluff. After going into politics, Huckabee remained alert to racial disparities in criminal cases. "He saw that everyone makes mistakes, everyone can be rehabilitated," says Cory Cox, Huckabee's clemency adviser for two years. "He believed racism is real, especially for people sentenced in the 1960s and 1970s who got disproportionate sentences based on the color of their skin. I think he thought he would be derelict in his duty if he didn't see justice was done."

Huckabee's three immediate predecessors in the governor's mansion were Bill Clinton, Frank White and Jim Guy Tucker. Collectively, they granted clemency 507 times in seventeen-and-a-half years. Huckabee? By himself, he granted twice that many: 1,033. Clinton might have pumped those numbers up, had political consequence not intervened. In his first stint as governor, Clinton commuted the sentences of 67 inmates in two years. One of them, a murderer, went on to kill again. Made to pay politically, Clinton lost re-election. The next time around, he apologized and told voters he'd learned his lesson. Clinton returned to the governor's office—and, in ten years, commuted only 8 sentences. Huckabee? In his ten-and-a-half years, he commuted 163. Clinton became so determined to shuck any soft-on-crime label that, in 1992, while running for president, he refused to halt the execution of Ricky Ray Rector. Rector had killed two men, including a police officer. Afterward, he shot himself in the head. The bullet destroyed his frontal lobe, performing, in effect, a lobotomy. At his final meal before execution, Rector told jailers he was saving his pecan pie "for later."

Huckabee's willingness to risk voter backlash made him a source of inspiration to many legal scholars who specialized in clemency. But in Arkansas, opposition mounted. That's predictable, to an extent. But unfortunately for Huckabee—and unfortunately for the cause he championed, clemency vigorous and true, not pale and scared—the criticism wasn't all of the knee-jerk variety. Much of it was grounded and fair; it was also avoidable, had Huckabee simply handled matters differently.

Outside Arkansas, Huckabee would eventually develop an image marbled with enviable attributes. People would remark on how kind he was. And charming. And self-effacing. He was a man of faith, without the self-righteousness, a man of belief, without the heat. "I'm a conservative, but I'm not mad at anybody about it," he would say. But in Arkansas, some people saw a different man. Petulant, bordering on childish. Churlish—quick to take offense, and to strike back. And secretive, slow to disclose records, wont to destroy them. In Huckabee's handling of clemency applications, these unflattering traits came to the fore.

For years, Huckabee refused to explain why he granted clemency in particular cases. He said if he did, other inmates would tailor their applications accordingly. This stance maddened prosecutors and victim-rights groups. It also made little sense. If Huckabee found certain qualities laudable—for example, exemplary behavior in prison—why shouldn't other inmates know? Why shouldn't they emulate those qualities? Huckabee's silence had the benefit of not boxing him in, of letting him slide away from attacks of cronyism or inconsistency.

The *Arkansas Democrat-Gazette* published an investigative story in 2004 that analyzed Huckabee's 111 commutations up to that point. Based on interviews and previously undisclosed records, the newspaper's research suggested that inmates seeking clemency from Huckabee stood a better chance if:

"The justice system treated them more harshly than most.

"They know a person who has known the governor.

"They worked at the Governor's Mansion.

"A minister intercedes for them."

Huckabee rejected more than nine out of every ten clemency requests. But anecdotal evidence gave skeptics plenty to work with. He granted clemency to James Maxwell and Willie Way Jr., convicted murderers who worked as trusties in the governor's home. He granted clemency to Donald Clark, a burglar whose stepmother worked in the Governor's Office. (Huckabee refused to say when he had learned that Clark was related to a staffer—but said if reporters reported the things he wanted them to report, maybe he'd reconsider.) He granted clemency to Keith Richards for a long-ago reckless driving conviction, after meeting the famed guitarist at a Rolling Stones concert. He granted clemency to Eugene Fields, a wealthy developer and major GOP donor. Fields was in prison after being convicted of driving while intoxicated four times in less than five years. When a Mothers Against Drunk Driving official wrote Huckabee and questioned his decision, he chided her for making the letter public and for fanning "the flames of controversy that have been stirred in this case by the unusual curiosity of certain media members." After being freed, Fields was arrested twice more for DWI; each time he nearly hit an oncoming vehicle, one of them a police car.

In his book *From Hope to Higher Ground*, Huckabee wrote: "Fortunately, no one to whom I granted clemency got out to commit murder, but obviously anyone who violates again can be a real embarrassment."

People couldn't help but notice how Huckabee repeatedly granted clemency in cases where church leaders made personal appeals. Four ministers interceded on behalf of John Henry Claiborne, a murderer granted clemency by Huckabee in 2004. One, the Reverend Charles Williams of the Covenant of Zion Cathedral Church, said he helped win "many, many" clemencies from Huckabee. In 2004 Huckabee said he planned to grant clemency to convicted murderer Glen Martin

Green, who beat an eighteen-year-old woman with nunchucks, drove over her head with his Ford Thunderbird, then dumped her body in a creek. The Reverend Johnny Jackson called Green a "wonderful Christian man" and told Huckabee that he had investigated the case and had become convinced the killing was an accident. Jackson didn't read the police file. Nor did he interview the case's lead detective, Don Egelhoff. "As far as I'm concerned, the good reverend is full of shit," Egelhoff told an Arkansas newspaper. In the Green case, Huckabee reversed himself once criticism spiraled.

But the case that would most haunt Huckabee—his first Willie Horton moment, in one commentator's words—was that of Wayne DuMond, a man convicted in 1985 of raping a distant cousin of Bill Clinton's. Everything about the case was steeped in political intrigue, doubt and whispers. While DuMond awaited trial, masked men broke into his home and castrated him with a knife. At least that was DuMond's account. (Some folks wondered if he mutilated himself.) The sheriff placed DuMond's testicles in a jar and showed them off, before flushing them down the toilet. The conspiracy-minded took up DuMond's cause, calling him an innocent victim of Clinton's political influence. Taking office, Huckabee said he intended to commute DuMond's sentence, calling the evidence of guilt "very questionable." After a public uprising, Huckabee reversed that decision. But in 1997 the parole board agreed to release DuMond; at least two members later said Huckabee lobbied them on DuMond's behalf in a private meeting that appeared to violate the state's freedom of information law. Huckabee denied applying any influence.

DuMond moved to Missouri in August 2000. The next month he sexually assaulted and murdered thirty-nine-year-old Carol Sue Shields. He was also suspected of killing a second woman but died in prison before those charges could be filed. Afterward, Huckabee said he now believed DuMond was guilty of the Arkansas rape and wished he hadn't been released. "Absolutely," he said. "How could you not?" Deborah Suttlar, a member of the parole board during the DuMond controversy, says Huckabee made the case a litmus test for the people in charge. If a parole-board member didn't support DuMond, Huckabee would not re-appoint that person to the board—and the job is a plum, paying close to seventy thousand dollars a year. "That changed the process," Suttlar says. "It is an independent board, and then it is not."

For Huckabee, the controversy surrounding specific cases threatened to muffle his legitimate concerns about the criminal justice system. He cringed at the state's prison numbers. In his decade as governor, the inmate population vaulted from about eight thousand to fourteen thousand. "It's not our goal to just lock people up," he said. "It is our goal to unlock their hearts, minds and souls so while they're here they can learn the skills that most of us take for granted." He couldn't stomach the unfair advantages that accompanied money and class. "If you have Johnnie Cochran as a lawyer, you're probably going to turn out better than if you have some public defender," he said. And when he chastised prosecutors who embraced rigid formula—for example, never supporting clemency for violent offenders—he had a point. Clemency is all about exceptions. A public official who makes no room for them weakens his voice.

But other people had equally legitimate concerns about Huckabee's approach to clemency. Too often, his announcements were met with surprise. People who should have been notified about a clemency request—and asked for their input— would be overlooked or ignored. The board that made clemency recommendations did a lousy job of screening cases; the basis for its vote would typically be reduced to a few cryptic lines, scribbled by hand and forwarded to the governor. Huckabee's lack of transparency left people to guess at his motives and criteria. But when these concerns were voiced—and they were voiced often—Huckabee responded with playground tactics. He made it personal, dismissing critics as publicity seekers. When one prosecutor, Robert Herzfeld, wrote Huckabee about flaws in his handling of clemency cases, Huckabee's chief aide wrote back: "The governor read your letter and laughed out loud. He wanted me to respond to you. I wish you success as you cut down on your caffeine consumption."

Herzfeld filed a lawsuit in 2004 challenging Huckabee's grant of clemency to Donald Jeffers, a convicted murderer who had beaten a man to death with his own prosthetic leg. Herzfeld claimed the state failed to solicit input—as required by law—from the local prosecutor and that the victim's family hadn't been notified. The state's attorney general conceded the error, and Jeffers' clemency was voided. Afterward, Huckabee announced he would change his ways. From now on, he said, more attention would be paid to notifying people and inviting input. The board would improve its investigation of clemency requests. And Huckabee would explain his reasons for granting mercy. "As I review the whole hullabaloo over this thing the past few months, the truth is I could have handled it better; I should have handled it better," Huckabee said.

Huckabee released criteria he would consider while reviewing clemency petitions and listed these reasons for granting clemency: "remarkable signs of rehabilitation" … compelling evidence showing "an injustice committed at trial" … "a terminal or substantially debilitating medical condition." He also left room for other reasons left undefined. If a petition showed merit, Huckabee would consider other factors—among them, the chances that the inmate would commit another crime.

When Huckabee reviewed Maurice Clemmons' application in early 2000, those changes in procedure were not yet in place. Instead, Clemmons' request traveled a path marked by cryptic notes, private files, unspoken criteria and a string of personal connections.

The seven-member parole board investigated clemency petitions by dispatching a single member to interview the petitioner in prison and to review the inmate's prison history. The board member who interviewed Clemmons was August Pieroni, a retired sheriff of Union County, which is in the state's southern reaches, bordering Louisiana. Other board members viewed Pieroni as moderate-conservative—not an easy mark for someone selling tales of redemption or victimhood. "Pieroni was tough," fellow board member Deborah Suttlar says. Whatever Pieroni discussed with Clemmons inside the Tucker prison—and Pieroni is now dead, so there's no saying—Pieroni came away believing Clemmons' sentence should be commuted. When Pieroni presented his recommendation to four other members of the board, they all went along, including Suttlar. "I know why the board voted in favor: August Pieroni sponsored it," Suttlar says. "And he took it seriously. Whatever he saw in the interview, it convinced him."

But while the board supported Clemmons' request, the paperwork it forwarded to the governor provided little explanation for the 5-0 vote. On a worksheet, the board reduced the basis for its recommendation to these handwritten words: "cousin—brother—present—said he was sixteen years at the time—been in eleven years—would have a job—judge recommends." This worksheet was silent on such matters as which cousin and brother it was, and what they said, if anything. On another matter the form misled. "Would have a job." Prison records said this was something that still needed to be arranged. Maybe Clemmons would have a job, maybe he wouldn't.

The packet from the parole board was also thin in other respects. Under Arkansas law, copies of a clemency application were supposed to be filed with the sheriff of the county in which the crime was committed; the prosecutor; the circuit judge who presided at trial (or that judge's successor); and the victim of the crime or the victim's next of kin. But the records forwarded to Huckabee included no correspondence with the prosecutor, sheriff or Clemmons' victims. Pulaski County's top prosecutor, Larry Jegley, subsequently searched for any evidence his office had been notified—and came up empty. Had Jegley been apprised of Clemmons' plea, he almost certainly would have objected. He had a standing policy of opposing clemency for all violent offenders—a category that would have encompassed Clemmons.

The only response in the file came from a circuit judge—and the judge wasn't Floyd Lofton, the man who had presided at four trials for Clemmons, but Marion Humphrey. Clemmons' luck went beyond the man now in the Governor's Office. It extended to the man now sitting in Pulaski County Circuit Court, in the seat once occupied by Lofton. Lofton retired in 1992. Humphrey, by election, took his spot—and, in accordance with Arkansas law, received the notice of Clemmons' application. What would Lofton's response have been, had he still been on the bench? "In this case I would have objected strenuously," Lofton says. He would have written the parole board and pointed out that Clemmons was a habitual offender—and that he had been given repeated chances to negotiate a plea but had insisted on his innocence. "If he wanted less time, he had an opportunity to get less time. The offer was always there, and he refused it. He refused to mitigate his own damages," Lofton says. "It became apparent that Mr. Clemmons never learned his lesson."

Over the years, Humphrey has held a remarkable array of positions. Newspaper reporter and editor. Arkansas assistant attorney general. Aide to former Congresswoman Shirley Chisholm. Intern for former U.S. Senator J. William Fulbright. In the 1990s Humphrey considered joining the race for U.S. Senate; had he run and won, he would have been Arkansas' first black U.S. senator. He has also held a number of religious posts. Associate minister of Pleasant Hill Baptist Church in Roxbury, Massachusetts. State director for prison fellowship in Arkansas. Chaplain of the Judicial Council of the National Bar Association.

Although Humphrey didn't preside at Clemmons' trials—he wasn't the judge when Clemmons threw the lock and made threats and hid the metal hinge in his sock—Humphrey had become familiar with the cases during Clemmons' appeal. It was Humphrey who had ordered a new trial on two felony counts, only to be reversed by the Arkansas Supreme Court. When Humphrey received notice of Clemmons' clemency application, he wrote back: "I favor a time cut for Maurice Clemmons. Mr. Clemmons was 16 years of age when his cases began in this court. I do not know why the previous judge ran his sentences consecutively, but concurrent sentences would have been sufficient."

Humphrey also had connections to the parole board. The board's chairman, Leroy Brownlee, was an elder in Humphrey's church. Humphrey says he "very well could have" talked with Brownlee about the Clemmons case. Because Brownlee rarely grants interviews about his work on the board—and he refused to answer questions in this instance—his role and possible influence can become fodder for speculation. And that's what has happened in the Clemmons case. Max Brantley, editor of the alternative weekly *Arkansas Times* and a longtime political observer, says: "Why did the parole board let him go? Why? Everyone thinks it was Brownlee."

The state's restrictive public-records laws make it difficult to know just what Huckabee saw when he reviewed Clemmons' petition. The governor's staff prepared summaries of clemency applications for Huckabee's review—but under the banner of executive-records exemption, Arkansas placed such files outside the public's reach. At the time, letters sent directly to the governor—and not to the parole board—also received confidentiality, allowing personal appeals regarding clemency petitions to be made in private.

But Clemmons' own writings remained a matter of public record. When he filled out his clemency application, Clemmons indicated he was seeking a commutation, not a pardon. The form listed four reasons that might support a sentence reduction and asked him which applied. Clemmons checked three: "I wish to correct an injustice which may have occurred during the trial"; "I want to adjust what may be considered an excessive sentence"; "My institutional adjustment has been exemplary."

The form asked: "What is your reason for requesting executive clemency at this time?"

"Mercy," Clemmons wrote.

Clemmons also wrote a letter to Huckabee, as part of his application. He started with: "There is absolutely no excuse/justification whatsoever for my past criminal behavior." Clemmons emphasized his youth at the time of the crimes. "I succumbed to the peer pressure … and fell in with the wrong crowd." He said he came from "a very good Christian family" and was "ashamed to this day" for what he'd done to his family's name. He wrote in rhyme, saying "where once stood a young sixteen-year-old misguided fool, whose own life he was unable to rule," now stood a twenty-seven-year-old man who had learned to "respect the rights of others … and not to follow a multitude to do evil." He wrote: "The angel of death has visited and taken away my dear sweet mother." He wrote: "I have never done anything good for God, but I've prayed for him to grant me in his compassion the Grace to make a good start. Now, I'm humbly appealing to you for a brand new start." He wrote: "I Pray you will be compassionate to my situation and have mercy upon me … God Bless You for your time and consideration. It is so prayed!"

Writing to Huckabee, Clemmons played the same notes he had summoned while writing to Humphrey two years before, a hymn of the remorseful Christian in search of mercy. He also glossed over his prison disciplinary history: "My institutional record will reflect that I have had problems. Yet, nonetheless, it will also reflect that change has occurred."

Because the parole board had forwarded next-to-nothing on Clemmons' background to Huckabee—no abstracts, summaries, disciplinary totals—it would have fallen to the governor and his staff to sift through the prison system's enormous file on Clemmons to test the credibility of his plea. That kind of search would have revealed how ludicrous it was for Clemmons to check the box: "My institutional adjustment has been exemplary." His institutional adjustment had been abysmal. And his claim that he had turned himself around? Underwhelming. When Clemmons filled out his clemency application in June 1999, his last disciplinary episode was only eighteen months in the past. A search of Clemmons' file would also have revealed how his letter's expressions of shame and referrals to prayer were such rare and recent phenomena. His exclamation points did not usually follow "It is so prayed!" They followed: "The whole thing was a conspiracy against me!" "I'm tired of being held down!" "Hell No!"

In years to come Huckabee would be asked how much he knew about Clemmons' prison history while weighing his request. Huckabee would tell CNN: "I read the entire file ... It was a file this thick ... I looked at the file, every bit of it." Every bit of it? That seems unlikely. By 2000, Clemmons' prison file already exceeded a thousand pages. But if Huckabee did read every bit of it, he would have seen a record—dated October 21, 1999—that boiled Clemmons' stay in prison down to this damning score sheet:

Disciplinaries: Twenty-nine times
Achievements: None

Clemmons' application would have presented Huckabee not with a clear choice but with a confounding mix of good and bad.

These factors worked in Clemmons' favor: His sentence, without question, seemed not to fit the crimes he'd committed. Even under the state's Byzantine formula for parole eligibility, he wouldn't have been a candidate for release until he was in his forties or fifties. Also: His background would have resonated with the governor. When Huckabee talked of sentencing disparities traceable to paid-versus-public defense and to class and neighborhood—and that's one word Huckabee liked to use, "neighborhood," a soft synonym for race—he could have offered Clemmons' sentence as Exhibit No. 1. Plus: Clemmons had Humphrey's support. He could hardly have asked for a better endorsement. Humphrey was both a judge *and* a minister.

And working against him? His disciplinary record, along with the venom in so many of his prison letters. Huckabee told reporters he looked for evidence of "true remorse" and rehabilitation: "It's more about what the inmates do in prison than about what they say." By that measure, Clemmons would have failed. No testimonials from prison guards or wardens—no letters saying, *I'd be happy to have him live next door to me*—accompanied Clemmons' application to the parole board. When Huckabee commuted the sentence of convicted rapist James "Bubba" Scott, Scott had only one disciplinary violation in thirty-plus years. Scott could claim rehabilitation. Clemmons, by comparison, had twenty-nine violations in just eleven years.

In Arkansas, mercy is a two-step process. First, the governor declares his intention to grant clemency, giving the public the chance to respond. Then, if there's no change of mind, the governor signs a proclamation making it official. In the Clemmons case, Huckabee announced his decision on March 30. His answer was yes. He planned to commute Clemmons' sentence. But *announced* might be too strong of a word. This was no high-profile case. There was no throng awaiting word. The same day Huckabee acted in the Clemmons case, the governor signed a proclamation summoning the state legislature into special session to decide how Arkansas would spend its tobacco-settlement dollars. Plus, the capitol building caught fire—a small fire, extinguished by water sprayed down a utility shaft. Those events made the newspaper. Clemmons did not.

Floyd Lofton, the judge who had presided over all those trials, didn't know Clemmons was about to receive clemency. He wouldn't learn that until nine years later, when he received a telephone call from a newspaper reporter in Seattle.

The clemency became official on May 2, 2000, when Huckabee signed an order that commuted the sentences for four of Clemmons' eight felony convictions. Those four accounted for 95 of the 108 years that Clemmons had been ordered to serve. The effect was to make Clemmons immediately eligible for parole. Again, nothing appeared in the newspapers. Coverage was instead devoted to Arkansas' first execution of a woman in 155 years—an execution that took place the same day Clemmons received mercy. The woman, Christina Marie Riggs, hadn't asked for mercy, saying she didn't deserve it. Instead, she'd begged for forgiveness.

Ten days after Huckabee signed the clemency proclamation for Clemmons, the governor attended the annual ceremony at the state's memorial for fallen law-enforcement officers. He expressed thanks that no new names were added this year. "The loss of even one officer is too many," Huckabee said. "We can all sleep safely in our homes because law-enforcement officers go out each night to patrol our streets. We remain safe and free to live our lives because of those willing to put themselves in danger on our behalf."

For Clemmons, one obstacle remained. He still had to convince the parole board to release him. Two weeks after Huckabee signed that proclamation, Clemmons received a certificate showing he had completed an anger-management program. It took him eleven years, but now he could offer at least one achievement.

The parole board—the same board that earlier recommended clemency—now asked the prosecutor's office for its input on Clemmons' potential release. Jegley's office responded with three words: "Object to parole." It didn't matter. In July, the board agreed to parole Clemmons. The vote was again 5-0. Cryptic as ever, the board's handwritten comments were: "Said he just wants the opportunity. Is not same person he was when he came in." Clemmons' Uncle Ray—Maurice's childhood friend who grew up to be a prison guard—would have agreed with that assessment, although maybe not in the way the writer intended. Those eleven years in the Arkansas prison system changed Maurice, Ray says. "He was a different guy. Maurice had a prison mentality. He grew up in prison, where you got to be a man or a girl."

The same month the parole board voted for Clemmons' early release, a corrections employee filled out a parole risk-assessment form for Clemmons. The form listed fourteen predictors and assigned a numerical value to each. For having a prior theft conviction, Clemmons received three points. For having a prior burglary conviction, four points. For being so young when he was first arrested, three points. The list went on and on. Clemmons finished with thirty points—putting him in the scale's highest category of risk, scoring him among those most likely to return to a life of violence.

He was released from prison the following month.

4

A NEW LIFE UP NORTH

MAURICE CLEMMONS HAD HIS SECOND CHANCE, courtesy of the governor and the parole board. But making something of that chance was another matter. Clemmons faced all the choices and challenges that await the newly released felon—fall back or go straight, and if you go straight, how? Clemmons' adult years had been spent in prison. Without so much as a GED, he had few credentials to offer the workforce.

After being paroled from the Arkansas prison system in August 2000, Clemmons landed a job at a slaughterhouse, working on the kill floor. But the job lasted only months. Clemmons told state officials that he quit, without saying why. He may also have held other jobs in Arkansas—tow-truck driver, auto-body worker, dishwasher—from what he wrote on employment forms.

In 2001 Clemmons traveled to the Puget Sound area of Washington. By then he had lots of family in Washington, lots of people to visit. One night he chanced upon an attractive woman, in her late twenties, while in a nightclub in Seattle's Pioneer Square, a historic neighborhood with an edgy nightlife. Her name was Nicole Smith. A graduate of West Seattle's Chief Sealth High School, Smith had two children—a twelve-year-old son and a four-year-old daughter—and a work history that included stints at a transmission rebuild center and as a manicurist. Like Clemmons, Smith took fierce pride in doing whatever it took to get by. In candid moments, talking to Clemmons on the phone, she'd allude to a past that involved making money in ways that went beyond filing and shaping nails. "I did what I had to do to get the fuck ahead. ... I had them kids, they are mine. I'm gonna get out there and do what I gotta do, whether it be boosting, hustling, whatever. I'm gonna do it." Clemmons and Smith hit it off. Their relationship endured even when Clemmons returned south—and it wasn't long before they were telling people they were engaged.

By spring of that year, Clemmons was back home in Arkansas.

On April 22, 2001, Taurus Fletcher was in her living room in Camden, a small town in the southern part of Arkansas, in Ouachita County. Her small child was with her. So was a man named Vincent Moore. At a quarter till midnight, someone knocked. "Jay-Jay," the visitor said. Fletcher opened the door. A black man wearing white—white pants, white shirt, gloves and a fishing hat—charged into the home. He pointed a gun at Fletcher's head, then at Moore's. The gunman ordered Moore to the floor and told Fletcher to gather up all the jewelry and money in the home. She handed the gunman a plastic Walmart bag with $10,000—money she'd been given by her grandmother, according to what Fletcher later told police. The gunman ordered Fletcher outside, to start her Buick. The robber sped off in Fletcher's car, but not before Fletcher noticed a Chevy Suburban nearby, sort of lurking, if lurking is a word that can be used for a vehicle as big and indiscreet as a Suburban.

Once notified, police issued an immediate alert for both vehicles. At 12:19 a.m., a patrol car spotted the Buick and gave chase. The Buick's driver, dressed all in white, ditched the car and fled on foot into the woods. About forty minutes later, police spied the Suburban and pulled it over. The passenger, dressed all in white, was Maurice Clemmons. From Clemmons' left front pocket a deputy retrieved a Walmart bag with $10,000. Clemmons' other pockets turned up Vincent Moore's jewelry. Questioned by police, Clemmons described himself more as a banker than a robber. He said Moore owed him money for drugs, so he took the cash, jewelry and car—as collateral.

Ouachita County prosecutors charged Clemmons with two counts of aggravated robbery. And they weren't the only prosecutors with Clemmons in their sights. In March 2001—the month before the Camden holdup—a man and woman were robbed in Little Rock, part of Pulaski County. The armed robbery netted video equipment and cash. Clemmons emerged as a suspect, and Pulaski County authorities got a warrant charging him with two counts of aggravated robbery. But they had yet to serve it.

In the man-in-white case, Clemmons pleaded guilty to a single count of robbery and was sentenced to ten years. Just like that, he had validated the correctional system's prediction that he would return to crime. By September 2001 Clemmons was back at the Cummins prison farm, back on hoe squad 4, back in barracks 13. But this time, unlike his first stretch in prison, Clemmons kept his head down. He got in trouble only once, and that was for not shaving, a violation of grooming policy.

Clemmons had learned how to do time. His rules were: Don't woof. Don't disrespect. Concentrate on getting out. "In the penitentiary you don't do no talking," he'd say. "You just handle your business. Lay low, don't bother nobody, and nobody gonna bother you." If he saw some young inmate talking big, saying what he was about and what he was going to do, Clemmons would shake his head. "Everybody wants a reputation. But that gang-banging stuff, somebody gonna be waiting on him with steel." Carry yourself right, and words weren't needed. "People know a big dog. They can tell. They know who real and who ain't. It's like a dog in a yard. The others are gonna know, don't mess with that one. They'll mess with the one that's sleeping." His second go-round in prison, Clemmons secured his GED. He racked up the good-time credits and capitalized on vocational training, earning a certificate in plumbing. Clemmons also planned for his release, collecting the paperwork he'd need to move to another state.

In September 2003, the Pulaski County prosecutor's office objected to Clemmons getting parole. The office's first objection, back in 2000, had failed to sway the board. This second dissent proved just as ineffectual. In November 2003 the parole board voted 5-0 to approve Clemmons for early release. Its handwritten explanation was a confusing mishmash: "Mrs. Rodgers—Mentors in—Fiancee— Said when he left the first time he was not ready. Doesn't want to die in prison. Mrs. Rodgers said that he will try to do the right thing." Cryptic as it was, the form did make one thing clear: Clemmons would likely become another state's problem. A checkmark indicated that Clemmons was to be transferred out of state, and in the margins someone wrote "Firm," and underlined the word.

Deborah Suttlar, a former member of the Arkansas parole board, says the board took a shine to petitions from inmates who promised to leave the state. Sometimes, an inmate received parole on that basis alone.

Clemmons wanted to move to Washington state. That's where his Uncle Joe had settled a quarter century before, building a pipeline since traveled by siblings, nephews, nieces and cousins. Clemmons saw Washington as a place to escape the racism he associated with Arkansas. Washington also happened to be the home of Clemmons' fiancée, Nicole Smith. The couple's engagement had survived Clemmons' return to the penitentiary.

Washington and Arkansas belonged to an interstate compact that governed the movements of parolees between states. At first, Washington refused to accept Clemmons, saying he needed an in-state sponsor. Rickey Hinton, Clemmons' half brother, stepped into that role—and Washington signed off, even though Hinton had a rap sheet of his own, with convictions for three felonies and more than twenty misdemeanors.

Arkansas released Clemmons in March 2004, even earlier than the norm. Clemmons benefited from a law that allowed the state to exercise emergency powers and speed up release dates when its prison system reached 98 percent of capacity. By 2004, the state's penitentiary population exceeded 100 percent of capacity; more than eight hundred inmates, the overflow, were housed in county jails until extra beds became available.

The same month he left Arkansas, Clemmons checked in with a community corrections officer in the Seattle area. Now on parole, Clemmons needed to keep Washington authorities up-to-date on his whereabouts and doings. Clemmons said he wanted to find a job in plumbing and hoped to move in soon with his fiancée.

In June, Clemmons returned to Little Rock. With Nicole Smith at his side, he dropped by the Pulaski County courthouse—the same courthouse where he had stood trial so many times and been convicted so many times, the same courthouse where he had been sentenced to 108 years. This trip to the courthouse represented a chance to start anew.

By the spring of 2004, Smith was thirty-two years old. With her kids now fifteen and seven, she struggled financially; twice, she had declared bankruptcy. She couldn't pay her rent. Her car had been repossessed. Her debts approached sixty thousand dollars, with some bills four years past due. "I know what it is to have nothing," she'd tell Clemmons. "I lost everything twice." For Smith, Clemmons offered the promise of escape from all those financial worries. He'd tell her: "As long as you got Maurice, you got a gold mine. You understand, love?"

At the courthouse, Clemmons sought out Marion Humphrey—the judge and minister who had championed Clemmons' request for clemency. Humphrey believed in second chances: "We're a country that says we believe in mercy. And one of the things about our lord and savior, Jesus Christ, is that he promoted mercy. And that is a part of the makeup of some of us who serve on the benches, who serve on parole boards, who serve in the governor's office." Clemmons had blown his second chance, but Humphrey didn't know that. All he knew was that Clemmons had appeared at his chambers, with a license in hand, a woman by his side, and a simple request: That Humphrey do the honors and declare them husband and wife. "He seemed like he was a person who had gotten his head on straight," Humphrey says of Clemmons. "He was making an effort to do right." Humphrey obliged. Afterward, the newlyweds had their picture taken—Maurice in a white T-shirt with a small Nike swoosh, Nicole in a tank top adorned with the Playboy bunny.

One month after the wedding, police in Little Rock took down a robbery report. The victim of the holdup—which took place July 8, 2004—told police he'd met a man in the lobby of a Comfort Inn and struck up a conversation. The man invited the victim to "hang out" in his room, No. 212. But once there, the man pulled out a black pistol and stole a gold watch, gold ring and fourteen hundred dollars in cash. The robber then jumped into a car with another man and took off.

The crime's planning left something to be desired. When police checked with the hotel, they learned that the robber had paid for Room 212 with cash. That was smart. But then the man did something stupid. He showed the front desk his Washington state identification. The name on the ID? Maurice Clemmons. This was four months after Clemmons' second release from prison. Still, Clemmons managed to escape charges. When police asked the victim if drugs were involved, he bolted. "The victim was a drug addict and he was not a good witness, and they could not make a case against Clemmons on that one," says Little Rock police Lieutenant Terry Hastings. "The victim was the only witness, and he just wasn't a good enough witness."

For Clemmons, the breaks just kept coming. On August 9, 2004, a brief hearing was held in the courtroom of Pulaski County Circuit Judge Barry Sims. The subject was a different robbery—the one that occurred in Little Rock in 2001, the one where Clemmons was suspected of stealing video equipment and cash. When Clemmons was a teenager getting hammered with 108 years, he'd been represented by a public defender. But no more. For this case he hired Stephen Morley, a former traffic judge in North Little Rock.

Stephen Morley's family was fairly prominent in the state's legal circles. Morley's father, Dean, was a district court judge in Pulaski County. Both of Dean's sons, Stephen and Randy, had followed him onto the bench; the two brothers even wound up endowing a $10,000-a-year scholarship at the University of Arkansas at Little Rock School of Law, for students planning to practice in Pulaski County. But in 1997 the state's judicial commission filed formal disciplinary charges against Stephen Morley. He denied the charges, calling them "absurd," but then agreed to resign from the bench. Morley was accused of threatening to kill a process server ("I will find you and I will kill you, you motherfucker ...I'll hunt you down ... I will get your ass, you piece of shit"); smoking marijuana; sniffing cocaine; beating two of his wives; filing a fraudulent insurance claim; forging a signature; and lying to police. That's a partial list. After threatening to kill the process server, Morley also stuck his tongue out at him, according to the charging documents.

In this case, Clemmons was facing two charges of aggravated robbery. But Morley asked the judge to throw the charges out, arguing that authorities had all but abandoned the matter. The arrest warrant had been issued in 2001 but wasn't served until three years later, when Clemmons was getting out of prison. "An unreasonable delay," Morley's motion called it. How was Clemmons—three years after the fact—supposed to remember his exact whereabouts on March 26, 2001? Say there were witnesses who could provide Clemmons an alibi. How was he to find them now? At the hearing, the Pulaski County prosecutors agreed to drop their charges. Larry Jegley, the head of the office, says the delay in serving the warrant was one factor. But there were others, too. "We had trouble finding witnesses, and there were other proof problems that I don't care to get into," he says.

Clemmons skated. And now he had a lawyer to turn to if he got into trouble again.

When Clemmons moved to Washington in 2004, he was a thirty-two-year-old parolee with nine felony convictions, working on chance No. 3. His first job was an unlikely one. Metro Bail Bonds in Tacoma hired him to be a bounty hunter—to track down criminals who had skipped court, leaving Metro on the financial hook. "I read him as a guy that was in prison most of his life, but he wasn't too bad of a guy," says Dave Regan, the company's owner. Clemmons lasted only one month. Bringing in bail jumpers requires a certain finesse—an ability to persuade—and Clemmons was not a subtle man.

Updating his community corrections officer, Robert Martin, Clemmons described skipping from job to job. He pulled seats out of buses, worked as a plumber (a job Martin couldn't confirm), and recycled metal. He bought a Ford Econoline van to lug around equipment and started washing moss off roofs and leaves out of gutters. In early 2005 he landed a job at Nortrak, a Seattle rail-supply company. Martin checked with Clemmons' bosses and heard good things. "Doing a good job ... gets along well with other employees ... pleased with work performance." Clemmons reported working six or seven days a week, putting in seventy or eighty hours, pulling down raises and paying off debts. But after ten months or so, he quit. He was on to something new, a business to call his own, and in December 2005 he showed Martin the business cards he'd ordered. "Owner: Mr. Maurice Clemmons," the card said at the top.

Sea-Wash
Pressure Washing/Landscaping
Licensed Bonded and Insured
Residential, Commercial, All Cement, Gutters, Siding, Houses, Landscaping,
Clean Ups and More

Picturing a tractor in one corner and a palm tree in the other, the card looked good, though what a palm tree had to do with the Pacific Northwest was anyone's guess. The company's Web site enhanced the sense of professionalism, assuring customers that Sea-Wash took pains to protect their sensitive financial information, saying the data was "encrypted and transmitted to us in a secure way." "He was determined to be successful," says Chrisceda Clemmons, an aunt of Maurice's who lived in Seattle. "He was making up for lost time. He wanted to be a happy, successful person." It's hard to say how well Sea-Wash fared over the years. Clemmons talked up the business to his community corrections supervisor, but a sheriff's detective couldn't help but notice a lack of equipment and other obvious signs of a flowering enterprise.

Clemmons also managed to catch the fever consuming financial markets in those years. He shoved his money into real estate, a late comer to an investment boom fueled by lax lending standards and a belief that property values would forever rise. In 2006, Clemmons paid $244,950 for a three-bedroom house in Parkland, south of Tacoma. That marked quite a turnaround for someone out of prison for only two years. In January 2008 he paid almost $180,000 for another house, a rundown rambler on 132nd Street South, just blocks away. He planned to rent that property to family. Four months later he bought a third house, for $265,000. His sister LaTanya moved in there.

In two years Clemmons bought $690,000 worth of real estate. In the early morning hours of July 5, 2008, fire destroyed Clemmons' house on 132nd Street. Clemmons attributed the blaze to the accidental discharge of fireworks—an explanation that investigators accepted, paving the way for a big insurance payout. His windfall in hand, Clemmons hired Beach Wood Homes to construct a one-hundred-thousand-dollar custom replacement. "It seemed like Nicole was in charge and running the show," says Beach Wood owner Garrett Alwert. "She was picking out colors for carpet or countertops." One subcontractor, Keith Bernasconi, talked with Clemmons while finishing the house's gutters. Clemmons told Bernasconi and his daughter, Melissa, they could relax in a small outbuilding on the same property. The place was decked out with a new pool table, black leather couches, a big-screen TV. "I was thinking, 'Wow, he's a high roller,'" Melissa says.

But however sunny the picture painted by those property records, another set of records, more obscure, hinted at darkness beneath and troubles ahead. These records were kept by the community corrections officers supervising Clemmons and included daily notes of tips received, phone calls made, suspicions aroused.

In late 2005, the FBI called Martin and said Clemmons might be in contact with Gerard Wells, a convicted felon and federal fugitive wanted for conspiracy and trafficking in stolen car parts. Martin confronted Clemmons—and, sure enough, Clemmons had seen Wells within the last month and a half. Clemmons had even helped buy a plane ticket for Wells to leave the area. Wells planned to use a false name while traveling, Clemmons told Martin.

As a parolee, Clemmons should have avoided the company of ex-cons. One reason he'd cited for wanting out of Arkansas was to escape the corrupting influence of all the felons he knew there. But in Washington, Clemmons was surrounded by trouble. Wells wasn't an exception. He was more the rule. There was Rickey Hinton, the half brother who served as Clemmons' sponsor. There was Darcus Allen—"Dorcus," to some of his friends—a man convicted of murder in a liquor-store holdup; Clemmons and Allen had served time together in Arkansas before reuniting in Washington. And there were Eddie Lee Davis and Joseph Pitts, cousins of Clemmons' who had likewise made the move north.

To hear Clemmons tell it, his embrace of Davis and Pitts was an act of familial charity. The two were getting into trouble in Arkansas. Clemmons' grandmother wanted Maurice to take them in, to set them straight. Clemmons let them live on one of his properties and gave them work. But if the goal was reformation, as Clemmons claimed, the move misfired. Davis picked up his first felony drug charge in Washington at the age of seventeen. At eighteen he was charged, along with Pitts and three other men, with dealing marijuana, Ecstasy and cocaine. For Clemmons, Davis became a personal go-fer, albeit a hapless one, never quite able to get things right. Talking to law-enforcement officers, Clemmons explained his cousins' criminal entanglements with this: "I've been trying to change them. But the past can't get away from them."

About the same time the FBI called Martin, so did a police detective. The detective had news even more disturbing: Clemmons was being investigated on suspicion of dealing drugs through the mail.

Beginning in 2005, postal inspectors and police agencies spent four years investigating a possible network between South Dakota and Washington, with drugs and cash going back and forth courtesy of the U.S. Postal Service and private mailing companies. The investigation netted four arrests. Clemmons wasn't among the indicted, even though his name and address appeared repeatedly on suspect packages. Police searched a house in Sioux Falls, South Dakota, and found a parcel, mailed by DHL, that held a Tupperware container with two-and-a-half pounds of marijuana; the marijuana was heat-sealed in layers of plastic, a type of packaging that can throw off drug-detection dogs.

Another time, police seized a UPS package because of dubious math. The package cost ninety dollars to mail, but, according to its sender, held a pair of tennis shoes worth twenty-five dollars. A trained dog reacted to the package in a way that heightened suspicions. The package, it turned out, did hold shoes, but inside the shoes was $5,500 in cash.

For postal inspectors, this investigation proved frustrating. Most of the suspect packages were sent by express mail, limiting the opportunities to secure a search warrant. If a package was held too long before delivery, the recipient might guess something was up.

In 2005, a police dog named Gunner, a four-year-old Weimaraner, alerted investigators to a package that was being mailed to Clemmons' home. A postal inspector expedited a search-warrant request, a U.S. magistrate signed off and the package was opened. Gunner's nose misfired. The search turned up "three large jerseys," according to court records. "We did see things going back and forth from him in packages that we believed to be narcotics," says Jerry Styers, a postal inspector in Washington. "We couldn't hit on it."

The tips about Clemmons kept coming. Four years after the postal investigation started, the roles reversed; instead of some police officer calling Martin with a lead, Martin reached out to Clemmons' newest community corrections supervisor.

In April 2009 Martin was watching the local TV news when he saw a Pierce County Crime Stoppers sketch of a serial robbery suspect. The sketch bore a striking resemblance to Maurice Clemmons—the parolee Martin had supervised from 2004 until 2006. Hold the sketch up to a mug shot of Clemmons taken the same year, and about the only thing missing is a mole on Clemmons' left cheek.

Martin sent an e-mail to Houth Thiem, Clemmons' current Department of Corrections supervisor. Thiem, in turn, called the Crime Stoppers hotline. But from there, the tip breathed its last, never making its way to the detectives who might have capitalized on it. Thiem's notes say the operator told him that Crime Stoppers had "received too many tips/leads already. He refused to take any more tips from DOC." Lauren Wallin, a Pierce County sheriff's analyst who coordinates the Crime Stoppers program, says: "That doesn't make any sense. We take all tips that come in unless a suspect is apprehended." Thiem should have contacted the Sheriff's Office directly, a sheriff's spokesman would later say, because the Crime Stoppers hotline is intended for anonymous tips. He also said he believed the robber may have been somebody else.

The description used for the sketch came from witnesses to the armed robbery of an AutoZone store in Lakewood, a Pierce County town not far from where Clemmons lived. Detectives spotted similarities between that robbery and ten others committed between April 2008 and April 2009, all in the Puget Sound area, all executed by a pair of men. Three of the other robberies were also at AutoZone stores. In a holdup of a Lakewood sports pub, a customer was grazed by a bullet.

When a KFC in Shelton was hit, the robbers bound some employees with duct tape while ordering another to empty the register and a safe. The robbers covered their faces and wore gloves. "They weren't amateurs. They knew what they were doing," says Paul Campbell, a Shelton police detective. "They walked in and controlled everybody." A year afterward, the robbery remained unsolved. Campbell wishes he'd been notified of the similarity between Clemmons and the sketch: "I'd have definitely gone down that road if it had been brought to my attention."

To hear Clemmons tell it, his first five years in Washington told a story of redemption, a story of a man who had gone straight and built a successful business on initiative and drive. That was the story he offered up in public anyway. But in private telephone conversations with close friends he would tell a different story—one showing that those postal inspectors and police detectives and probation officers had every reason to be suspicious. Much as he explained that one armed robbery in the language of a loan officer—*I was securing collateral for a debt*—Clemmons saw little to distinguish between crime and commerce. Money is money. It wasn't until the spring of 2009—when he became convinced that he was the focal point of an epic spiritual battle—that he would begin to worry about where his money came from.

Maurice Clemmons
at age five.

His grandmother's house in Marianna, Arkansas.

Clemmons grew up in this neighborhood in Marianna, which is part
of Lee County. At the time, forty-four percent of the county's
residents lived in poverty. Only seventeen percent had graduated
from high school. Clemmons left Marianna as a teenager and
attended high school in Little Rock.

Mike Huckabee,
the Arkansas governor,
received Clemmons'
plea for mercy in 2000.

Clemmons' mother, Dorthy, visits him in an Arkansas prison.

Clemmons and Nicole Smith, with Judge Marion Humphrey,
on their wedding day in 2004. Humphrey had supported
Clemmons' petition for mercy from the governor.

A house in Parkland that Clemmons bought in 2008. After a fire,
Clemmons added a studio apartment and allowed his cousins to move in.

A house in South Tacoma that Clemmons rented to his sister LaTanya.

The home in Parkland where Maurice and Nicole lived. Surveillance
cameras with floodlights monitored all approaches to the house.

A bank robber in Little Rock, April 2009, believed to be Darcus Allen, Clemmons' friend and prison mate from Arkansas.

Sketch of a Puget Sound serial-robbery suspect, next to a mug shot of Clemmons. Investigators have not ruled out Clemmons but also have other suspects.

Quiana Williams, a Clemmons girlfriend who had a baby with him.

On May 9, 2009, Clemmons went on a rampage outside his Parkland home, smashing eighteen windows on cars and houses. He fought with two deputies who answered a 911 call. "Shoot me, shoot me," he said as one deputy pulled a gun.

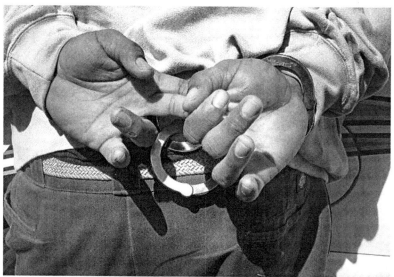

Deputies needed to use two sets of handcuffs to keep Clemmons under control after his May 9 arrest. Talking to a deputy, Clemmons called himself "The Beast" and said: "White people will be killed if they do not right their ways."

5

FOUR DAYS IN MAY

May 9, 2009

DWAIN CLINE JR. WAS SITTING WITH HIS WIFE, eating lunch, when the first rock flew into his home. He didn't see the rock. But he heard the glass explode. Then he heard a second explosion, just like the first. Cline was sixty-nine, and not in the best of health. He went to the front of his house and saw that two of his bay windows had been shattered.

Cline lived across the street from Maurice Clemmons, a man he considered friendly enough, a guy who didn't seem to cause trouble. Their neighborhood was in Pierce County, south of Tacoma, in a patch of sprawl dotted by 1950s ramblers and an occasional junker on cement blocks. By Puget Sound standards, the neighborhood was affordable, none of those pricey lots edging up to the water or mountains. McChord Air Force Base was nearby. So was the Army's Fort Lewis.

Cline walked outside and saw two men standing in front of Clemmons' garage. What's going on? Cline asked.

He's really upset, one man said. He'll pay for the damages.

Cline didn't know what to make of it. He turned for home, only to have Clemmons emerge from his house and approach. Clemmons asked Cline something about Jesus. What the question was exactly, Cline could not remember later. But whatever it was, Clemmons didn't wait long for an answer.

Clemmons threw a rock at his neighbor—a man he'd never had words with before, a man who simply wanted to know why rocks were crashing through his windows. Cline managed to swat the rock away. So Clemmons threw a second rock. This one sliced Cline's hand, making it bleed and swell. Cline turned and ran, but Clemmons threw a third rock, which thudded into Cline's back. Cline staggered into his house, and his wife called 911.

That call came in just before 1 p.m. on this Saturday in spring. But other calls were coming in, too—all from the same neighborhood, all about some crazy bald man, and rocks, and allusions to the divine.

Cindy Raihl was leaving the neighborhood after visiting her nephew. Driving down 131st Street South, she noticed two cars with their windows smashed out. As she neared the street's end, a bald man ran out from a driveway and threw a brick at her Mitsubishi, breaking the right rear window. Raihl wasn't about to stop and inquire. She punched the gas, rounded the corner, and, when she was a safe distance away, pulled out a phone. "I was just in shock," she says. "The look in his eyes is something I will not forget."

Raihl's nephew, alerted to what had happened, drove down the street in his Honda to investigate. Seeing Clemmons, he stopped and asked if he knew who was throwing rocks. Clemmons walked up to the Honda and asked: "Do you know the Lord Jesus Christ? Do you have the Lord in your heart?" A passenger in the Honda saw a rock in Clemmons' hand. "Go!" she told Raihl's nephew. But he was too slow. A rock smashed into the Honda's side window. As the car sped off, another rock cracked the window in back.

Within minutes, Clemmons went after other neighbors and passersby, throwing rocks the size of softballs. The police's incident report would go on for twenty-five pages, tallying all the damage: eight cars, three houses, eighteen windows. "Carnage," one deputy called it.

Now thirty-seven, Maurice Clemmons didn't much resemble that seventeen-year-old who had entered the Arkansas prison system two decades earlier. Those 156 pounds had turned into 240. His head was shaved. Now, to go with the scars, he had a tattoo of a bulldog, inked on the left side of his chest. Nine years had passed since he'd received clemency from Governor Huckabee, and in those nine years he had found plenty of trouble. But today's had nothing to do with robbing or stealing. Today's was all rage and madness.

David Christian, a thirty-year-old Pierce County sheriff's deputy, was the first to respond to the 911 calls about some bald man throwing rocks. About 1 p.m., Christian turned off Tenth Avenue and headed west on 131st, a short street that dead-ended in a matter of blocks. There was no questioning he had the right location. A house on the north side of 131st Street had a window broken out. Shattered glass littered the street. Victims approached, trying to flag Christian down, but he waved them off, indicating he'd talk to them later. Christian pulled up to the house where the callers said the bald man lived. In front of the house, No. 1118, the deputy saw three cars with smashed windows. He also saw two men, neither of them bald.

Where's the bald guy who did this? Christian asked.

He's inside, one man said. He lost his composure, but it's OK now. He'll pay for everything.

I still need to speak to him.

He's sleeping.

I don't think so, Christian said.

It had taken Christian four minutes to get here. He figured there was no way someone could crash that fast, going from fury to slumber in just a few minutes. The deputy started walking toward the house.

Private property, one of the men said.

The two men in front of the house were Eddie Lee Davis and Joseph Pitts. Both were cousins of Clemmons' and had criminal records, for drug charges. They spent lots of time with Clemmons, much of it at this house, a low-slung L-shaped home with a circular drive and a sophisticated surveillance system. "High-tech, low-res, eight cameras, every angle," is how Clemmons described it.

Davis told Christian to leave.

Christian told Davis he was investigating a crime. He asked Davis for help. But Davis refused to give; he just stood there, in the deputy's way. Christian tried to move past him, but Davis swatted the deputy's hand. Don't touch me, Davis said. The two began to tussle—grabbing, pushing—and then Pitts joined in. Christian managed to notify dispatch of what was going on, but before help could arrive, Clemmons burst out of the front door, rushed the deputy and punched him straight in the face. Then he grabbed the deputy's left leg, trying to take him to the ground. Christian fell onto the hood of a car parked in the driveway. Clemmons threw more punches, connecting one, two, three times, bloodying the deputy's lip, blackening his eye, cutting his nose.

A second deputy arrived. As he ran up to help, Clemmons lunged for him. The deputy, Heath Page, grabbed his flashlight and cracked Clemmons over the head. But Clemmons kept fighting, and so did Davis, so did Pitts. Page broke free from the scrum, drew his gun, and ordered the three men to the ground. Davis and Pitts complied, but not Clemmons, Clemmons kept fighting with Christian, Clemmons, seeing the gun, told Page to go ahead, *shoot me, shoot me,* his words a command.

Christian, outweighed and out-muscled, resorted to training and leverage. He slipped around to Clemmons' back and applied a choke—a "sleeper hold" in common parlance, a lateral vascular neck restraint in the police vernacular. Clemmons started to give. His legs began to buckle. He went to the ground and Christian handcuffed him, using two sets of cuffs. As Christian escorted Clemmons to the patrol car, Clemmons had unkind words. "He expressed a certain disdain for law enforcement," Christian wrote later.

With Clemmons and his two cousins secured, Christian talked to Clemmons' wife, outside the house. Nicole Smith told the deputy that she had recently discovered her husband was cheating on her. And it wasn't just an affair. Clemmons had a baby with the other woman. Nicole had confronted Maurice about this, and that's what set him off, she told the deputy. Two of the cars with smashed windows belonged to Nicole, although she didn't want to bring charges.

Christian went back to Clemmons. He read Clemmons his rights, and Clemmons said he understood. Then Clemmons said, "Here's what I want your report to say: President Obama. He's my brother."

Christian thought maybe Clemmons was talking emotional kinship. But he wasn't sure.

Clemmons continued: "White people will be killed if they do not right their ways. This will happen in the biblical sense."

Clemmons called himself "The Beast." Then he said: Oprah is my sister. LeBron James is my brother. T.I. is my favorite rapper.

In his report, Christian said Clemmons "acknowledged the assault as an unfortunate but necessary occurrence."

The deputies hauled Clemmons and his cousins off to the Pierce County Jail. After the patrol car pulled up to the sally port at 2:45 p.m., Clemmons began to yell—"loudly," according to reports—while being pat-searched. He kept it up in the pre-booking area and when his handcuffs were removed. Clemmons refused to cooperate with the booking process. He became increasingly agitated and hostile, yelling at jail staff: "I'll kill all you bitches."

At the jail, Clemmons' criminal history warranted a security classification of Level 2. But a booking sergeant, wary of Clemmons' threats and his earlier attack on the deputies, overrode that classification, bumping Clemmons up to Level 1, "High Maximum." "Staff should use caution when dealing with him," one jailer wrote, noting that Clemmons might be facing a third strike and a possible life sentence. The jailers put Clemmons in a cell away from his two cousins. As afternoon turned to evening, they conducted cell checks at fifteen- or thirty-minute intervals, and jotted staccato descriptions on a watch sheet.

Awake.

Sitting.

Refused dinner sack.

Awake.

Refused to dress out.

Sitting on bench.

Awake.

Yelling.

Awake.

Standing at door.

Yelling.
Yelling.
Around 7:30 p.m., Clemmons threw a roll of toilet paper into the toilet bowl. To avoid flooding, staff turned off the cell's water. At 10 p.m., Clemmons finally agreed to change out of his clothes and into the jail oranges. The jail checks continued until midnight.
Standing at door.
Awake.
Awake.

The origins of Clemmons' religious delusions remain something of a mystery. But if one incident eclipsed all others, it was an incident that happened earlier in the spring of 2009. The exact day is unknown. So is the full name of a man who figured prominently in the story. But however light the story's details, the event's impact was accorded substantial weight by Clemmons and his family and friends. Even Clemmons' Uncle Ray—Maurice's close friend from childhood, living in Arkansas—heard reports about how Clemmons believed he had been cursed by a "devil worshipper."

The man's name was Mark. Clemmons couldn't remember his last name. But Clemmons would say it was Mark who had brought all this about—or at least Mark was the vessel. Mark lived in a mobile home on one of Clemmons' properties. In the spring of 2009, Clemmons went to the mobile home and found a bizarre scene. Mark was acting crazy, tearing the place apart. Mark told Clemmons that the devil had jumped out of the oven and attacked him, with flames flying and everything. Clemmons believed him. Clemmons believed the devil had invaded Mark and taken his body over, as punishment for some evil in Mark's past. Mark's talk of flames cinched it. "The devil is fire," Clemmons would say. Clemmons also believed one other thing: That for the devil, Mark was but a way station. "The devil jumped out of him and jumped in me," Clemmons would say.

That's how Clemmons—in private, anyway—would explain all the horrible things he did on this weekend in May. *The devil jumped out of him and jumped in me.* Clemmons would tell Nicole to take pictures of that oven door ripped from its hinges. Take pictures of all the ways Mark ransacked the trailer. Clemmons became convinced that if jurors saw those pictures, if jurors heard Mark's story, Clemmons would be held blameless, that jurors would acquit him of any charges prosecutors might bring. "The truth is going to set me free," he'd say.

In the meantime, Clemmons would lie. To authorities, his official story would be: I didn't throw those rocks. Eddie threw those rocks. Why are you coming after me? Clemmons would also manufacture grievances from this day. In private, he'd admit throwing those rocks, he'd admit hitting his neighbor, Dwain Cline. But he'd pick at certain details in the police reports and work himself into a rage, missing the forest for the trees. "Man, I had a blue cap on the whole day. Ain't nobody could have seen my bald head that day." He'd insist that Deputy Christian had no grounds for trying to enter his house. "That wasn't right." And he'd rail against his neighbors for calling police. *Snitches,* he'd call them. If only he'd been white, he'd say, no one would have dialed 911. "We ain't even supposed to be in the neighborhood," he'd tell Nicole, and Nicole would say, "If we do, we supposed to be kissing ass," to which Clemmons would answer: "No matter what we do, it's always going to be held against us. That's why things have to change."

May 10, 2009

After midnight, the jail staff continued its checks on Clemmons.

Awake.

Standing.

Awake.

Awake.

At 2:40 a.m., they were able to finish up the booking process—taking his fingerprints, shooting his picture. This was twelve hours after he arrived at the jail. Clemmons' booking photo radiates menace—eyebrows pitched, eyes locked on the ground, tight and angry.

Clemmons may have finally fallen asleep after this, but it's hard to say. The notations stop at this point.

May 10 was a Sunday, Mother's Day. In lots of places that would have meant Clemmons was out of luck if he wanted to bail out. The courts close on weekends—and without a judge to set bail, someone might have to stew in jail until Monday. But Pierce County wasn't like most places. Pierce County had a system that allowed people to post bond without ever facing a judge, if it happened to be a weekend or holiday.

Called "booking bail," the system works according to formula. Each criminal charge is assigned a dollar figure; the more serious the charge, the greater the amount. By making bail available, the system eases jail overcrowding and saves money. For some guy arrested for being drunk in public on a Friday night, the system seems fair, sparing him two days in jail when he's likely to get no worse than a fine and probation. But booking bail also has a disadvantage: It treats people indiscriminately, like factory parts in a production line. "When it's booking bail, it doesn't take into account particular details like somebody's history," says Pierce County Prosecuting Attorney Mark Lindquist. "And that's problematic. It's one of the dangers of booking bail."

Another danger arises from the formula's figures, which are set by Pierce County Superior Court. Some numbers, to put it charitably, seem low. The bail for second-degree murder? $50,000. First-degree kidnapping? $50,000. A drive-by shooting? $10,000. Distributing child pornography? $5,000. A Seattle television station, KING 5, investigated Pierce County's booking-bail system and uncovered hundreds of cases where people suspected of homicide, rape or felony assault had been released without any review by a court. One man, freed on $50,000 bail for second-degree murder, later went before a judge; the judge took into account the suspect's long criminal history and reset bail—at $1 million.

Had Clemmons' history been taken into account, he would not have fared well. All those felony convictions out of Arkansas would have raised alarms. So would the possibility that he was staring at a third strike and a mandatory life sentence. But with booking bail, what mattered were the charges on the booking sheet. Clemmons had been booked on four felony charges—two for assault, two for malicious mischief—and, by formula, his bail was set at $10,000 per charge, for a total of $40,000.

Clemmons' wife needed to find a bail-bond agency. In the Puget Sound area, she had dozens to choose from. Bad Boy Bail Bonds. Bail Rite Bail Bonds. 24-7 Bail Bonds. Goodfella's Bail Bonds. Scottfree Bail Bonds. You Walk Bail Bonds. Even Acme Bail Bonds, a name inextricably linked to Wile E. Coyote. She settled upon Aladdin, one of the West's largest bail-bond agencies. With fifty offices dotting the landscape from Southern California to the Pacific Northwest, Aladdin helps secure the release of more than ninety-thousand people a year. "We get you out," its Web site says. "We get you through it."

Like most bail-bond outfits, Aladdin charges customers 10 percent of the bond. (Unless the person belongs to a union, or has served in the military, or has hired private counsel. Then Aladdin provides a discount.) That 10 percent is the company's to keep. That's how it makes a profit. But most bail-bond agencies also demand collateral for the remaining 90 percent. That's how the company manages its risk—and motivates its customers to show up in court. For large bonds, customers often put up the equity in their homes.

In this instance, Aladdin gave Nicole Smith a discount because Clemmons had private counsel; that knocked the bond's price down to $3,200. Even then, Smith didn't have to pay all of it upfront. Unbeknown to most of the public, bail-bond agencies operate in an open marketplace in which competition is intense and everything is negotiable, even with public safety in the balance. Some judges, setting bail, assume the defendant will have to pay 10 percent of the figure before posting bond, meaning a high bail will keep the average defendant behind bars. But the bail-bond agencies in Washington have shed such hard-and-fast rules, waging a race for whatever money a defendant might have. They calculate risks

and come up with creative ways—in some cases, tethering a GPS bracelet to a suspect's ankle—that will discourage clients from skipping town. With Nicole,
Aladdin agreed to a payment plan, allowing her to put up a mere $1,700 at the out-
set. The rest she would cover with two later payments.

Aladdin also elected not to demand any collateral. Smith didn't have to put up
any property—not a house, not a car. Aladdin's chief executive officer would later
say this was due, in part, to Clemmons having a good credit rating and no known
criminal record. And how did Aladdin determine that Clemmons had no criminal
record? The company limited its search to Washington. By not checking records
for Arkansas—the state where Clemmons had spent almost his entire life—
Aladdin missed all nine of Clemmons' felony convictions.

In exchange for the $1,700 upfront, Aladdin posted the $40,000 bond—and
Nicole's husband was freed. Clemmons was released from the Pierce County Jail
at 12:15 p.m., not quite twenty-four hours after he smashed eighteen windows and
busted up Deputy Christian's face and demanded to be shot and called himself
"The Beast."

Now he could go home.

This was not good news for the other people staying at Clemmons' house.
Nicole's twelve-year-old daughter—Maurice's stepdaughter—lived there. So did
a more distant relative, an eleven-year-old cousin of Maurice's stepdaughter. The
eleven-year-old had moved in a couple of weeks earlier, because of problems in
her own family. Now she wanted out. She saw how strange Clemmons was acting,
and it scared her. Before Clemmons was released from jail on Sunday, the eleven-
year-old asked Nicole to take her home. But whatever Nicole's answer, the girl was
still at Clemmons' house when Clemmons was freed.

Clemmons described it as an awakening. He'd never been one for church, never
been one to study the Bible. But in the spring of 2009 he was awakened. He
became convinced that spiritual forces were alive in him. He read *The Spirit of
Liberation*, written by Bishop E. Bernard Jordan. Using big bold letters, the book
provides ninety-six prophetic principles.

Creation began in Africa!

We were the true originators of the Word of God—Not the white man!

Jesus was a black man!

Freedom cannot exist without wealth!

The gospel has been polluted by Europeans!

Jordan writes: "The law serves the oppressor and enslaves the oppressed. ...
We have a police department in our city that has nothing better to do on Sunday
mornings than to ticket law-abiding citizens' cars parked in front of the church.
Think about the psychology of this. They're letting you know that they think you

are in the wrong neighborhood." Jordan writes: "If you have been walked on you are a candidate for the anointing! ... Grapes become valuable when they are crushed."

Clemmons believed he was anointed. "I've been suffering my whole life." He became convinced we had entered revelation—and that he was Jesus Christ after Jesus was crucified but before Jesus ascended to heaven, and that everything was preordained, that every moment had already played out "hundreds of thousands of billions" times before, that France's president, Nicolas Sarkozy, was the devil and New York City was Babylon and the fifth trumpet blast was sounding and that God was "lining up all his soldiers in the penitentiaries." In time, Clemmons accumulated followers.

May 11, 2009

The two girls—the twelve-year-old and the eleven-year-old—were in the den, playing on the computer. It was in the pre-dawn hours of Monday—past 1 in the morning, closing in on 2. Maurice Clemmons walked into the room and left. Then he walked in a second time, and this time he was naked.

Come with me into the living room, he said.

In the living room, Clemmons told the twelve-year-old, his stepdaughter, to sit on a stool and take off her clothes. He told her to touch his penis. She didn't want to, but was afraid he'd hurt her if she didn't. Clemmons made the eleven-year-old do the same thing.

Afterward, the girls went to their bedroom. Clemmons said he was going to go to sleep.

But not long after, Clemmons came into the girls' room. He started touching his twelve-year-old stepdaughter and doing other vile acts, and as he kept going, the girl began to fear he would rape her, and she told him no. He said OK and left, but then he returned again, and touched her again, and left again, but not before saying don't tell anyone about this or he would go to jail for a long time. When he left, the girl stayed in bed, crying.

Clemmons went into his bedroom. Around 3 a.m., he awoke his wife. He told Nicole he wanted to have sex. "Trust me," he told her. Then he left their bedroom and retrieved Nicole's twelve-year-old daughter. When the girl entered the room, she saw her mother on the bed, naked and crying. Clemmons told the girl: Your mother is Eve and I am Jesus. Nicole pleaded with her husband, please don't hurt her, she doesn't need to be here, but Maurice said: Trust me, the world is going to end soon and I am Jesus. He asked the girl: Are you afraid? Yes, she said. The girl left the bedroom and telephoned her nineteen-year-old brother, told him what was happening, and asked him to drive over to the house and get her.

I'm on my way, he said.

The nineteen-year-old was Maurice's stepson. When he pulled up, the other girl, the eleven-year-old, fled the house and jumped into his car, desperate for a ride to anywhere else.

He went inside, saw his sister, and told her to come on. What about mom? the girl asked. So he went to the bedroom to get their mother, and he saw his stepfather, standing there, naked.

Why are you doing this?

I'm fine, Clemmons said.

You're not fine, his stepson said. You need help.

Clemmons talked of worlds colliding, of heaven coming to earth and the devil, too.

The stepson wanted to leave, but Clemmons wouldn't allow it. The only way out now was to fight; the stepson was afraid, he knew he couldn't take his stepfather. Clemmons said it was time for a family meeting. He told his stepson to take off his clothes. He told his stepdaughter to do the same. He said they were "the first family." He said they must be naked, all of them together, at 4 in the morning—"on the dot," because that was God's number. He ordered them to pray and to look in the mirror and be proud of their bodies. Everyone went along. Everyone was afraid. This went on for five minutes, maybe longer. Clemmons talked of how beautiful it was, that they could share this moment.

Then Clemmons let everyone get dressed. The stepson grabbed his sister and left, but when they got to the car, the cousin was gone. Where she went, no one knew. She was an eleven-year-old child, ninety-five pounds, in black shorts and a black T-shirt, lost to the night.

The sheriff's deputies began arriving just before 5:30 a.m. This was two days after deputies Christian and Page had arrived at the same house and been assaulted by Clemmons. But this time, Clemmons was gone.

The lead investigator was Teresa Berg, a forty-five-year-old sergeant-detective. She had been with the Sheriff's Office for more than twenty years and had been investigating child-abuse cases for fourteen of them. Berg arrived at 5:45 a.m. and stayed with the case late into the night. She interviewed the twelve-year-old, and a great aunt, and Nicole, and the nineteen-year-old stepson. Berg had no doubt that the family's account of the night was true: "It was just so bizarre of a story. For everybody to get it consistent, there's just no way." The twelve-year-old was shaking and crying, Berg says. "She was scared to death of that guy. The details of what she was saying, without hesitation, she didn't make that up." Berg wondered where the eleven-year-old was. Relatives were searching the neighborhood, looking for her. The family told Berg that Clemmons had been acting "crazy," that he hadn't been eating or sleeping for days. He said he could fly—and they had seen him in the backyard, jumping. He said the Secret Service was coming to get him, because he had written to President Obama, and that Obama was also coming, in order to confirm that Clemmons was the Messiah.

Another deputy interviewed LaTanya Clemmons, Maurice's half sister. LaTanya said Maurice was not in his right mind. She talked about how he'd busted up all those windows Saturday, and how Nicole had bailed him out Sunday, and how she figured some mental-health professional would have evaluated him while he was in jail. She also wondered how he would react when confronted by police.

For investigative purposes, officers wanted to sketch the home's layout. But Nicole worried about police rummaging through the house. She let Berg go halfway down the hallway—and that was it. Nicole told police they could take no pictures inside the home. She refused to fill out a handwritten statement.

Berg told Nicole that she should take her daughter to the hospital. But Nicole hesitated. She didn't want to leave her house. A great aunt began yelling at Nicole, saying she needed to accompany her child, she needed to get her priorities straight. Nicole relented. She took her daughter to a hospital in Tacoma, where medical staff examined the girl and took a rape kit. Berg told Nicole that Maurice was to have no further contact with Nicole's daughter. Nicole said she understood.

That evening, Berg finally found the eleven-year-old. The two talked on the phone. The girl told the detective she had run from Clemmons' home to a nearby gas station, where an attendant let her use the phone. The girl called her godmother, who lived in Renton. Her godmother picked her up and took her home.

But Clemmons was still nowhere to be found. He was last seen fleeing the neighborhood on foot. The Sheriff's Office tried using dogs to track him, but the dogs were unable to pick up his scent.

May 12, 2009

At 1:30 p.m., Clemmons was supposed to show up in Pierce County Superior Court to be arraigned on charges stemming from all the rocks and punches he had thrown three days earlier. By now, prosecutors had reviewed the police reports and filed formal charges. Clemmons faced two felony charges for assault and five others for malicious mischief.

But when a court official took a roll call of the courtroom gallery, Clemmons was a no show. Three hours later, at the close of the court's day, he still wasn't there. A judge issued a bench warrant, calling for Clemmons' arrest for failure to appear.

Clemmons was on the run from seven felony charges. Once prosecutors looked at the latest batch of police reports, they would file an eighth, this one for child rape.

Berg, the detective, worried about this case more than most. She had investigated hundreds of cases—cases with the kinds of details that can induce long sleepless nights—but this one, it was way up there on the red-alert meter. Berg worried about the safety of Clemmons' stepdaughter. About the safety of law-enforcement officers. About the safety of anyone who crossed Clemmons' path. "We're like, 'Look, he's going to hurt somebody. It's so easy to see. It doesn't take an expert to see this.'" The signs were everywhere—the assault on the deputies, the threats toward the jail staff, his bizarre and awful behavior with his family. "I was really worried that we wouldn't find this guy and what he would do next," Berg says. She told the patrol officers looking for him: *You have to be careful.*

6

THANK YOU, GOD

ON JUNE 12, 2009, ABOUT THREE HUNDRED PEOPLE attended a prayer service at Bishop E. Bernard Jordan's church in New York City. It was a balmy Friday evening, in a church alive with possibilities. Zoe Ministries, on Manhattan's Upper West Side, occupied a space that once belonged to the Master Theater, an off-Broadway venue. True to those roots, the church offered performance along with its ministry; congregants might hear reggae, hip-hop or rap, not the kind of rap that reveled in violence or misogyny, but rap that celebrated Jesus and forgiveness. Over the years, the musicians who played at Zoe Ministries included Lionel Hampton, Salt-N-Pepa, Billy Preston. The church's ministers were also an eclectic, electrifying group; they included the Reverend Run—also known as Joseph Simmons, also known simply as Run, from the famed rap duo Run-DMC. Simmons credited the church with helping him to find his way, saying that after meeting Jordan, he "stopped going to the racetrack, stopped smoking reefer and started walking the straight line."

Jordan was a self-proclaimed prophet since the age of fifteen. In the spring of 2009, he was on the cusp of his fiftieth birthday, a minister who wore long dreadlocks and preached a blend of spiritual soul-searching and entrepreneurial self-enrichment. His church was a "prosperity ministry." In chat rooms and in streaming video, Jordan offered prophecies ($365 for a year's worth), one-on-one coaching with a "prophetic midwife," and $7-a-bar "prophetic soap" ("This is a soap that helps bring protection and gives you a greater ability to function with greater intuition and insight," Jordan's Web site says). For $3,000, you could be part of Jordan's "inner circle." Despite Jordan's commercial success, the religious mainstream largely ignored him. "I believe that it is because of race," Jordan once said. "They hate to see a Negro get a dollar."

According to the church's Web site, Bishop Jordan could not only see someone's future, he could shape its contours. "Like Nostradamus ... the accuracy of the gift that operates in Bishop Jordan will astound you! He is known to predict exact names, dates, and times of events both individually and globally! ... As a prophet, he can truly decree a thing and see it established—just like the prophets of the Scriptures! He is not one just to give information, but he is also known to create miracles and circumvent events merely by the power of his speech!"

On this evening, the congregation at Zoe Ministries included an unlikely member—someone who shared Jordan's enthusiasm for exclamation points, but who happened to be far from home. As the prayer service was in full swing, Maurice Clemmons stood up and asked—loudly—for a glass of water. Jordan had no idea who Clemmons was. But he knew that this disruption of the service was strange and inappropriate. "Everybody knew something was not quite right," he would say later. Clemmons sat back down. But then he stood again—and disrupted the service again, by saying he was sorry for interrupting the first time. Later this same evening, Clemmons rushed the stage. Two men from the church intercepted him and escorted him outside. But Clemmons hung around the church. He eventually returned to the service, and, when the time came for offerings, approached the pulpit and pledged about eleven hundred dollars to Jordan's ministry, writing down his credit-card number and dropping off an envelope.

The eleven hundred dollars may not have represented much to Jordan—his church often received larger donations from others—but to Clemmons, the expenditure came at a time when he needed all the money he could get. Whatever his sources of income, by the spring of 2009, they appeared to be drying up. In May, a subcontractor had filed a lien on Clemmons' custom-built house; five more subcontractors would follow.

From the information provided on the pledge, Jordan could tell Clemmons had come from the West Coast.

How did you get here? Did you fly? Jordan asked Clemmons.

No, Clemmons said. I drove.

Clemmons said he'd made the trip with Dawson Carlisle, a friend from the Seattle area.

What brought you here? Jordan asked.

God told me to come, Clemmons said. I've been running away from the police. The police have been knocking at my door, and I've been running ever since.

You've come here with a lot of worries, Jordan said. When you go back home, God is going to set your mind free.

Jordan's question, *What brought you here*, was a good one. Clemmons told Jordan that this was the first time he'd ever set foot in a church. In his thirty-seven years, about the only time he'd turned to religion was when he needed an alibi (*I wasn't having sex with that other inmate; I was in the Island of Hope chapel, praying*) or when he needed something from Marion Humphrey or Mike Huckabee, two ministers with the power to set him free (*In closing, I declare under the watchful eyes of our Lord that I will do all in my power as a man to live a drug-free, crime-free life to the end of my existence).* But something in Clemmons had changed. Even his Uncle Ray in Arkansas took note: "Maurice was all about getting, all about having. He was all about money. Then, suddenly, he was all about God." Clemmons had discovered Bishop Jordan on cable TV and while scouring the Internet—and the draw was immediate and powerful.

When Clemmons had failed to show up in court back in May, his community corrections officer visited Clemmons' wife. Nicole told the officer that Clemmons had withdrawn $700 from an ATM on May 11 and she hadn't seen him since. This news prompted the Washington State Department of Corrections to ask Arkansas to file an "absconder" warrant, for fleeing. Clemmons, after all, was still Arkansas' parolee, not Washington's.

Arkansas filed the warrant on May 27, citing all the felony charges pending against Clemmons, his failure to report to the Washington Corrections Department, and his failure to tell the department that he had changed addresses. The warrant was good for a no-bail hold in all fifty states. But Jordan's appeal was apparently so great that Clemmons crossed a good number of those states when he and Carlisle went on a three-day road trip from Tacoma to New York, twenty-eight hundred miles away.

For Clemmons, Carlisle became acolyte No. 1, although Clemmons was more likely to refer to Carlisle as his wingman. The two made the strangest pair—and they knew it. Friends called Carlisle "Boo Man," a nickname that said more about his reaction to the world than his effect upon it. Ever meek, Carlisle traced his timidity to his youth, when he crashed on his bicycle, messing up his teeth, scratching the skin from his face. He stayed in the house the whole summer, longing to heal, desperate to avoid ridicule, his mother slathering his scars with cocoa butter. "I never got over that emotionally," he'd say. "With women, I will pick anyone who will pick me."

Clemmons and Carlisle crossed paths because Carlisle was dating Nicole's sister. When the two men first met—Clemmons showed Carlisle the rims on his car—Clemmons had asked Nicole if Carlisle was "retarded." Clemmons mocked the broad cuffs on Carlisle's pants, saying he looked like a "swashbuckler," a "pirate." Clemmons called Carlisle a skateboard geek. "You didn't get cool until you started messing with me," Clemmons would tell Carlisle. One day in spring, not long before their road trip to New York, Clemmons summoned Carlisle to his home. Carlisle recounted the day like this: "I was in the back yard. I spoke to him. I could tell he wasn't the same person. He was totally different. The very same day I saw my friend stop the wind and I saw angels before us." When Clemmons said he was Jesus Christ, Carlisle believed him. Clemmons gave Carlisle a name:

"Gabriel, my most trusted messenger." "We went from Boo Man and Maurice to Jesus Christ and Gabriel. It's beautiful, you know what I'm saying?"

Clemmons began studying the Bible, and when he'd butcher some word—he pronounced Job, the man, as "job," as in employment; Psalms became "Palms"; and Pontius Pilate became "pilates," the exercise that strengthens torso muscles—Carlisle would say nothing, or maybe find some roundabout way to say the word right. In conversation, Clemmons' voice would sometimes change, the register would drop, words would elongate, and Carlisle would forever affirm Clemmons' new identity, saying thank you God, thank you God, thank you God. And everywhere Carlisle looked—*miracles*. A charge went through on a maxed-out credit card? *A miracle*. Carlisle's printer worked after he shook the cartridge? *Another miracle*. One time, as the two men talked on the phone, Carlisle told Clemmons he had just witnessed the clouds parting.

"The sun is hitting me right in the face."

"Because what I'm telling you is the truth, little brother," Clemmons said.

"It's beautiful, it's beautiful, the sun is beaming, thank you God."

"The truth is glorious. It is glorious," Clemmons said. "The sun ain't never shined on you when you was living a lie. ... We command the suuuuuun. We command the raaaaaain. We can make the earth shaaaaaake. We can turn the sea into bloooooood. We can make the stars fall out of the skyyyyyy."

"Amen, amen."

At Zoe Ministries in New York, Bishop Jordan's introduction to Clemmons had been peculiar enough. But the day after that prayer service, the minister saw Clemmons' behavior become even more bizarre.

On June 13, Jordan celebrated his fiftieth birthday. He marked the occasion with a gala—suggested donation, $250 per person—at the Grand Hyatt, a three-hundred-dollar-a-night hotel in midtown Manhattan, next to Grand Central Station. That evening, Clemmons emerged from the Midtown traffic and entered the Hyatt's lobby, looking resplendent in a black tuxedo and crisp white shirt. His head was shaved and gleaming, his small goatee neatly trimmed. He sauntered past the bronze columns and towering flower vases and went up the escalator. At the top, he tapped Carlisle as emissary, dispatching him to approach the party's reception desk and announce their arrival. Carlisle leaned over the table.

"My friend over there, Maurice Clemmons?" Carlisle said. "That's Jesus Christ."

Jordan, wearing a microphone headset, paused, taken aback. "We're all Jesus, sir," Jordan said, grinning. Neither Clemmons nor Carlisle had been invited to the gala, held in the Hyatt's three-thousand-square-foot ballroom with twenty-four-foot glass windows overlooking Lexington and East Forty-second. But Carlisle meant it—Maurice Clemmons was Jesus Christ—and the more Carlisle persisted, the more frustrated Jordan became.

"I don't know what you are trying to communicate, okay?" Jordan said. "He is Maurice Clemmons to us. We are not going to call him Jesus Christ."

Jordan went on: "Serious. We do not tolerate stupidity"—at this, Carlisle nodded—"and we are not going to have that type of stupidity. If you are decent human beings, you are going to enjoy yourselves. If you are not, then we'll escalate it to another level. But that's not what our guests come here for. If there's some mental problem, then you need to find an institution."

As the pleasantries deteriorated, Clemmons came over, a white handkerchief folded in the pocket of his tuxedo. Jordan grinned again.

"You didn't RSVP, did you?"

"I don't know nothing about that," Clemmons said.

Jordan checked the seating list, knowing he would not find Clemmons' name. "We're all full inside, so we're going to have to put you in the overflow."

"That's no problem. No problem, bro," Clemmons said.

"I wish you had RSVP'd."

"I didn't know."

"Then how did you know to come?" Jordan asked.

"You did a live chat." Clemmons paused. "And uhm, you know … God called me."

Jordan started laughing. "Okay, Maurice. Take it easy."

Later that night, a video producer dropped by Clemmons' table. He found that Clemmons was now in shorts and a T-shirt bearing the name of Clemmons' business. The tuxedo had disappeared. Asked where his suit went, Clemmons told the producer, "Yeah, one of my friends wanted to get married, so I gave him my tux."

To Jordan, Clemmons' problems were evident. "Who goes around saying they are Jesus?" he would say later. "This was a functional man, who also needed mental help. … He was a sick man, torn apart within himself, trying to heal his wounds. That's not a sane man. That was a sick man. … He should have been in a room with padded walls."

In addition to its brick sanctuary, Zoe Ministries was a cyber-church, allowing congregants to seek the guidance of prophets through the Internet. Clemmons, despite all his years in prison, was not intimidated by the computer age. He had a Twitter account on which he followed a strange assemblage of sources and voices: the U.S. Centers for Disease Control and Prevention, liberal MSNBC host Rachel Maddow, San Francisco Mayor Gavin Newsom, basketball icons Shaquille O'Neal and Michael Jordan, the United Nations Refugee Agency, Southwest Airlines, the CEO for Zappos (the nation's largest online shoe company), and the Reverend Al Sharpton. In mid- and late June, after his meetings with Jordan, Clemmons tweeted several times. "Looking for bishop jordan," he wrote in one message. Another time he wrote: "Reginald Robinson man of God, looking to start a Church hopefully with the blessing of Zoe Ministries! radical teachings."

Not long after the birthday gala, Jordan called Clemmons on the phone. He encouraged Clemmons to turn himself in to police. He encouraged Clemmons to talk to his lawyer, to get a mental-health evaluation, to get treatment. "I don't want to go to the police, I don't want to turn myself in, I don't want to go back to prison," Clemmons told Jordan. But however much Clemmons protested, something changed his mind. He may have had no intention of returning to prison, but he was at least willing to confront the consequences of the decision he'd made to blow off court and skip town.

When a deputy called her with the news, Detective Teresa Berg experienced one feeling first and foremost: relief. Berg knew how dangerous Maurice Clemmons was, how unbalanced he had become. For seven weeks he'd been on the run. And now? The Sheriff's Office had learned that Clemmons would be showing up at Pierce County Superior Court, to try to get his failure-to-appear warrant quashed. Clemmons' lawyer had filed notice, down to the place and day. Deputies no longer had to look for Clemmons. He was coming to them. It was a gift falling from the sky.

Sure enough—on July 1, about 1:15 p.m.—a sheriff's sergeant spotted Clemmons in a second-floor courtroom. The sergeant, accompanied by Berg, another detective and several deputies working courtroom security, approached Clemmons in the courtroom's public-seating area. You're under arrest, the sergeant said. Officers handcuffed Clemmons and took him away. (At least that's the low-on-drama account rendered in police reports. Clemmons later relived the scene with Carlisle, who was also in the courtroom. "Man, they had their guns drawn," Carlisle said. "Yeah," Clemmons said. "Weren't they scared of me, man? Hey, you hear me call them cowards? Look how deep they came for one man, scared of the man, scared like a motherfucker. One man." Clemmons chuckled when recounting the show of force.)

Berg had Clemmons brought to the interview room at sheriff's headquarters, which was on the first floor of the same complex. There, she told him what this was all about—that he was under arrest on a charge of raping his stepdaughter—and asked if he'd be willing to talk about the case.

No, Clemmons said. There's nothing to talk about.

Clemmons told Berg that he had hired a lawyer, Daniel Murphy, from the Washington city of Federal Way. He was supposed to meet Murphy in the courtroom, Clemmons said.

Berg began filling out a jail booking form. As she took information down—Clemmons' date of birth, his address, the place of his arrest—Clemmons told her he'd come to the courthouse with his wife, Nicole, and with his minister, Reginald Wayne Robinson from the Universal Church. Clemmons told Berg that he was now a minister himself—that he had been in New York, getting ordained. He'd returned home to his family four days ago, Clemmons said.

Have you seen your stepdaughter? Berg asked.

Every day, Clemmons said.

For Berg, that news hit hard. So much for Nicole saying she'd keep her daughter away from her husband.

You have a middle name? Berg asked.

In the name of the Lord Jesus Christ, Clemmons said.

Berg didn't write "In the name of the Lord Jesus Christ" down as Clemmons' middle name. She didn't write anything down. Clemmons saw—and became angry.

Write it down, he said.

No. This form is for someone's legal name.

You're not a believer, Clemmons said.

Berg went on with the form. Any medical conditions? she asked. "No." Mental-health issues? "No." Are you suicidal? "No." Clemmons told Berg: "Life is precious." The detective agreed.

Afterward, Clemmons was escorted to the Pierce County Jail, where the staff was directed to use caution in dealing with him. "He has little regard for authority," one jailer wrote.

Berg returned to the second-floor courtroom where Clemmons had been arrested. Seeing Nicole, she approached. You remember me? Berg asked. Nicole said she did. Berg asked if they could talk. Nicole agreed but said she wanted her brother and another woman to accompany her. The group headed one floor down, to a small conference room in the sheriff's headquarters.

What's going on here? Nicole asked.

Berg explained that Clemmons had been arrested on suspicion of raping Nicole's daughter. And then the detective had a question of her own. She wanted to know what Nicole was doing with Clemmons, since Clemmons was a wanted man.

I hadn't seen him until just now, Nicole said.

Then one of you is lying, the detective said. Either you're lying or he's lying. Which is it?

Nicole looked startled.

The detective told her what Clemmons had said about being home with his family for four days—and about seeing Nicole's daughter every one of those days.

Nicole admitted that was true. But she said Clemmons' lawyer was planning to file papers with the prosecutor's office, asking for the rape charge to be dropped.

That's not likely to happen, Berg said.

But my daughter lied.

No, she didn't.

My children will do whatever I tell them to do.

That I believe, Berg said. And that's what concerns me.

The detective laid it out for Nicole: Your daughter didn't lie to me that day. Your son didn't lie to me that day. You didn't lie to me that day. What you said that day—what all of you said that day—was the truth.

But Nicole insisted. It was all a lie, she said.

Berg didn't know it, but by early summer 2009, Nicole Smith had begun to believe her husband's claim that supernatural forces were at work. Clemmons summarized the events of May by saying that if his physical being was guilty, his spirit was innocent, because how could he be held responsible for anything the devil made him do?

"Satan was in me, the head motherfucker," he'd say.

In some ways, Smith seemed an unlikely person to extend anyone an easy pass. She worked hard, making call after call—to free her husband, to keep their house in order, to protect their finances from ruin. "Nicole has worked like a Trojan," one lawyer told Clemmons. She showed little patience for people who were lazy or looking for a handout or quick to make excuses.

But she was also a receptive audience to claims of higher powers and the need to look for signs. She didn't call her husband Jesus or God or Lord, but when he talked of what was happening, how he had been anointed, how miracles were all around them and the world was in revelation, she would say: Yes, it's real. Reviewing footage captured by their home's elaborate surveillance system, she saw an image on camera No. 5 that was half sun, with a beam of light, and half red flames, with black in the middle, and she took it to be angels and demons at war, just outside her house. She attached meaning to dates. Clemmons was born on a Sunday. She was born on a Sunday. She attached meaning to numbers. To Smith, those three straight 6's in her husband's Department of Corrections number (866697) were no coincidence. She balked at calling one bail-bond company because three straight 6's appeared in the company's phone number. She calculated two-thirds as a decimal, came up with .66666, and said, "Hmm, that's weird." She attached meaning to names. *That jailer? Did you notice? His name was Jesus.* Upon hearing a conspiracy theory, she would search the Internet, find confirmation, and her doubts would dissolve. In a world of relentless sensation and overwhelming information, she walked without filters.

You're selling out your daughter to keep your man, Detective Berg told Nicole.

I don't need him.

Maybe you need him to pay your bills.

No. I have my own money.

You don't work.

My money is from somewhere else.

Nicole said her family wouldn't testify against Clemmons—to which the detective said, if you're subpoenaed, you'll testify or face arrest. Nicole said she didn't care. When the detective asked if that meant Nicole had filed a false police report back in May, Nicole said yes, and when the detective told her that was a crime, Nicole said: I'll take the rap. Berg brought up the warning she'd issued in May, about Nicole keeping Clemmons away from Nicole's twelve-year-old daughter. Now I'll be contacting Child Protective Services, Berg told Nicole. Your actions could cost you your child.

That can't happen, Nicole said.

We're done talking, the detective said.

She showed Nicole the door.

The following day, July 2, was a Thursday. Since it wasn't a weekend, there'd be no booking bail, no resorting to formula to attach a dollar figure to Clemmons' release. Instead, Clemmons appeared before a judge in Pierce County Superior Court.

By now, Clemmons had been charged with eight felonies. Seven stemmed from May 9, when he was accused of throwing rocks at cars, houses and people, and assaulting the two deputies. The eighth charge—second-degree child rape—traced to May 11, when he was accused of sexually assaulting his twelve-year-old stepdaughter.

Clemmons' lawyer had been licensed in Washington for six years; he handled a range of criminal cases (DUIs, drugs, juvenile, felonies) and personal-injury matters (you name it: automobile; motorcycle; semi-truck; boat/RV; bicycle/pedestrians; road construction). Clemmons had found him in the phone book: "Daniel J. Murphy, Jr., Attorney at Law, Call 24/7." He offered free consultation: "Home, Hospital, Jail." Murphy's Web site provided a touch more detail: "Aggressive, personalized, affordable legal representation. We serve the citizens of the state of Washington against oppressive governmental bodies and insurance companies …" *Oppressive governmental bodies.* With Clemmons, Murphy was preaching to the choir.

At the hearing, Clemmons pleaded not guilty to all eight charges. Then the subject moved to Clemmons' possible release. "I would request bail, as it is presumed," Murphy said.

In Washington, bail is indeed presumed. That principle is grounded in the state's constitution, which says "all persons charged with crime shall be bailable," with the exception of capital cases. Washington law also says a judge can't insist that bail be posted by cash only. If a defendant has sufficient collateral to secure a bond, that's good enough.

At the hearing, deputy prosecutor John Cummings asked for $300,000 bail. He cited Clemmons' lengthy criminal record in Arkansas and said Clemmons might be facing a third strike, increasing the risk he would flee. Murphy proposed a much lower figure, $40,000, and challenged the prosecution's evidence: "On the rape charges, there may be a recantation anyway."

The judge, John McCarthy, was concerned that Clemmons had failed to appear in court two months earlier. But Murphy said Clemmons "did not have notice" of that hearing. "He also has a medical condition that was occurring right at that time," Murphy said, without specifying what that condition was.

In Pierce County, more than five thousand felony cases get filed each year. This hearing was routine. It lasted maybe ten minutes. McCarthy settled upon bail of $190,000 — with $150,000 for the child-rape charge and $40,000 for the other charges. From his experience on the bench, McCarthy considered the figure to be high. Some people charged with similar crimes were released on their own recognizance.

To secure a bond, Clemmons would have to come up with $19,000—10 percent of the bail—unless he could negotiate a cut rate or some kind of delayed payment plan with a bonding company. Most people can't afford that kind of money. Besides, Clemmons was already in the hole, having agreed to pay $3,200 to secure his previous $40,000 bond, and then throwing the money away by skipping his court date back in May. When Clemmons had been taken back into custody, the Aladdin bail-bond agency asked to be taken off the financial hook. The court granted the request—so Clemmons was now starting from scratch.

Cummings, the prosecutor, hoped the bail amount wouldn't matter anyway. Clemmons' recent run-ins in Washington had allegedly violated his parole in Arkansas. Now charged with being a fugitive from another state, Clemmons could be held without bail. At Cummings' request, McCarthy ordered just that: No matter what happened with the Washington charges, there'd be no bail on the fugitive warrant.

But Clemmons' lawyer told the court that he was hoping to clear up that fugitive matter. "I've contacted his former attorney down in Arkansas who is working on this," Murphy said.

The day after this hearing, Clemmons placed a call from jail to Stephen Morley, his old lawyer in Arkansas. Morley, in his car at the time, answered the call on his cellphone.

"Hey, man," Morley said.

"Hey, what's up, Steve?"

"Well, not much. I was sorry to get that call yesterday. I talked to that lawyer. I'm going to do what I can around here to help you on the deal. Gosh, dog."

"It ain't bad as you think, man," Clemmons said. "This is what happened. My bitch ass wife, Nicole, she found out that I had an affair with another woman and had a baby. So, what she try to do, she know I'm on fucking parole, and she throw the gauntlet at me."

Nicole thought he was going to leave her, Clemmons told Morley. And he kept telling her: This other thing was just a mistake.

"Yeah," Morley said. "I know, I know. Everybody makes fucking mistakes. You gotta learn to forgive."

"She didn't forgive me until it was too late," Clemmons said.

"God damn it," Morley said.

After implicating him, Nicole had signed some kind of recantation, saying she'd been angry and told a lie, Clemmons said.

"God damn it," Morley said. "$150,000 bond, all this heartache and bullshit, all for a fucking lie."

Clemmons and Morley had known each other for at least five years. Morley was the lawyer who had helped Clemmons in 2004, when Pulaski County prosecutors had agreed to drop two aggravated robbery charges against Clemmons. Morley worked out of a low-slung complex of brown buildings in North Little Rock, a few blocks north of the muddy, slow-moving Arkansas River. About five feet seven, he had thinning blond hair and a jaunty walk. An Arkansas Razorbacks rug decorated his office, along with a fish tank. On his desk Morley displayed two buck knives.

Clemmons told Morley he was in danger of losing his houses and landscaping business "all because of some fucking adultery."

"You feel me?" Clemmons asked.

"I do, buddy," Morley said. "I've suffered a lot from fucking around on my ex-wife, and, you know, it cost me a bunch of money, but not like this."

Morley's cheating had indeed cost him. Adultery comprised two of the twenty-six disciplinary charges that had been filed against him as a judge. Charge No. 6 was cheating on wife Bonne with girlfriend Kathy. Charge No. 7 was cheating on Kathy—former mistress, now wife—with girlfriend Wanda. Morley was also accused of punching both wives in the stomach while they were pregnant. He was accused of hitting Kathy in the head and face, and of choking her, and of trying to push her down the stairs, and of calling her "every name in the book." He was also accused of telling her that if he lost re-election, he would kill her.

After leaving the bench, Morley had prospered in private practice. He represented all kinds of liquor retailers in permit disputes. He'd been elected secretary/treasurer of the Arkansas Association of Criminal Defense Lawyers. He also remained active politically—donating to Democrats Mike Ross for Congress, Mark Pryor for the U.S. Senate, John Edwards for president, and joining a political action committee determined to elect more lawyers to the Arkansas legislature.

Clemmons told Morley how important it was that he get out of jail—and get out soon. He needed Arkansas to lift its warrant. To that end, Morley offered Clemmons hope.

"I've got a real, real, real good connection out at the Governor's Office," Morley said. "So, you know, I feel like we can get a fair disposition real quick on this. Real quick."

"You can't just make it disappear?"

"I think I can, that's what I'm saying."

"Yeah, well, that's what I need, Steve. *Today*. Like I said, I'd rather spend as much as I can—right now—instead of losing everything."

"Well, do this," Morley said. "Do this. See if you can shoot me about five down here and I'll put it in the trust account. ... If we can do this easily then it's not much. If it gets to be kind of a tug-of-war, then, you know ..."

"Here's what I'll do, Steve. Listen."

Clemmons told Morley that he was in the middle of refinancing one of his houses—and that he planned to borrow $170,000 against the home's equity.

"Here's how I need you to work with me," Clemmons said. "Let me send you a deed to a house I got in Arkansas with a check for $20,000. But post-date the check and let me get out—so that way we can go to closing and I can get that money. Then, I can deposit the money in the account."

"That's OK with me," Morley said.

Morley told Clemmons that he already had a call in to his friend at the Governor's Office. He'd left a message on her cellphone.

"We're working on it," Morley said. "It's not going to happen over the weekend, though. I've got to tell you, I'm not going to lie to you. ... I mean, she's up in Fort Smith, and maybe over in Oklahoma at the casinos. So ..."

"So what you think?" Clemmons said. "The early part of next week or what?"

"I do. I mean that sincerely."

"So you just gonna make it disappear where I can bond out?"

"Yup."

That settled, the two men switched subjects. Morley was also defending Maurice's half brother, Timothy Mack Clemmons. Timothy Clemmons was charged with dealing cocaine, Ecstasy and marijuana; with shooting and wounding a man in Little Rock; and with shooting his eight-year-old daughter in the back, breaking a rib and collapsing a lung. That shooting occurred in a drive-by in which Clemmons was accused of opening fire on his former girlfriend's house, blasting out a bedroom window. Pulaski County prosecutors convinced a judge to revoke Timothy Clemmons' pre-trial bond, saying he posed too great a risk to the public's safety. So at the same time Arkansas held Timothy Clemmons without bond, Washington strived to do the same with his brother. Timothy Clemmons was eventually convicted of shooting his daughter and sentenced to seventy-two years.

But whatever jeopardy his brother might be in, Maurice Clemmons now felt a whole lot better about his own future.

"Hey, I appreciate it, Steve," he told Morley. "You a lifesaver, man."

"Well, you all have always been good to me, and I appreciate it. I don't forget my friends."

Clemmons hung up the phone. But then he picked it right back up and dialed Nicole's number. Getting Arkansas off his back was one thing. But he also had other problems to deal with—chief among them, an angry wife. He would make thirteen calls from jail on this day, working the phone for three-and-a-half hours.

The relationship between Arkansas and Washington—the former, a place that rid itself of a problem citizen; the latter, a place that took the problem in—is as old as crime and geographic boundaries. In the United States, the interstate movement of felons on parole has long created tension and bitterness. Up through the 1920s, state laws often prevented ex-convicts from leaving the state where they were convicted. But enforcement was lax, due, in no small part, to an obvious lack of incentive by most everyone involved. An ex-convict had ample reason to want to make a fresh start elsewhere. And the state where he'd been convicted had ample reason to let him go. Waving goodbye allowed him to become someone else's problem. There was even a term for it—"sundown parole," as in, be gone by sundown, and never come back. But however expedient this arrangement—and however cinematic (picture the marshal, telling the gunslinger to hit the trail)—the result amounted to pawning a dangerous individual off on another jurisdiction, which, suspecting nothing, exercised no special oversight and often paid the price.

In 1934, Congress tried to impose some semblance of order, authorizing interstate compacts to regulate the transfer of parolees. The first compact was struck three years later. Under this system, states would agree—under defined circumstances—to accept each other's ex-convicts and to supervise them. A lexicon developed: a "sending state" was the one that shipped the ex-con out. A "receiving state" accepted him. A sending state would "retake" the ex-con if he violated his parole in the receiving state.

Although an improvement, this system also generated problems. Receiving states often complained that sending states passed along insufficient information about parolees. Correspondence occurred by mail, creating long gaps in communication. New forms of punishment—such as deferred sentences, or those requiring mental-health or substance-abuse treatment—complicated transfers, as each state had its own rules and resources. The system staggered in the 1980s and '90s when the U.S. prison population exploded. Overworked parole officers often denied legitimate transfer requests, violating the 1937 compact. Some officers lost track of their cases, allowing ex-cons to move without warning to other states.

In 1995, a murder in New Jersey epitomized the system's shortcomings. A member of the Warlocks motorcycle gang, Robert "Mudman" Simon (he'd earned his nickname eating a sandwich containing feces), shot and killed a police sergeant in Franklin Township. At the time, Simon was on parole from Pennsylvania, where his record included armed robbery and the murder of his nineteen-year-old girlfriend, shot in the face for refusing to have group sex with other Warlocks. In the aftermath, New Jersey blamed Pennsylvania for paroling Simon after only twelve years. Pennsylvania blamed New Jersey for not enforcing Simon's parole conditions. But both states also accepted some measure of fault, and Pennsylvania overhauled its parole system. The year before Simon murdered the police sergeant, Pennsylvania granted 72 percent of parole petitions; the year after, the figure was 38 percent, causing prison populations to swell.

The controversy also spurred reform on a national level. In 1997, the National Institute of Corrections convened a committee to find a more orderly system of interstate transfers. The result was the Interstate Compact for Adult Offender Supervision—or ICAOS, an unfortunate acronym that captured the very element states wanted to avoid. The system set up a central authority with the power to enforce well-defined rules in federal court. Receiving states could not turn away offenders who had close ties to their state, and sending states had to retake offenders who committed new felonies or proved to be repeat scofflaws. A secure Internet-based network eliminated cumbersome delays in communication. And if arguments among states arose, the compact provided a dispute-resolution process. Between 2000 and 2005, all fifty states, plus the District of Columbia, Puerto Rico and the Virgin Islands, signed on to the compact. Arkansas joined in 2001, while Huckabee was governor. Washington signed on three months later.

The system has not been trouble-free. Shortly after ICAOS was ratified, a sex offender from Pennsylvania got permission to move to Tennessee. Because he had family there, the man was a "mandatory transfer" under ICAOS. But Tennessee law required the man to undergo a psychological test first, and he refused. So Tennessee refused to accept the transfer. The dispute landed in federal court, where, in 2005, a judge sided with ICAOS, ordering Tennessee to assume supervision. "We're in a box, and we put ourselves in there because of this compact," said Bill Dalton, a member of the Tennessee Board of Probation and Parole.

By 2010, the number of interstate transfer cases managed by ICAOS had reached 116,000—still a small fraction of the 5.1 million adults nationwide who are under criminal supervision. Nearly all of the ICAOS cases are so-called mandatory transfers—ex-convicts moving to be near family or jobs. That was the case with Clemmons; his half brother Rickey Hinton pledged to support him. States have little incentive to accept discretionary transfers. Who'd want to add to the workload and risk?

The compact has produced winners and losers—the winners being states that ship out more parolees than they take in, and the losers being those that take in more parolees than they ship out. Think of it as an import-export list. On the loser list, Washington ranks No. 4. During the 2009 fiscal year, Washington exported 1,046 parolees while importing 2,527—or about two-and-a-half times as many, placing a disproportionate burden on the state, now required to supervise all of these additional individuals. One of the biggest winners was Virginia. It shipped out 7,211 parolees while taking in 3,101.

The import-export ratio of ex-convicts is, in fact, a point of pride in some quarters. That is especially true for the criminal justice system's most common pariahs—sex offenders. The chairman of New Jersey's parole board, Peter Barnes, bragged in a 2007 press release that New Jersey's tough laws had made it a place that sex offenders wanted to avoid: Twenty-one convicted sex offenders moved to New Jersey, versus eighty-six who moved away.

"What's wrong with you?" Clemmons asked Nicole.

"A lot."

"Come up with it."

"You know, Maurice, I figure it like this. I've been so true and faithful to you, it's fucking unreal. And for you not to come clean with me, it's really hard to be …"

Clemmons tried to cut her off. "Look here, Nicole …"

"And I'm not talking about the bullshit you told me. I'm talking about the bullshit you haven't told me."

In May, Clemmons had confessed to having a child with a woman named Quiana Williams. But now, Nicole knew his cheating went even further.

"Come clean," she told her husband.

"What is there to come clean about?"

Nicole threw another woman's name in his face.

"Look here, man, I ain't have no relationship," he said.

"That's bullshit. I heard the bitch on the phone. You've been talking to her for five years."

Nicole said she'd recently overheard Clemmons' cousin Eddie on the phone, talking to this other woman. So she put Eddie on the spot. She made Eddie ask the woman questions that plumbed the depths of Maurice's affair with her, while Nicole listened in. For Nicole, the details cut. In June, Maurice had met this woman at a Holiday Inn in Renton; that same day, at the same hotel, he had met Nicole for a husband-wife getaway.

Clemmons, busted, stopped denying the affair. But he refused to provide his wife with an explanation.

"All the shit I've been through with you, I deserve an explanation!" she said. "Ten toes down, even through all this. I'm still taking care of all the business. Everything. I don't deserve an explanation?"

"Okay, listen to this here. You hear me? I'm focused on my freedom."

"And I am, too. That's why I'm calling Morley, all this other stuff."

Nicole pressed. Clemmons dodged. "Listen, Nicole, you're starting to make me hate your guts"—"really," Nicole said—"yeah, for the simple fact, I'm facing a life sentence."

As soon as they hung up, Clemmons was on the phone with Eddie.

"God damn you. How'd you let that happen?"

"She went on the computer and checked the phone records," Eddie said.

"No, you bitch ass nigger, she said she heard you talking on the phone to her."

Eddie hemmed and hawed. He said he'd tried to keep the phone call secret from Nicole, talking to Clemmons' girlfriend in a separate bedroom. When Nicole caught on, he'd tried to trick her, claiming the woman had been sleeping with one of Clemmons' friends, not Clemmons himself. Whatever Eddie's efforts, Clemmons wasn't impressed. He later told a friend that he planned to "close both his eyes and bust out some teeth." In the end, Clemmons and Smith both turned their anger on Eddie. Nicole blamed Eddie for trying to keep the secret; Maurice blamed Eddie for failing.

Clemmons sometimes called Eddie his "wingman." He attached the same label to Carlisle. They were Wingman 1 and Wingman 2. But Clemmons rarely had kind words for his cousin. He rarely had kind words for any of his family or friends. *Not real bright*, he'd say. Talking to other people, Clemmons would run down his sister LaTanya, his uncle Ray, his friend Darcus Allen. "Darcus is retarded," he'd say. Talking to Nicole, Clemmons would run down his half brother Rickey. "Retarded, my brother is retarded." Talking to Rickey or Carlisle, Clemmons would run down Nicole. "When I get out, I'm gonna whip that bitch with a belt. That bitch will be obedient to me, man." Talking to Nicole, Clemmons would run down Carlisle. "His mind is real weak." Nicole encouraged Clemmons to be kind to Boo Man. "Everybody can't be you," she'd say, and Clemmons would agree, "Everybody can't be me."

On July 3—the same day he talked to Morley, and to Nicole, and to Eddie—Clemmons called Carlisle. Clemmons had problems beyond his infidelity. Getting the Arkansas hold removed was but the first of his obstacles. Even if Morley's connections proved as good as advertised and Arkansas rescinded its fugitive warrant, Clemmons was still too broke to make bail in Washington. Nicole had been trying to refinance one of their houses, to pull out $170,000 in equity, but the lender was balking because Nicole didn't have a job, and Clemmons—whose name was on the mortgage—was locked up. They had just a few thousand dollars in savings, and their credit cards were starting to max out.

But Clemmons had a plan. He told Carlisle to get on his computer, go to the Zoe Ministries' chat room, and begin typing a message.

"Okay, write this down," Clemmons said. "… tell them the man of God is locked up …"

"… okay, man of God is …"

"… locked up, and he is ready to reap his harvest, and give them both bank account numbers."

"… he is ready to reap his harvest …"

"Yeah, and have Nicole give you both bank account numbers. The Chase account number and Bank of America."

Clemmons wanted Carlisle to ask the church's followers to post his bail.

"They know who I am, right?"

"Yes, they do."

"They doing everything in Lord Jesus Christ's name, right?"

"Yup, everything in Jesus Christ's name."

"They know I'm Jesus Christ. Then pay me my goddamn money! Right or wrong?"

"Right," Carlisle said.

"I'm the Lord, nigger," Clemmons said. "What part of that don't you understand?"

Clemmons zeroed in on the dollar figure he expected from Bishop Jordan's followers. "Tell them 37 billion in the Chase account …"

"Okay, hold on. Thirty-seven bill-i-on, billion with a b, in the Chase account."

"Make sure you say billion."

"I'm gonna say billion … in the Chase account. I'm writing it down."

"And, um, um, um, 7 million in the Bank of America account."

Carlisle wrote that down, too. Clemmons, feeling generous, told Carlisle that he should also provide his own bank account number—and ask for another $7 million in donations to be deposited into it.

Carlisle told Clemmons he would carry his word: "I'm gonna follow it out because I'm the messenger."

"Right, you got the message straight from the Lord," Clemmons said. He burst out in laughter. "Ain't that a trip?"

"Yeah, it's a trip, it's a trip."

Her voice was so thin, so retreating, so scared, he had trouble making it out.

"Your momma say you ain't even been asking about me," Clemmons said.

It was July 5. Clemmons wasn't supposed to have contact with his twelve-year-old stepdaughter—the child he was accused of raping—but here he was, talking to her on the telephone. He called her "peanut head" and said he wanted to know why she hadn't been asking about him.

"I was hurt," Clemmons told the girl. "I said I know she wouldn't do me like that. You wouldn't do me like that, would you?"

"No."

"Huh?"

"No."

Washington's Child Protective Services already had an open file on Clemmons. Teresa Berg, the Pierce County sheriff's detective, had followed up her threat to Nicole and called CPS. Nicole may have recanted her claim about Clemmons molesting her stepdaughter, but the initial complaint was good enough for CPS to start asking questions. CPS could enforce the no-contact order by removing the girl from Nicole's care. If CPS found that Nicole allowed Clemmons to see or talk with the girl, the agency could go to court and ask that the child be moved to foster care or, more likely, sent to live with a relative.

But despite those options—and despite the severity of the alleged abuse by Clemmons—CPS pursued this case with little vigor. Months passed before the assigned social worker even scrounged up a copy of the girl's interview with Detective Berg. Nicole later agreed to take her daughter to counseling and to call 911 if Clemmons saw the girl. But on this day, there was no call to 911.

Clemmons told the girl he'd be out of jail in a few days.

"All right," he said. "Put your momma on the phone."

She handed the phone to Nicole.

7

THE GOLD PACKAGE

IF THERE'S ONE INSTITUTION THAT CAPTURED the greed and short-sightedness that crippled the U.S. and world economies in 2008, that institution was Washington Mutual, a small savings and loan that became a really big bank, acquiring other banks from California to Utah to South Carolina to New York, and diving headlong into subprime loans, writing loan after loan under the marketing banner *The Power of Yes*, writing loans that offered small promise of ever being repaid (Little income? Insufficient collateral? *Just say yes*), then bundling those loans and selling them off as securities, injecting the financial markets with a ticking time bomb of bad debt. Washington Mutual epitomized the fallacy of something for nothing, symbolizing a time in which money lost its meaning.

So it was only fitting that it was an old Washington Mutual branch, since gobbled up by JP Morgan Chase, that Nicole Smith prepared to visit on the morning of July 7, 2009, holding a check for $150 million. Her check possessed as much value as many of the loans Washington Mutual once wrote with such gleeful abandon. About the only thing real were the zeros.

Nicole had been informed of the plan that morning, when her husband had called from jail, waking her up, saying, "I got something for you to do." Write yourself a personal check, he said, for $150 million. Make it a Bank of America check, so the funds will be drawn from your account there. Take the check and deposit it in your account at Chase. But first: Anoint the check. Take oil and trace a cross on the front of the check and another on the back. Also: Pray seven times. Five times before you leave the house. Once in the car. Once as you walk up to the teller.

"Okay," Nicole said.

Nicole didn't balk, she didn't challenge. About the only thing she asked was where he got the figure of $150 million.

"From God," Clemmons said.

"Oh."

"He said this is the seventh day of the week, and this is the seventh month. He said deposit 150 in the Chase account and He said anoint the check."

Clemmons told Nicole that if she believed, if she brooked no doubt that the funds would be there, then God would provide and the funds would be there. "You have to walk on faith," Clemmons told her.

That morning, the two talked three times before Nicole headed to a Chase branch in Tacoma, on Seventy-second and Pacific. Clemmons turned these conversations into a pep talk, trying to instill as much confidence as he could. First, he drew on his own experience.

"See baby, I'm gonna tell you something, and this is how you gotta look at it. This is all faith is. When I was going to hit them licks, I had faith I was going to be successful at it. That's all it is. I had faith that every lick I hit, I was going to get away with it. You see what I'm saying? And I used to get away with them. It took courage to go do what I did."

Hit them licks. That's slang for robbery.

Then Clemmons drew on Nicole's experience. As Clemmons talked, Nicole listened to gospel music. She also had spent the morning reading the Bible, looking for calm, telling herself: "The money is in the bank. I am a millionaire. Manifestation."

Clemmons reminded Nicole of times in her past when she would cash "bogus" checks, knowing she didn't have the money.

"I used to do that shit a lot …" Nicole said.

"Exactly."

"… when I was writing them hot checks."

Clemmons told her this was basically the same thing, only this time God was saying the check is real, God was saying He would cash it for her.

"You been doing these things, but you been doing them the other way," Clemmons said.

"Really, I been trained to do it," Nicole said.

"Yeah. The whole time. Right or wrong?"

"You right," she said.

Clemmons told Nicole to cast away all worry.

"What you need to do, go and eat your cookie, you hear me?"

"Well, see, that's what I did yesterday and then it started playing mind tricks on me," Nicole said.

Clemmons reiterated how bold he had been in his life of crime.

"OK, then. If you my woman, you got to be bold."

"I am bold, Maurice. I done did some wicked shit in my life. Crazy stuff. Crazy and everything else."

"Be crazy for the Lord now, then."

She laughed. They both laughed.

This telephone conversation was nothing all that unusual for Clemmons. Even though his words were taped—all of them, every word—he peppered his calls from jail with an astonishing array of admissions and allusions. He would talk about maybe selling their new house, the one around the corner from where they lived, the one built with insurance proceeds after fire destroyed the previous dwelling. "I look at it that God know how I got that house," Clemmons told Nicole. "You follow me? So He probably want us to get rid of it, period, anyway." Clemmons mulled the possibility of wrecking his cars for insurance. Another time he talked of their current roster of houses.

"If I have to, I burn every last one of them down, for the insurance," he said.

"No, don't talk about that on the phone," Nicole replied.

To Carlisle, Clemmons talked of how God had helped with armed robberies: "All them licks that I done hit, they were meant for me to hit. He had them set up. That's why they were so easy. I should have been shot up like a mother." He talked of how he'd made a living selling, or "slinging," drugs. Cocaine. Marijuana. Ecstasy. He spoke of this in the past tense, but while Clemmons was in jail, he and Nicole would sometimes hush their voices and make weird references to "trees" and "cookies" and "batter," references that made no sense until they tripped up and let slip that a cookie wasn't a cookie, a cookie was a blunt, a cigar-sized stick of marijuana. The same morning the two talked about depositing that $150 million check, they had one of these conversations seeded with code.

"So, was I not supposed to, uh, do anything with them trees?" Nicole said.

"Why?"

"Because I, uh, twenty dollars."

"Oh, you making twenty dollars?" Clemmons said. "Yeah, you can do that. But you got them from the cookies."

"Oh, OK. Got you."

"Keep them batches of cookies. … Gonna be hard to find some good stuff."

"I wasn't sure, because I started thinking about it, and I know you said you weren't going to be doing anything anymore …"

"I got 'em from the cookies," Clemmons said. "He give us the green herb. The herb ain't like all the other stuff. You know what I'm saying. We got it just for the cookies. You still got some of that batter, make it up already, huh? … You ain't gave away my cookies, have you?"

"Nah, I gave Dorcus one, but there's still some out there. That's all I gave him, just the one. And I had a couple. They ain't yours, they're ours."

"Yeah, you know what I'm saying."

Clemmons talked to Nicole of how they used to get fast money, and "fast money go fast." But now they would be getting "God money."

"I ain't one to stay in no game for forever anyway, Nicole."

"In what?"

"In the game."

"Yeah, I know that. I didn't want that either."

"We were tired of it."

"Been tired of it."

"Exactly," Clemmons said. "Tired of looking over our shoulder, tired of all that. You know what I'm saying? But what got us was, we thought that we were going to come out of it on our own terms."

Instead, Clemmons said, they were coming out on God's terms, on supernatural terms, whether they were ready or not.

To Clemmons' mind, what he and Nicole were up to now, trying to deposit this $150 million check, was a switch in direction, a way of going straight. But with Clemmons and his circle of friends, the lines often fuzzed between crime and commerce, between a legitimate enterprise and a con. Clemmons referred to his friend Reggie Robinson as a minister. That's how Robinson portrayed himself when he visited Clemmons in jail—a sight that amused Clemmons to no end. "He was looking like Elvis Presley the Third," he told Nicole. Robinson may have picked up a minister's certificate but more notable was his criminal record, which included a string of theft charges in Washington. Robinson told Clemmons that he planned to get a booth at Sea-Tac Airport and solicit donations for the church he'd created. "I'm just gonna post up, man … because they don't know me from nobody else."

Clemmons lived in a world of predators and prey, and while he was usually the predator, he was sometimes the prey, a big fish getting nibbled at by even bigger fish. For many Americans, banks became Public Enemy No. 1 for deceptive loaning practices that contributed to the tumble in the real estate market. Clemmons himself complained of how one of his houses was "upside down"—meaning he owed some bank more for the house than the house was now worth. But Clemmons was always eager to turn things around. While in jail he tried to refinance another home, in order to pull out some much-needed equity. When the bank objected to his family's insufficient proof of income, he and Nicole arranged to make up a fake job for her.

After Nicole arrived at the Chase branch, Clemmons dialed her cellphone. She told him she was just sitting there, in front of the counter, waiting for word on the check.

"They're having a hard time entering it into the computer," Nicole said. "There's too many zeros."

"You gonna be all right," Clemmons told her. "God got you. He got angels around you and everything."

Clemmons told Nicole they had been trying to win the lottery for years, and now God was just going to give them the money straightaway. "This is His lottery, and He's the boss of all the banks."

"I love you, Nicole," Clemmons said.

"Do you?"

"I really do. I'm glad God made you for me, because we fit. Don't you think we fit?"

"And I love you."

After a long, long wait, the bank gave Nicole a receipt for her deposit, but told her it would take days or weeks for the check to clear. She would just have to await word.

For Daniel Murphy (Clemmons lawyer No. 1: Washington) and Stephen Morley (Clemmons lawyer No. 2: Arkansas), the challenge was to get Clemmons out from under the Arkansas fugitive warrant. To do that, they would have to overcome the protestations of Washington.

As far as Washington was concerned, Clemmons was now Arkansas' problem. Because the "absconder" warrant made no allowance for bail, Washington's Corrections Department staff saw two scenarios: Either Clemmons would be held in jail until convicted on the assault and child-rape charges—and then sent to prison for a long time, possibly for life. Or Clemmons would be acquitted, but still returned to Arkansas because he'd fled in May, violating his parole. Either way, Washington's supervisory division was done with him. The state sent notice to Arkansas that it was ending supervision and closing its file on Clemmons.

Murphy and Morley talked on the telephone at least twice during the first week of July. Murphy worked on getting records to help Morley make Clemmons' case. He talked with Nicole about her recantation. He also met with a counselor who had begun seeing Clemmons; the counselor wrote a letter about this treatment, and Murphy faxed it to Morley.

In the meantime, Morley worked on identifying the players involved in the issuance of the fugitive warrant. In telephone calls with Clemmons, Morley said he'd found out that the person in charge of ICAOS cases for Arkansas was a woman named Linda Strong. She worked for G. David Guntharp, the director of the Arkansas Department of Community Correction. Morley told Clemmons that Strong had not been receptive to his initial approach. "About as blind as a bat about a lot of that stuff," he said. Strong had wanted details on Clemmons' mental-health treatment, Morley told Clemmons.

On July 8, Morley wrote a letter to Strong, downplaying Clemmons' problems in Washington. Clemmons was facing new charges, yes. But, according to Morley, those charges "may be dismissed in the near future." Morley also challenged the propriety of Arkansas' "absconder" warrant. Washington's Corrections Department had gone years without requiring Clemmons to report, Morley wrote. If Clemmons wasn't required to report, how could he have absconded? "It is my belief there is some confusion concerning Mr. Clemmons' status," Morley's letter said.

Morley's interpretation of "abscond" was decidedly narrower than the basis cited by Washington when it had requested the warrant. When the warrant had been issued, Clemmons was on the lam. He'd failed to show up for his arraignment on felony charges. His wife said he'd left home. He wasn't supposed to change residences—or even stay away overnight—without Corrections Department permission.

On the morning of July 9, Morley spoke again with Strong. But he didn't appear to be making much headway with her. "She was kind of tepid about it," Morley told Clemmons later that day. Even so, Morley remained upbeat. He told Clemmons:

"I believe there's calls being made to David Guntharp. ...

"I've already called my friend out there and she's talking with David Guntharp. ...

"I believe that you'll get out tomorrow."

Clemmons may also have had another emissary making his case to the head of the Arkansas parole system. Arkansas records say that Clemmons' wife, Nicole, made a personal appeal to Guntharp. But Guntharp later said he did not recall talking with anyone from Clemmons' family.

The counselor who had been treating Clemmons was Timothy Bean, a forty-year-old practitioner who worked at Crossroads Counseling in Lakewood, Washington. Clemmons had started seeing Bean in the spring, after the twin incidents that generated all those felony charges. It was Bean who had met with Murphy concerning Clemmons' current predicament.

On July 9, at a few minutes after noon, Clemmons called Bean from jail.

"Hey, Maurice, how are you?"

"I'm all right."

"Hey, I apologize that my letter didn't help," Bean said. "I thought that it would."

"Ain't no problem," Clemmons said. "Certain things meant to happen certain ways."

In a profile available online—in a therapy directory produced by *Psychology Today*—Bean says his focus is to help people "overcome their fears and learn to live with grace and dignity within their economic reality. ... I believe each of us has a true center that contains the wisdom needed to grow and heal. Using a foundation of Humanistic therapy the healing wisdom of each client is explored in a respectful and compassionate way. ... I believe that much of our society is asleep and seeking to awaken. I have an interactive style that supports and respects the power of each individual to grow and heal. The journey of each individual is sacred and unique."

Clemmons called Bean his "psychological and spiritual adviser." Bean called Clemmons a charismatic man, beloved by his family, who was dealing with a "spiritual crisis" rooted in the 108-year sentence he'd received in Arkansas as a youth. To Bean, Clemmons was "trying to solve the hole within him—the great injustice that occurred when he was sixteen years old. All his choices led him back to solve that crisis."

On the phone, Clemmons told Bean that upon arriving in jail he had asked for a Bible. The first page he turned to said be faithful to your wife and be faithful to God—and that very day, Clemmons' wife discovered an affair he'd been having for four years.

"Oh, boy."

"Yeah. So, you know, everything is real."

"Yeah."

Being locked up, he'd had time to think and to read the whole Bible, Clemmons said. "I know He pruning me right now, He cutting off all the rough edges—you know, preparing me for whatever it is to come. You know?"

"Absolutely. Absolutely."

Clemmons told Bean: "Once the story is told, all the witnesses that was involved come forward and tell what they saw, the things they saw me capable of doing, like me stopping the wind, and, you know, these balls of light appearing, you know, things like that, then the truth got to be told. Too many people saw what I saw and experienced what I saw. And, you know, everything that happened was supernatural. You know?"

"Yeah."

"So I'm just gonna let God guide my footsteps, I'm gonna stop fighting it and, you know, I'm gonna obey all his commandments and just do what I know I'm supposed to do, what He created me to do."

"Absolutely," Bean said. "And He created you to do great things."

Clemmons said: "Even my wife, she finally coming around to it. People run from the unfamiliar and what they don't know. ... For things to happen to me the way they happened to me, it was really mind-blowing. ... It's amazing, though, huh?"

"It is," Bean said.

Bean told Clemmons: "Well, I think the biggest part of this lesson, Maurice, is that you have to begin to live without fear. And once you can start living without fear, you won't have to run from anything. Fear is a tool of the devil." Clemmons told Bean he wasn't scared of the devil ... he wasn't scared of any man ... he would stand toe-to-toe with anyone ... he no longer worried about material things, and Bean said *good, good, good, excellent.*

When Clemmons began thinking he was Jesus Christ, he received what he interpreted to be affirmation from all kinds of sources. Other people may not have been lining up and saying "yes, you are Jesus Christ," but that's what Clemmons was hearing. He believed he had convinced other inmates at the jail, including one who said, *I can tell you've been anointed,* and another with the biblical name of Luke. He believed he had convinced the jail chaplain. While reading, Clemmons would seize upon random details as proof of his true identity as Jesus. "He had four other brothers. Just like I do. Because we one and the same." And some people actually were saying *yes, you are the Messiah.* Clemmons' Aunt Chrisceda picked up on this weird vibe. When she called Clemmons' home, Eddie Davis, the young cousin, answered the phone with: "Aunt C, you know that Maurice is your lord savior Jesus Christ." "It was kind of like a cult thing, as far as I can tell," Chrisceda says. "He was believing what Maurice was telling him, that he was God. Eddie was going along with Maurice's program, as crazy as it was."

Clemmons also took assurance in the prophecies that he, Nicole and Carlisle were receiving from Zoe Ministries, prophecies communicated by phone, mail or Internet. Clemmons belonged to the Trailblazer program, which, according to the church's Web site, provides twelve months' worth of prophecies at a cost of $365. The prophecies the three received could be general—a blessing awaits you, don't procrastinate, you'll have a new awareness—or as specific as go into real estate or buy a new car. Clemmons could always find something in his life to confirm the prophets' words. One prophecy declared that on the twenty-ninth, he'd be able to buy some stuff. And what had happened on the twenty-ninth? He'd ordered some stuff from the jail commissary. Another prophecy declared that in a particular month, he would need to have patience. "Well," Clemmons said, "what better way to have patience than in jail?"

Requests for money often accompanied these prophecies. The church called these donations tithes or "sowing a seed." Sow a seed for $388, one of Clemmons' prophecies said, and that will "unlock gold potential for you." Clemmons and Carlisle made a practice of tithing, diverting 10 percent of certain checks that came their way. They also bought Zoe products—purchasing, for example, an MP4 player of the master prophet's teachings, at a cost of about four hundred dollars. Clemmons based one decision after another on the latest prophecies received, while drawing comfort from their unfolding. When Carlisle praised Clemmons after an extended oration on the power of love, Clemmons said: "My prophecy said that in the month of July, I would be going to another level. And that's what you just said, right? That I've gone to another level. So God doesn't lie, right?"

Clemmons had a plan. He had lots of plans, but his plan for today was real estate.

While Clemmons was in jail, Nicole and Carlisle attended a workshop on real-estate investments sponsored by Trump University, Donald Trump's online business school. For Clemmons, the Trump name carried such caché he could not resist. Clemmons and Carlisle had earlier attended a ninety-minute seminar presented by the same institution and elected afterward to sign up for the $1,495 three-day workshop. With Clemmons in jail, Nicole took his place. "Look," Clemmons told her on July 10, the workshop's first day. "You going to the best school for real estate that money can buy. Now ain't that a blessing?"

Any advice that flowed under the Trump name, Clemmons absorbed in a way that was stunningly literal. "Convenience is the enemy" became, for Clemmons, a directive to sell his residence, because having a house to live in was nothing if not convenient. For Clemmons and Carlisle, the seminar and workshop fired dreams of wealth. Clemmons said that once he made bail, the two would go into business together, "the nerd and the gangsta." They would invest in distressed real estate—in Michigan, in Georgia, in every state you could think of—and cash in when prices spiked. "We gonna do a fifty-state strategy," Clemmons said. They would travel in luxury RVs, towing a car behind, wearing thousand-dollar tailored suits. Their company, Clemmons said, would "outpace Google and Microsoft until they want to buy it out for at least $100 billion."

"Who knows what the next day gonna bring?" Clemmons told Carlisle from jail. "Today I'm sitting in here, looking at this wall. Tomorrow we could be multimillionaires. Just look at how quick it flips. You never know."

Clemmons also had other businesses he planned to launch. He and Carlisle would invest in GM and customize "old-school Buicks" with fiberglass bodies—"It'll get 25 to 30 miles per gallon," Clemmons said—and high-end DVD players. "Black folks will eat them up like candy." Clemmons' mind became fevered, his mood giddy, as he ordered Carlisle to lay the groundwork for one enterprise after another. "Write this down," he'd say. "We're going to make us a bottled water company, and we're gonna name it Revelations. Because ain't nobody's water gonna be good but our own." Clemmons told Nicole they would start anew in Michigan and spend their winters on snowmobiles, wearing goggles, dressed in thermals, kicking up snow. They'd move to Ann Arbor, to "new neighbors, new scenery, everything, then we'll be around more black people." (Ann Arbor is 9 percent black, a smaller percentage than in Tacoma.) Clemmons and Carlisle would buy Bentleys, the quarter-million-dollar sticker price be damned. Nicole would get a Mercedes-Benz.

Carlisle became skeptical of the Trump enterprise, saying the ninety-minute seminar seemed designed to get people to sign up for the $1,495 workshop, and the workshop seemed designed to get people to sign up for an even pricier mentorship program. The mentorship program would separate the wannabes from the gonna-bes, is how the sales pitch went. Each step of the way, Carlisle told Clemmons, the program offered enough information to spark interest but not enough to act upon. "So it's a hustle," he said. But Clemmons and Nicole weren't discouraged. Describing the mentorship program, Nicole told Maurice: "It's the gold package. It's like 29 percent off. It's normally $47,000. They're giving it to people for like $35,000." The couple didn't have the $70,000 needed to sign up two people, so Clemmons told Nicole to offer a post-dated check. That was Clemmons' answer to most financial pinches—a post-dated check or swiping a maxed-out credit card and hoping the charge went through. Clemmons told Carlisle: "No, what it is, bro, it's not a hustle, it's the truth. You gonna need mentorship."

Clemmons planned to buy or lease office space for his fledgling real-estate enterprise, but when one of the Zoe prophets called Nicole—"He asked if we had an office at home, and I said, 'Yeah, in the back,' and he said, 'God is touching the office and blessing it'"—Clemmons decided a home-based business was the way to go. "That's a good prophecy about the office being blessed, we'll set up there." Clemmons was convinced they would become rich—and by ways not wicked, but holy and godly and right. The idea so delighted him that he laughed and laughed, a man in jail, joyous at what lay ahead.

"Hey, what's up girl. Tell me some good news."

It was July 14—two weeks after Clemmons turned himself in and was returned to jail. Nicole, his wife, did indeed have good news: "Steve Morley called me yesterday evening and said he went over that lady's head, straight to the head of the parole board in Arkansas, and they said it will take until Wednesday to recall the warrant."

"Wednesday? Well, that's a blessing," Clemmons said.

Morley, the lawyer in Arkansas, had come through. The fugitive warrant was going to be lifted. Nicole had tried other means to free her husband. She'd reached out to Marion Humphrey, the judge who had supported Clemmons' petition for clemency years earlier and who had married them. But Humphrey told Nicole that the fugitive matter fell outside his jurisdiction; however, he would pray for Clemmons, he would hope for the best. In the end it was Morley who had swung matters Clemmons' way. On the phone, Clemmons repeatedly asked Nicole to relate this story, *tell me again*, exulting in how his lawyer had gone over Linda Strong's head. Nicole would relate how Morley had gone straight to the head of the parole system, how he had dealt with "some lady who speaks directly to the governor." Nicole recounted how Linda Strong was described as a bureaucrat—"she's gotta go by the books"—and how Morley had said he didn't want to step on toes, but he had to go over her. "He sounded confident," Nicole said of Morley. "He was laughing."

"That's why I say we have to have Steve," Clemmons told Nicole. "Steve know people. They try to go through the proper chain of command and it didn't work."

Clemmons had nothing but hostility and suspicion when it came to police and prosecutors and parole officers. But he liked his lawyers. "Steve a good dude," he'd tell Nicole. "That's one white man there that we can trust." Clemmons had equal words of praise for Murphy, his lawyer in Washington. "Daniel is down. You hear me? That dude is a good lawyer. I'm talking about he real righteous, he been telling them folks how they been messing around. ... I put him in the same category with Steve Morley ... You know Steve is a righteous guy. ... Daniel and Steve, them's some real finds there. God truly blessed me to hook me up with them two cats."

Morley and Murphy both talked a language that resonated with Clemmons—occasionally profane, often tough, typically sympathetic to whatever was grinding away at Clemmons at a particular moment. Clemmons didn't much care for bail-bond companies. Murphy told him: "Bail-bonds people are dirty people, all they care about is money. They don't give a shit about people, all they care about is money, money, money, money." Talking strategy with Clemmons, Murphy would talk of the prosecutor this way: "I don't want him knowing anything. I want to ambush that son of a bitch next week if we have to." Clemmons believed that without his two lawyers, he would have been "railroaded," that the Arkansas warrant would never have been lifted.

Morley gave Clemmons the news himself on July 15: "I talked with the parole board and you're all approved. It'll go in the computer and you should be cleared by tomorrow." And indeed it did—and indeed he was. On July 16 Arkansas rescinded its absconder warrant on Clemmons. The state sent word to Washington to re-open its supervision of Clemmons and to notify Arkansas once the criminal charges were resolved. If Washington considered Clemmons to be Arkansas' problem, Arkansas was now saying: He's yours until further notice. In an e-mail to Linda Strong, a co-worker said the decision to lift Arkansas' hold had come down from David Guntharp: "This is the case the Director requested the abscond warrant be recalled to allow this offender to bond out."

When Morley touted his "real, real, real good connection" in the Governor's Office, he was referring to Amy Click-Horoda, Governor Mike Beebe's liaison to the Arkansas parole system. Click-Horoda knew Morley through legal organizations as well as mutual friends in Fort Smith, Arkansas, where Click-Horoda lives. Click-Horoda would later decline to sit for an interview about the Clemmons case. But through a spokesperson, she said she often spoke with Morley about criminal cases, although she didn't remember calls specifically about Clemmons. If there had been such calls, she said, she would have referred Morley to David Guntharp or Linda Strong. Guntharp says: "It was not unusual for her to call. Usually, if there was an issue to be resolved on interstate compact, she would tell them to contact me or Linda Strong. I don't recall getting any calls. She could have, in terms of seeking information. What she'd say is, 'Check into this and see what you think.'"

As for Morley, he won't talk about anything he might have said to anyone regarding Clemmons. He told a reporter: "I don't discuss clients, living or dead." Then he slapped the reporter on the back and wished him a nice stay in Little Rock.

Arkansas' decision to rescind the abscond warrant baffled and angered Washington's Corrections Department staff. Administrators traded e-mails expressing dismay. One called the situation a "major malfunction." The agency simply had not anticipated that Arkansas would withdraw the warrant; the staff could not remember that ever happening before.

The Clemmons case, it turned out, slipped into a crack between two ICAOS rules. One rule, 4.112, said Washington could end its supervision when Clemmons fled and Arkansas issued an absconder warrant. This rule recognized that Arkansas had a duty to take back its parole violator. But a second rule conflicted with the first. Rule 5.102 said if Clemmons was convicted of a new felony, Arkansas had to retake him—but only after Clemmons had served out his prison term in Washington for the new crime.

Within hours of learning of Arkansas' decision, Marjorie Owens, an ICAOS administrator for Washington, puzzled over the conflicting rules. With no Arkansas warrant to hold him, Clemmons could now bail out. And if he did, Washington no longer had authority to supervise him, having closed his file.

On July 23, Owens wrote an unusually blunt e-mail to her Arkansas counterparts: "Please provide your justification for cancelling the abscond warrant. Cancelling the warrant appears to be in violation of ICAOS rules. ... At this point, without clarification justifying your actions, Washington is not going to reopen this case and resume supervision. Hopefully this offender will not get out. I'm concerned that you have no problem releasing your offender into our community, based on his behavior. I thought ICAOS was all about community safety."

Arkansas officials took nearly two weeks to respond. The reply, from Linda Strong, was terse: "The warrant was rescinded. When the pending charges are adjudicated we will reconsider the case."

For Washington, another option existed. Harry Hageman, the executive director for ICAOS, sat in his office in Lexington, Kentucky, willing and able to intervene. Under the compact's rules, Washington could have requested a hearing to resolve the dispute. The conflict with Arkansas could even have been sent to arbitration, with the matter decided by a neutral panel drawn from three other states. A binding legal opinion could have been had within weeks. In early August,

Owens called Hageman to complain about Arkansas and its handling of Clemmons. Do you want me to give Arkansas a call? Hageman asked. Hageman had previously led Ohio's parole department and knew supervision cases could go awry. No, don't do that, Owens told him. Hageman did not hear about the matter again. "Neither state involved the commission to do what was needed," he says. "Both states felt comfortable in their position and let it go."

On July 18, Clemmons called Nicole from jail. She was stressed about gathering money for his bail and dealing with unexpected home repairs. She also continued to burn about her husband's cheating.

"I just want you to know, I love you and really respect you," Clemmons said.

"And, uh, things gonna get better with us, and our relationship will get back to the plateau that it once was on. Our love gonna take off in a new direction. We gonna grow, we ain't gonna shrivel. We gonna grow, you know what I'm saying. Like you said, ain't no quitting in you and ain't no quitting in us. We gonna fight for our marriage to be, you know, holy and beautiful, you know what I'm saying. And let our love roll, get our relationship back with the kids and get everything back stable, you know what I'm saying. We gonna have some tough days ahead of us but at the same time, with me pulling and you pulling and we pulling together and things like that, we gonna overcome anything that come before us. Because like I said, you got love in you and I got love in me and we got God in us. And both of us doing what we doing, we can overcome anything that comes in our path."

After a long pause, Clemmons said: "You hear me, love?"

"I hear you."

Moments later, Nicole handed the phone to Rickey Hinton—Clemmons' half brother, the man who had agreed to be Clemmons' sponsor when he had left Arkansas and moved to Washington.

"Guess what," Hinton said. "And this is bad. Little mama is pregnant."

Yet another woman—Clemmons' mistress No. 3—had told Hinton she was pregnant with Clemmons' child.

"She acting kinda sad about it, bro," Hinton said. "I told her, don't say nothing. She strong, but I said, this is on your head. Don't tell nobody, your sister or nobody. Because she said you all did it without a rubber and all that, right. I said I don't need no details."

"That's the truth, brother," Clemmons said.

Clemmons asked if she was showing yet. Hinton said no.

"Look," Clemmons said. "Listen. I gave her one hundred dollars and told her to go get the thang, man. Just like the other broad."

By late July, the Clemmons case had become a labyrinth for employees at the Washington Department of Corrections. How they had gotten here—that was confusing. Where they should go now—that was confusing. Officers and supervisors and administrators passed e-mails back and forth, debating the situation: "You guys are confusing me ... This is a messy situation ... Would you please explain this to me?" In dealing with Clemmons, the department may not have made the best decisions—a matter that remains in dispute to this day. But any missteps could not be attributed to bureaucratic indifference. The case received attention up and down the ladder of command.

The agency's recent history explained why. In 2006, three law-enforcement officers were killed in the Puget Sound area within four months. Two were Seattle police officers, the third a King County sheriff's deputy. All were killed by felons under Corrections Department supervision, and in each instance the department had screwed up, setting the tragic events in motion. The missteps included overlooking an offender's outstanding arrest warrant or minimizing such parole violations as breaking into a car, testing positive for cocaine, and blowing off mandatory appointments with a corrections officer.

The three deaths prompted powerful blow-back. Governor Chris Gregoire ordered the department to drop the hammer on offenders who violated supervision. Community corrections officers were told to impose more jail time for violations. Arrest warrants were to be issued within seventy-two hours—not the weeks or months it took before. And a new law forced the department to focus on higher-risk offenders, causing thousands of lower-risk felons—often those with drug crimes—to be cut loose. The legislature's in-house think tank, the Washington State Institute for Public Policy, developed a new risk matrix, using criminal records to identify those offenders most likely to be violent. That matrix has been criticized by Corrections Department field staff because it accounts only for criminal history—not pending charges, not an offender's religious delusions, not the gut instinct of a well-trained corrections officer. That matrix found Clemmons to be "High Non-Violent"—meaning he was labeled a high risk to commit new crimes, but not to spill blood.

The department's problem with Clemmons was this: The agency had initially filed a report that accused him of violating his parole by committing all those felonies in May. If Clemmons was found at an administrative hearing to have committed those violations, he could be sanctioned with jail time, achieving the agency's goal of keeping him in custody. But when Arkansas had issued its abscond warrant—and Washington had responded by closing its file on Clemmons—all those alleged parole violations were dismissed.

"So, here we are," Lori Ramsdell-Gilkey wrote in an e-mail to seven Corrections Department colleagues. "[Clemmons] is in a local jail with no Arkansas hold and no Washington DOC hold and the offender may or may not be able to bail out. We don't want that to happen if we can help it." Ramsdell-Gilkey was a supervisor in the hearings unit, which handled alleged parole violations. She came up with an idea "to get some sort of rein back on this case," a way to "work around" Arkansas. She said the department should amend its original parole-violation report and add a new allegation—one that had not already been dismissed. The new allegation could be failing to report to the department. Or maybe absconding from the state's supervision. If a hearing officer found probable cause on the alleged violation, the department could recommend that Arkansas pick Clemmons up. "Then it is on them if the offender walks," she wrote.

When Ramsdell-Gilkey sent this e-mail, the only thing holding Clemmons in jail was the amount of his bail: $150,000 on the rape count, plus $40,000 on the other charges.

The bail bondswoman on the phone with Clemmons was gentle but firm: If I post your bond, you will go back to court for each hearing, right, Maurice?

"Nicole has tried so hard," said Lucille Fisher, the eighty-year-old owner of Seattle Bonding Company. "She has assured me over and over that you are an upright, upstanding person, that your word is your bond. She has assured me of that. I wanted to talk to you too, because, uh, this would wipe me out."

Clemmons' grand schemes from earlier in the month had gone nowhere. No $37 billion (*billion, with a b*) from Zoe Ministries. No $150 million in Nicole's Chase account. (The check didn't clear. Chase closed Nicole's account. Bank of America did, too.) No more talk of thousand-dollar suits and Bentleys and Benzes. Clemmons was still staring at $190,000 bail. Normally, a defendant would be expected to post 10 percent of the bail in order to bond out. But Nicole had found a bonding company—Lucille Fisher's company—willing to make a deal. Nicole had scraped together about fifty-two hundred dollars in cash and from credit cards. Clemmons was promising to make installment payments, and they were still working on refinancing one of their houses. For collateral, he would sign liens on at least two houses, including the one in Little Rock that Stephen Morley already held as collateral for his bill. Clemmons also offered to put in jewelry and to sell some of his vintage cars.

Fisher was anxious. If Clemmons fled again—as he had in May—her company would be on the hook for the full $190,000. Clemmons had to sell her on his reliability.

"I ain't got no reason to run," Clemmons said. "And, all you have to do is take whatever money she got now, and give me, give us until we refinance this other house I got and we'll pay the difference. If you'll just work with me, I'm a man of my word, you know."

Clemmons told Fisher that he'd had a "spiritual" revelation while in jail, and that he did not fear going back, if convicted. "Like I said, Ms. Fisher, I went to prison when I was sixteen years old, I did fifteen straight years. I was raised in prison."

In the end, Fisher agreed to post the bond for $5,200 down plus monthly payments for the rest. Her willingness to cut a deal—to let Clemmons out for so much less than 10 percent upfront—would have come as a surprise to John McCarthy, the judge who initially set Clemmons' bail at $190,000. McCarthy didn't know such negotiations were even allowed. He thought defendants needed 10 percent or they stayed behind bars. But lots of prosecutors in Washington were familiar with the bail system's resemblance to a bazaar—and they weren't happy about it. "There's no truth in bail," says Dan Satterberg, King County's prosecuting attorney. When defendants can walk on less than 10 percent of their bail, "that forces us to guess what amount of bail will keep them in jail and keep them from escaping the system or committing further crimes. When we guess wrong, bad things can happen."

In late July, Clemmons began to entertain doubts. Not about the criminal justice system—his mind had long since been made up on that, he was a victim, the system was crooked—but about the church he had turned to for support.

Clemmons' doubts could be traced two weeks back. The circumstances are hazy—the telephone conversations provide a sketch, but not details—but somehow or another a Tacoma-area branch of Bank of America had been presented with a check, for a large amount, that involved Nicole's account and made reference to Zoe Ministries. A manager told Nicole that employees had done a Google search on Zoe Ministries and had come away thinking the church was a scam, but Nicole would have none of it; she seized upon the bank manager's last name—Fath, or "faith without an I," as Nicole put it—as evidence the devil was at work, trying to sow doubt. When Nicole passed along the bank's suspicions to Clemmons, he dismissed any suggestion that the church was playing him for a sucker. "I refuse to believe that," he said. "I'm not retarded."

But on July 21 Clemmons called Carlisle and asked what he thought about Zoe and all those prophets on the phone and Internet. Carlisle hesitated, reluctant to express reservation, fearful this was some kind of test and he was in danger of failing. He turned the question back to Clemmons.

I've been reading the Bible, Clemmons said. The Scripture says to give to the poor—and Bishop Jordan isn't poor. With that opening provided, Carlisle said he had been reading the Bible, too. And he'd also been wondering. He couldn't help but notice that the Bible described Mannaseh as a bad man, but Bishop Jordan had named one of his sons Mannaseh, and why would a man so versed in Scripture do that? Clemmons and Carlisle mulled this over, Clemmons saying maybe it was time to ask these prophets some tough questions, Carlisle saying "the only thing they talk about is getting money, getting money, getting money." "They gonna have some explaining to do," Clemmons said. "We gonna be wary of wolves in sheep's clothing." He talked of all the money they had donated to the church, all the seeds they had sown: "We in debt and everything. We done gave them everything that we done had. Now we can't help nobody, we need somebody to help us."

The possibility that he had been taken advantage of—the thought that there were forces out there he might not understand—rattled Clemmons. As he and Carlisle talked, his fears fired off in all directions. Maybe Zoe was listening in on this phone conversation, he told Carlisle. He talked of how people could tell what channels you watched on TV, and how technology could be used to spy and torment, how bugs could be planted anywhere. He brought up the movie *Eagle Eye*, a thriller in which mysterious forces take over and imbue cellphones and traffic signals and video billboards with a sense of menace, and Carlisle said, "Yeah, that's real, that's real." Clemmons suggested Carlisle take their concerns to a chaplain they'd met, but he told Carlisle to avoid talking with him over the phone, do it face to face, make sure you're not even in a car when you're talking.

"We can't follow nobody blindly," Clemmons told Carlisle. "You feel me?"

Carlisle said he was relieved to hear about Clemmons' dawning suspicions. "You ain't gonna go for the okey-doke, and I admire and respect that. ... It's a trip. I'm rolling with a straight-up gangster."

With the fugitive warrant lifted, Clemmons had one last obstacle to clear: posting bail. He returned to Pierce County Superior Court on July 24, to ask that the $150,000 bail on his rape charge be knocked down. The judge, Thomas Felnagle, had been on the bench for seventeen years. In a survey conducted by the *News Tribune*, Tacoma's newspaper, local lawyers voted Felnagle the county's finest judge, calling him intelligent, eloquent, compassionate, decisive. Early in his career, he'd left his private practice behind to do volunteer work in Poland and Egypt. Felnagle had previously worked as a defense attorney and as a prosecutor, rising to the rank of Pierce County's chief deputy for criminal matters. He'd also served as counsel to Washington Governor Booth Gardner in the early 1990s.

Clemmons' lawyer, Daniel Murphy, asked Felnagle to reduce the bail on the rape charge to "something around the neighborhood of fifty thousand dollars." He argued: "Mr. Clemmons is not a flight risk. ... The threat to the community, I don't believe we have a problem with that. ... He has been seeing a counselor. ... He's the sole income earner for his family. ... He is a property owner of a number of different properties that need his attention at this point." As for the rape charge itself: "We believe that we have some good evidence on our side to disprove these allegations."

The prosecutor, Angelica McGaha, argued: Clemmons *is* a flight risk—he has ties to Arkansas, he just returned from New York. He *is* a threat to the community—his mental health appears to be slipping and he's been in contact with the twelve-year-old girl he's accused of raping. "If anything," McGaha said, "the bail should be raised from $150,000."

For Felnagle, this was not a difficult call. Citing Clemmons' "significant criminal history," citing the "serious allegations" against him, citing the way Clemmons had been "acting crazy," Felnagle denied the defense request to reduce Clemmons' bail. "The warning signs are all over the place," Felnagle said. "I think the bail is appropriately set, and I am going to decline to change it."

What Felnagle didn't know, what McGaha didn't know, is that Clemmons was already covered on the full $190,000, thanks to Lucille Fisher and the Seattle Bonding Company. Clemmons bailed out the same day of this hearing. The bond, stamped at 5:01 p.m. on July 24, allowed Clemmons to walk away from the Pierce County Jail, wearing the same black suit and pink shirt that he'd been arrested in twenty-three days earlier. He planned to take Nicole to the Oregon beach town of Seaside for a couple of nights. This was the second time in two months that he'd managed to elude efforts to keep him in custody, and it would not be the last.

But while Clemmons was now free, the Corrections Department didn't know it. It was still pursuing Ramsdell-Gilkey's plan to keep Clemmons in jail. On July 28, four days after Clemmons posted the $190,000 bond, a community corrections officer wrote to a colleague: "I was going to serve offender today only to find out he bailed out!"

8

I WILL BE CARRIED BY SIX

ON THE WARM BUT CLOUDY AFTERNOON OF AUGUST 20, Clemmons took Diamond, his young German shepherd, for a walk around the neighborhood. Clemmons was free—free to pursue any business opportunity that caught his fancy, free to plug into the prophets' chat line at Zoe Ministries, free to walk his dog. Clemmons talked a lot about reaping and sowing, and right now he was reaping. This was his reward for spending all that money to secure a $190,000 bond—and for hiring a lawyer in Washington, and for hiring a lawyer in Arkansas. He still had to beat all those criminal charges pending against him, but that was down the road. For now, he was free.

He strolled past the neighbors whose houses he'd vandalized a few months earlier, past an elementary school and over Clover Creek, a small stream where salmon spawn. Earlier in the day, his brother Rickey had seen a white van cruising through the neighborhood. Rickey saw it twice. Maybe it meant something, maybe it didn't. Clemmons noticed something, too. Walking along, he saw cars go past with dark tint on their windows. Unmarked police cars? Maybe, maybe not. Clemmons didn't give it much thought. The way he figured, he'd done nothing to draw heat since bailing out. He didn't have anything to sweat.

Clemmons headed up a thoroughfare—one of the few streets in his neighborhood that had a sidewalk—toward what was one of the few patches of green in his neighborhood, the campus of Pacific Lutheran University. It was a Thursday, with lots of students milling about. Earlier in the day, Clemmons had met with his counselor, Timothy Bean. Bean had told him: You have to understand, the enemy will be coming, you have to be careful. Clemmons was in the middle of a book, *The Spirit of Liberation*, by Bishop Jordan, and the book said messed-up stuff will happen in your life, but you have to make it through, you have to stay strong, and then it will be glorious.

As Clemmons neared a thicket of pine trees at the entrance to the campus, he saw a marked Pierce County sheriff's car. Maybe something was going on after all. Clemmons quickened his step, but it was no use.

Nick Weber, a young Department of Corrections officer, jumped out from his unmarked car, his gun drawn and nerves raw. Two other Corrections officers and four or five deputies screeched up in their cars. Students took in the scene, wondering what was going on.

We have a warrant, Weber told Clemmons. You're under arrest.

To Clemmons, it seemed like there were enough cops here to fill fifteen cars. Cops were jumping out of bushes, yelling commands, pointing their guns at him, acting jumpy.

Weber belonged to the Tacoma office of the Pacific Northwest Fugitive Apprehension Team, which included men and women from the U.S. Marshals Service, the Pierce County Sheriff's Office and the Department of Corrections. In law-enforcement circles, these officers are the equivalent of bloodhounds, hunting down people on the run. Weber, a six-year Corrections Department veteran with a quick laugh, knew to be wary of Clemmons. He'd hunted for Clemmons once before—in the spring, after Clemmons had failed to appear for a court hearing. At the time Weber had dropped in on Clemmons' house and been struck by the sophisticated surveillance system, the cameras covering all approaches, the flood-lights on motion detectors, the monitors inside the home. Weber had read the police reports about Clemmons' delusions of religious grandeur. And he knew how Clemmons had jumped those two sheriff's deputies in May. The officers had monitored Clemmons during the day, loath to arrest him in his home. This walk with the dog gave them the opportunity they'd been waiting for. "I didn't want him to look at this as a situation where he'd run or try and fight through," Weber says.

Clemmons didn't fight. A warrant? he asked. What kind of warrant? A Department of Corrections escape warrant, an officer told him. To Clemmons, that made no sense. But he said: If you had a warrant, why didn't you just come knock on my door? I've been right where I'm supposed to be. Why didn't you just knock on my door?

A sheriff's deputy drove Diamond home in a patrol car, and Clemmons, in cuffs, was stuffed into the back seat of Weber's car. Clemmons fumed, telling Weber: I need to put a restraining order on Pierce County and the Corrections Department. Weber tried to divert Clemmons' anger, asking him about restoring old cars. Clemmons wanted to talk about books he was reading—about getting rich, about prophecies. "He seemed to think he had a lot of control over his own destiny," Weber says.

After all the confusion and debate, the Corrections Department had come to grips with the obvious: Arkansas was not going to take Clemmons back. He was Washington's problem now. The day before Clemmons' stroll with his dog, the agency had obtained a special "secretary's warrant" for Clemmons' arrest, citing his failure to report to his Corrections Department officer after getting out of jail in May.

So Clemmons was back in the Pierce County Jail. And if he was mad before, he was furious now. For all the maneuvering he'd done to secure his release, for all the money he'd spent, he had received—what?—twenty-seven days of freedom.

On Thursday, the day he was arrested, Clemmons tried calling Murphy, his lawyer. No luck. He tried again Friday but was unable to get through. For Clemmons, it became clear that he'd be spending the weekend in jail. Clemmons did manage to reach Nicole, and, in the days that followed, he vented his frustration at the turn of events. "This is crazy. … It's ridiculous, it is ridiculous." He was angry they'd arrested him late in the week, rather than on a Monday, scuttling any chances of a quick hearing. "Malicious prosecution. … personal vendetta." He was mad they'd arrested him for something now that they could have arrested him for before—back when he was already in jail, back before he spent all that money on bail. "What they did is retroactive. They can't do what they doing." He was mad they had jumped him, their guns at the ready. He believed they wanted to spook him, to make him startle and flee, giving them cover to open fire. He directed Nicole to reconfigure their surveillance system to provide an even better view of the street. "Because the way they rolled down on me, they trying to kill me." He told her to call Timothy Bean, the counselor, and have Bean tell the Corrections Department it was messing with Clemmons' mental health.

In these phone calls, Clemmons no longer talked merely of freedom. He started talking revenge. He wanted to sue the department. He wanted to punch back. "They just ain't nothing but the devil. … Don't ever trust white people. Don't *ever* trust them. … Same thing make 'em laugh will make 'em cry."

Washington may have had Clemmons back in custody, but there was no guarantee he'd stay there. Clemmons had shown the ability to post a big bail. So the state took one more run at a no-bail warrant, one more run at seeking Arkansas' help. On September 1, Washington's lead administrator for ICAOS, Merlin "Lin" Miller, called his counterpart in Arkansas. Miller hoped Arkansas would issue another warrant to deny Clemmons the right to bail until all his felony charges were wrapped up. In an internal e-mail, Miller recapped the result of this request: "Arkansas will not reissue warrant."

But Arkansas later sent what is known as a "technical warrant." The warrant's purpose, however, was unclear—and would generate intense dispute in months to come. An accompanying coversheet provided checkboxes so Arkansas could state its intentions. Arkansas checked "Continue supervision and notify upon disposition of pending charges"—exactly what it had been saying all along. It did not check "Warrant issued. Keep us apprised of offender's availability for retaking."

Unlike the first go-round, Arkansas did not enter this second warrant into the National Crime Information Center database, used by police to learn if someone is wanted. Washington corrections officials insisted the warrant wasn't valid unless it was entered in NCIC.

Was the warrant good, or not?

Clemmons' community corrections officer noted the warrant in his computer file but did nothing with it. He didn't serve it on Clemmons in jail. He didn't notify jail staff or prosecutors. Nor did Washington's ICAOS administrators tell him to. For Washington, the second warrant delivered the same message Arkansas sent in July: Clemmons stays there. But Arkansas later insisted the warrant was good—and could have been used by Washington to hold Clemmons without bail. "The second warrant differs little from the first," says Rhonda Sharp, a spokeswoman for the Arkansas Department of Community Correction. "The second warrant was not entered into NCIC because Mr. Clemmons' whereabouts were known." David Guntharp was even more pointed: "Where the hell they're coming up with the fact that if it isn't in NCIC it isn't a warrant—that's crap."

Hageman, the ICAOS executive director, says the warrant's status was a legal question, and since neither state asked for a legal opinion, the question remains unanswered. But he wonders why Washington—so determined to keep Clemmons behind bars—didn't treat the warrant as valid. "Washington could have taken a copy of the warrant and given it to the jailer," Hageman says. "To me, the whole thing about NCIC doesn't make a lot of sense. You put it in NCIC so police know, and in this case, he was in jail. But different states do things differently. In some states, they want it done their way, even though it's not the only way. And the other state wants it done their way. And in the end, nothing is done."

For the Corrections Department, another option existed for extending Clemmons' time behind bars. The agency could hold a hearing accusing Clemmons of violating his parole by committing all those felonies in May—the felonies for which he had yet to stand trial.

When a parolee faces criminal charges, the department normally waits for the charges to run their course before pursuing parole violations. But in Clemmons' case, the department elected to act immediately, an unusual move that wound up creating all kinds of confusion.

Pursuing Clemmons, the department committed one misstep after another. The agency held a hearing August 31 and found probable cause on eleven violations. But the next day, the agency erased everything it had done the day before, saying it had misconstrued the case's procedural history and acted "in error." "This is kind of a mess with what's going on, and we're trying to get that cleared up," a hearing officer told Clemmons.

On September 10 the agency held another hearing for Clemmons. A new hearing officer presided—the third for Clemmons in eleven days—but this officer, Robert La Lanne, was no more confident of the department's direction in this matter than his predecessors. Within the department La Lanne had received conflicting advice. Yes, hold the hearing. No, don't hold the hearing. A colleague, in an internal e-mail, described La Lanne as a "stressed out mess over this."

La Lanne explained the proceeding to Clemmons. A community corrections officer would present evidence concerning ways in which Clemmons had allegedly violated parole. Since this wasn't a court proceeding—this was an administrative hearing—certain evidentiary restrictions would be lifted. If the department wanted to present hearsay evidence, fine. At the hearing's end, La Lanne would decide if Clemmons had violated his parole—and, if so, arrive at a punishment, which could include jail time. Afterward, Clemmons could appeal the sanction—that is, the punishment—but not any finding of guilt.

In Clemmons' case, parole-violation allegations that had previously been dismissed without prejudice—when the department initially closed its file on him—were now being resurrected. But only some of them. The department was going to hold in reserve three allegations related to the day that Clemmons allegedly raped his stepdaughter.

If the department was confused by all this—and it was—the confusion for Clemmons was many times greater.

"What do dismissed without prejudice mean?" he asked La Lanne.

The hearing lasted two hours. David Christian, the deputy Clemmons punched in the face, testified by telephone. So did Teresa Berg, the Pierce County sheriff's detective. La Lanne received police reports about Clemmons' rock-throwing rampage. Clemmons didn't have a lawyer present. But he was allowed to ask questions, raise concerns, present evidence. Clemmons left no doubt he believed he was being screwed. He complained of hearsay. Of double jeopardy. Of having this hearing before his trial instead of afterward. "I object to that paperwork," he said. When a community corrections officer mentioned the resemblance between Clemmons and the sketch of a serial robber, Clemmons said, "But it wasn't me," and added, with a laugh, "All black people look alike." Clemmons claimed his cousin Eddie Davis threw all those rocks and had even pleaded guilty to it. (This wasn't true; Davis had pleaded guilty to assaulting the other sheriff's deputy.)

Clemmons claimed the video from his security cameras would show the police were lying, but he said he didn't want to show the video just yet, he wanted to hold it back for trial. "Polices can say anything. You know, it's been proven that polices are human and that they can write what they want to write on a piece of paper. They not angels, you know. But the security system ain't gonna lie."

Why do you have such an expensive security system? a department officer asked.

"I have collector cars that been broken into," Clemmons said. "I have cars that are worth twenty thousand dollars apiece in my driveway. Several of them."

And like a loop on a tape, Clemmons kept returning to how he'd been burned when the department arrested him after he'd spent so much money to bail out. "I would of never bonded out of jail, period. … I would have wasted $19,000? … There's no way that somebody can say I'm a threat to the community. I ain't out there doing nothing to nobody. … You've got me spending all my money. … It's like you want me to go back to crime if I lose everything that I built up." And it wasn't just the bail money. Clemmons also talked of how much his lawyers cost. "The lawyer up here, $15,000. And the lawyer in Arkansas, $20,000."

La Lanne, the hearing officer, found Clemmons guilty of eight allegations, all involving the assault on Christian and the rampage in Clemmons' neighborhood. He ordered Clemmons to serve 120 days in jail. But, he said, Clemmons would get credit for time served since his arrest—and he could shave a third off his time by behaving while in custody.

The hearing officer also attached one last condition. He told Clemmons that when he got out of jail, he must report to his Corrections Department officer, in person, within one day of his release.

For Clemmons, the August 20 arrest changed everything. Gone was the sunny optimism that had surfaced in his earlier conversations with Nicole and Carlisle. Gone was the talk of moving to Michigan or Georgia. Gone were the pledges to go straight. The relationship between Clemmons and Carlisle—"Gabriel, my most trusted messenger"—reached an end. Clemmons told Nicole: "If you know the truth and you running from the truth, like what Boo Man did, they going to hell." Boo Man was out. Rickey was in. Months before, Clemmons had trashed his half brother at every turn—Rickey is lazy, Rickey is retarded, Rickey is pitiful—but with Clemmons' world collapsing around him, Rickey emerged as a precious source of support.

In late September, a month after his return to custody, Clemmons talked to Rickey from the Pierce County Jail, their conversations recorded just like the rest of Clemmons' calls. Clemmons told Rickey about his feelings toward police.

"At first the hatred died down when I had got out, but now it's back. Sometimes it burns me in my chest, man, I have so much hatred toward the police and stuff."

Clemmons said he was going to start riding with a pistol in his car.

"The next time a police pull me over and I ain't did nothing I'm gonna shoot him dead in his face. I swear it, bro. You know what I'm saying? If they come any- where near me, and I know I ain't did nothing, I'm gonna show 'em, if you bringing the trouble to me, and my family gotta be sad singing and stuff, then yours is gonna be sad singing too."

During these conversations, Rickey sometimes cautioned Clemmons to be careful about what he said, to be mindful that his words could be played back at him. Rickey also told Clemmons: "Keep strategy in your mind, bro."

"The strategy is gonna go, kill as many of them devils as I can, until I can't kill no more," Clemmons said. "That's the strategy." That strategy applied for every cop, man, woman or dog, Clemmons said. "A dude ain't no man if you don't make no stand."

Clemmons and Rickey played this conversation over and over, Clemmons making threats, Rickey preaching caution, Rickey talking about the need to "strategize."

"Look, Rick, listen, let me tell you, let me say it one more time, and you take this here, and you can take it any which way you want to take it, before I let them devils put me back behind some bars and railroad me, I will be carried by six. Now what part of that don't you understand?"

Clemmons said there would be no trial on the charges against him, "because I ain't gonna see the courtroom. ... When I touch down, we going to war. ... I ain't gonna play with them no more." Clemmons said there would be no repeat of what happened twenty years before, no repeat of him being sentenced to the penitentiary.

"Ain't gonna be no trial," he said. "I'd rather be carried by six than be judged by twelve. So. You know what I'm saying. As long as I got some company, I be all right."

"So you gonna take some with you, huh?"

"Yup."

Rickey tried to lower the heat. "We gonna pray to God that none of that has to take place." But Clemmons wouldn't let it go. "I feel sorry for the one that come knock on my door for nothing. ... I ain't gonna be living in fear and I'm not gonna look over my shoulder, if you look for me then I'm looking for you."

"Woe to the one that sees me first," Clemmons said.

Boo Man was out, Nicole was still in, but the way she and Clemmons now talked—the occasional tenderness was gone, replaced by bitter asides, mundanity and silence—there was no telling how long that would last.

On October 1, Clemmons and Nicole talked about power-steering fluid. "Piece of crap truck," Nicole said. They talked about Maurice's relatives. "Not very smart," Nicole said. "No, they ain't bright," Maurice said. They talked about the lottery. "You check Powerball? What's it up to now?" Clemmons said. Nicole went in search of the answer. Over the phone, Clemmons could hear paper shuffling.

Minutes later, Nicole said: "It's $193 million. So nobody won." Clemmons railed about being kept in jail: "They know they wrong, what they did to me. ... Straight railroaded. ... It's gonna make them cry in the end, sure is, their kids and everybody else. ... Same thing make 'em laugh is gonna make 'em cry. I ain't gonna show no mercy."

They talked again on October 2. "Yup, yup, yup, yup, yup, yup, yup, yup. What the Mega Millions up to?" Clemmons talked of how he would skate on the rock-throwing spree by Eddie taking the fall. "Well, Eddie pleaded guilty to everything. ... Somebody got to be innocent. You get what I'm saying? Does that sound reasonable?" Ten minutes passed. "Another day, another day. Can't wait to get some payback, though."

They talked on October 3. Nicole told Maurice that his dog Diamond was sick. "She got a heart murmur." The dog was dropping weight, she was down to forty-eight pounds, and if they did nothing the dog might die. X-rays would cost a couple of hundred dollars. Surgery might run fifteen hundred. "If it ain't one thing, it's another," Clemmons said. Nicole asked what he wanted to do. "I don't even want to talk about it," he said. "You know what I'm saying? Next subject." But then an idea came to him—maybe some charity would pay for the dog's treatment. "Gotta be some animal lover groups that chip in."

Clemmons ranted about the Corrections Department losing some paperwork connected to his case, delaying his appeal, making it likely that he'd serve all his time before they ever got around to deciding if he needed to. For Clemmons, this only fueled his belief that the system was hard at work, intent on screwing him at every turn. He didn't believe in incompetence. He believed in conspiracies.

"What's the Mega up to?" he asked.

"One-hundred and twenty-two."

"I feel sorry for the next one coming," Clemmons said. "I ain't going no more. I'm gonna stay packing. I swear to God, I ain't going no more. I ain't no more catch the cuffs. Oh no, catch this bullet. Everywhere I go, I'm gonna stay packing, stay ready."

"You're just saying that because you're upset right now."

"I put that on *dot*."

"Put your faith in God."

"That's what I'm gonna do. I'm gonna put my faith in God to kill every last one of them that come up on me. That's gonna be my faith, to kill every last one of them devils."

You have sixty seconds remaining—a woman's voice, recorded.

"I ain't going no more, unh unh, ain't gonna go, it ain't happening, because there ain't no such thing as justice, and if there ain't no such thing as justice then I'm gonna go the wild, wild west, there's only justice when it work against you, and that's it, oh no, I just ain't going no more." *You have thirty seconds remaining.* "Did it to me when I was young, now I'm a grown man, and it ain't happening no more. I'm gonna give 'em what they been looking for—a dangerous nigger."

He paused.

"I'll holler at you tomorrow," he said.

And he hung up.

They talked on the fifth. "What the weather look like out there?" he asked. They talked on the sixth. Nicole put Eddie on the phone. Maurice berated him for dirtying up the trailer where he was allowed to stay. "I'll hit you in the mouth and stomp you. You try me if you want to, you got that, nigger?" Maurice told Nicole to put him on speakerphone and to gather Rickey and Eddie around. Maurice told Rickey to keep Eddie in line. If Eddie strayed: "Take a hammer, a stick, a baseball bat, whatever you got to do, and bust his head to the fat beat, and then put him on the street. It's that simple. You follow me?" Don't wear my clothes, Maurice said. Don't wear my shoes. They talked on the seventh ("I'm going to kill these devils when I get up out of here") and the eighth (Powerball, "another day, another day") and the ninth (Mega Millions). They talked of being behind on house payments, and of Bank of America calling, wanting money, and of Maurice's dog, and of Eddie and Doug being mooches, and of maybe reaching out to the ACLU for help.

Clemmons was not only back to putting his hopes in the lottery, he was back in the fold of Zoe Ministries, placing his faith in the church's network of prophets. Whatever doubts he'd once had appeared to be gone. On the tenth, Clemmons told Nicole to call the church in New York. She dialed on her cell while Clemmons stayed on the other line.

"Tell them that Prophet Maurice Clemmons needs to speak to a prophet—say it just like that," Clemmons said.

"Do you want your prophecy from that one dude?" Nicole asked.

"Um, yeah, somebody."

New York picked up. Nicole asked for a prophet named Ralph but was told that he was at breakfast.

"Ask if any prophet is around," Clemmons said.

"No, they all at the breakfast today," Nicole told Clemmons.

Forty-five seconds passed, with nothing said.

"Check the Mega," Clemmons said.

They talked on the eleventh. Nicole said she bought some movies from a place that sells bootlegs. "You get five for $20." She bought *G.I. Joe, Transformers: Revenge of the Fallen, Angels & Demons.* The bootlegs are so good you can't tell, she said. Nicole told Maurice that a bank, IndyMac, sent notice that it's going to foreclose on one of their homes. "We just, what, a couple months behind?" Maurice asked. "Four," Nicole said. "They can't do that," Maurice said.

They talked on the twelfth. He asked her to call Zoe Ministries again. Nicole dialed the number. "I was trying to get in touch with a prophet, either Ralph Boyce, or Yasmin, or any prophet," Nicole told New York. No prophet was available, so she left a message. Clemmons told Nicole to see if any prophets were available by online chat. "Neither one of them are on here," she said. "What prophets they got on there right now?" Clemmons said. Nicole named more than a dozen: Devon, Robert, Michelle, Gloria, Crystal, Nazarene, Thomasine …

On October 14, two licensed psychologists, Melissa Dannelet and Carl Redick, went to the Pierce County Jail to interview Clemmons as part of a court-ordered mental-health evaluation. They were charged with answering these questions:

Did Clemmons have the mental capacity to understand the eight felony charges pending against him and to assist in his defense?

Did he present a "substantial likelihood" of committing future acts of violence that would jeopardize the public's safety?

Should he be evaluated by what the law calls a "designated mental health professional" to see if maybe he should be committed involuntarily to a treatment facility?

The psychologists interviewed Clemmons for one hour and fifteen minutes. A pre-doctoral intern sat in. So did Clemmons' lawyer, Daniel Murphy. The psychologists took Clemmons' history—family, work, beliefs. He provided them with a mix of truth and lies. He said he'd never been expelled from school (a lie) and that he'd been transferred among fifteen state prisons in Arkansas (a gross exaggeration). He said he had a landscaping business that was "going pretty well." (Detective Berg would have begged to differ: "That was kind of a sham. He didn't have any equipment. Where's the stuff?")

To the psychologists, Clemmons betrayed no obvious signs of mental disturbance. His speech and thought processes? "Intact." His affect? "Appropriate." Cognitive functioning? "Appeared normal." They found his capacity for abstract thought to be "adequate." Ditto for his insight.

The psychologists asked Clemmons about his appetite. "They don't feed me enough. I've lost twenty-five pounds." They asked about his energy level ("I pace the cell and read books"), his mood ("I'm real irritated by being here"), and his religion ("I believe in God").

For the two psychologists, the evaluation of Clemmons didn't end with the interview. They also reviewed jail health records, Clemmons' rap sheet, and documents provided by the prosecutor's office. One source they did not tap was the collection of telephone conversations—all recorded—that Clemmons had been making from the jail.

So when Clemmons answered their question about religion with "I believe in God," they were oblivious to the hours of conversation in which he expressed the belief that he *was* God. They were oblivious to the conversations in which Clemmons said his counselor and his jail chaplain had advised him to quit saying he was Jesus. Society wasn't ready for the truth, is how Clemmons replayed these conversations. If he continued to reveal himself for who he was, he'd get thrown into a "straightjacket," he'd get thrown into the "crazy house." So Clemmons elected to go underground. If asked about his religion, he would say he was a man of God, and leave it at that. That's what he did with these psychologists—and they were none the wiser.

To the psychologists, Clemmons denied harboring any thoughts of suicide. Asked if he thought of harming others, he said: "Sometimes I think about it—a person gets enough—everybody thinks the police can't lie …" Hearing that, one of the psychologists followed up with a more pointed question: You ever thought of hurting any police officers?

No, Clemmons said.

Clemmons said that back in May, he had experienced hallucinations, visual and auditory. He offered no details on whatever it was he'd heard. But what he saw? "People drinking blood and people eating babies." He saw scenes of lawlessness on the streets, with people acting like cannibals. When these hallucinations started, Clemmons said, he turned to a counselor, Timothy Bean, who treated him with hypnosis "and all kinds of things." After about three weeks, the hallucinations stopped.

The interview over, the psychologists left the jail. Now they had to write up a report, answering those three questions.

Clemmons called Nicole on the fifteenth. They talked about how their conversations were being tape-recorded—not that the threat of a permanent record did anything to temper Clemmons' words.

"Fuck the police," he said. "They ain't benefiting us. The only thing they good for is throwing us in jail. Fuck the police."

"Yeah, I hear you."

"Fuck the prosecutors …"

"But there's always a time to shut up and a time to talk," Nicole said.

"Yeah, I'm just saying. Fuck 'em. You know what I'm saying? Fuck whoever listening, too. Fuck your momma and your daddy."

"Sometimes there's no talking to you," Nicole said.

"I'm just saying. I just get sick of them bitches."

"Yeah, I understand that. But there's a time to shut up and a time to talk."

They talked on the sixteenth: "Another day, another day," he said. "Auto insurance is due on my car," she said. "Don't worry about it," he said. They talked on the seventeenth, "another day," and on the eighteenth and nineteenth, "another day, another day."

On the nineteenth, the two psychologists, Dannelet and Redick, finished their report for Clemmons' mental-health evaluation. They concluded that whatever issues Clemmons may have had in the spring—back when he racked up all those felony charges—by the time they evaluated him, "there was no evidence of a mental disorder." Their evaluation "did not reveal any evidence of psychiatric symptoms." What's more, Clemmons had "communicated clearly and articulately" when asked about the charges he was facing and what would happen in court. So their answer to the first question was: Yes. He could understand the charges against him and assist in his defense.

Question 2: Was he likely to be violent in the future? Their answer: Yes. "It is our professional opinion that he presents with increased risk for future dangerous behavior and for committing future criminal acts jeopardizing public safety and security." But they based this upon Clemmons' past—on his history of violence and his previous violation of court-ordered supervision. They did not base this upon a finding that he was, at present, mentally disturbed.

And because they did not find evidence of mental disturbance, their answer to question No. 3 was: No. "We have insufficient grounds to recommend a [designated mental health professional] evaluation for civil commitment at this time."

The upshot was: The criminal case against Clemmons could go forward—and, there would be no civil-commitment proceedings. If Clemmons could swing his release from jail before trial, he'd be free to go.

Two days later, Clemmons called his brother Rickey. Clemmons said he might be getting out on November 8. But he couldn't be sure.

"I don't trust the bitches," he said. "They devils. … It ain't no such thing as justice in America, not when it come to nobody black. When you black they do you the way they want to do you."

"Um hmm," Rickey said. "The whole system is white and racist."

"Exactly."

"Everybody black, they act like they scared of these bitches," Clemmons said. "Ain't nobody standing up—you know what I'm saying?—and fighting 'em. You know what I'm saying? So they do you any kind of way, and then you're basically powerless. …

"They messing with a real nigger now, though. You know what I'm saying? Watch a brother be victorious. I'm telling you"—Clemmons paused, laughed—"they messing with a thoroughbred. You know what I'm saying? My blood is true."

"Um hmm."

"They ain't no bitch in my blood, period. ... Like I said, I already got things lined out, how things going to play out. See, the worst thing they could of ever did was to put me in here where I can have a chance—*you have sixty seconds remaining*—where I have a chance to use my mind."

"Right."

"See, I can think of something, you feel me? They messing with a brother that know how to think. You know what I'm saying? What they did to me is gonna come back and bite 'em in the ass. ... It's a time and place for everything. Same thing make 'em laugh will make 'em cry."

"Don't let them get to your head, man," Rickey said.

"Ain't getting in my head, I'm a get to their head. ... I'm telling you, I'm telling you, before the month of November is up, they gonna have a whole different outlook on everything."

The day after that conversation between Clemmons and Rickey, another man set out to do what Clemmons had been threatening to do. Clemmons didn't know the man, and the two could hardly have been more different. But somehow they had arrived at the same place.

Christopher Monfort had what he needed. He had the bottles of propane, and the fuses, and the duct tape, and the liquid accelerant, and the messages that would explain why he had killed all these police officers. He didn't know what the body count would be. That would all depend on how many cops took the bait and fell into his trap.

He arrived at a Seattle police maintenance yard on October 22, 2009, in the hours that separate midnight and sunrise. It was 4, maybe 4:30. The sun wouldn't show for another three hours. He crept around the yard, crouching between the patrol cars and other police vehicles. The yard was off limits, so he had to be careful. An eight-foot fence, topped with razor wire, rimmed the yard, which was on the south side of Seattle, just a few blocks from where the Mariners and Seahawks played. He wore dark pants and a dark sweatshirt, the hood up. He carried a dark backpack.

Monfort's history did not form a straight line leading to this. He had no criminal record, no run-ins with police that had wormed inside his head and introduced rot. Nor did he have one of those spooky pasts spent with some paramilitary outfit shooting up the woods. He had no munitions training, but if there was one thing he excelled at, it was research, and he had planned this out, researching explosives, researching fuses, calculating the number of minutes that would pass before his improvised bombs, once set, would discharge, firing shards of metal every which way.

Monfort was forty-one years old, and in those forty-one years he had left about as light a footprint as a man can leave, with hardly a friend to speak of, with hardly an ambition fulfilled. He had a bachelor's degree from the Pacific Northwest's top university, but he'd done nothing with it. No matter where he was, or what he was doing, he wanted something more but lacked the stuff to grab it. Driving trucks, he talked of flying planes. Working security, he talked of being a cop. Taking undergraduate courses, he talked of Harvard Law. His whole life had been: One day I'll be a history professor; or an expert in constitutional law; or a probation officer; or maybe I'll be a great artist, or pick up the guitar. Monfort was a cipher, and if ever a quote captured a forgettable presence, it's this quote from a woman who knew him in college: "No one really liked Chris. But they didn't dislike him. He was an oddball. He had ideas, but no one was interested in them."

The maintenance yard housed all kinds of police vehicles, from patrol cars to a "mobile precinct," a fancy rig the size of an RV that could hold eight officers and came equipped with a restroom, computers and other police gear. Monfort took a knife—modified, with the handle now a metal flagpole attached to a three-by-five American flag—and drove it through the roof of a new police cruiser.

Using duct tape, he attached ten notes to buildings and cars around the yard. One referred to a case that had been all over the news, a case in which a King County sheriff's deputy had been captured on video, punching a teenage girl.

OCTOBER 22nd is the 14th National day of protest to stop Police Brutality.
These deaths are dedicated to Deputy Travis Bruner, he stood by
and did nothing, as Deputy Paul Schene Brutally beat an
Unarmed 14 year old Girl in their care.
You Swear a Solemn Oath to Protect US From All Harm, That includes You!
Start policing each other or get ready to attend a lot of police funerals.
We Pay your bills.
You Work for US.

His bait would be fire. Someone would see the flames, and a 911 call would be placed, and police would come screaming up at just about the time his bombs would go off.

Monfort set the "mobile precinct" ablaze. Flames erupted, illuminating the night sky. As he started to take off, Monfort saw that he had been spotted. Two men were coming toward him, and as they approached, he pointed to the mobile precinct, and then he ran, east, into the night.

One of the two men called 911. Four minutes later, the first police car arrived.

9

IN THE LINE OF DUTY

FOR A POLICE OFFICER, death can come in many ways, from a charging car driven by a drunken driver to a bullet from behind. Since 1792, about nineteen thousand law-enforcement officers have been killed in the United States, an average of one every fifty-three hours. The annual numbers rise and fall, reflecting the times. Crime recedes. Safety precautions advance. Then crime comes roaring back. The year with the most recorded deaths remains 1930, at the height of Prohibition and bootlegging and the kind of lawlessness symbolized by such figures of the day as Al Capone and Frank Costello and Bugs Moran. That year, 285 officers died in the line of duty. When Prohibition was repealed in 1933, the officer fatality numbers steadied and declined. But in the 1960s and '70s, violent crime exploded in the United States, and so did the number of officer deaths. Two hundred and seventy-nine officers died in 1974, the nation's second highest total. Innovation helped drive the numbers back down. Police departments began to use highly trained SWAT teams to handle particularly dangerous situations and started outfitting officers with light-weight bulletproof vests that could be worn at all times. By 2008, the number of officer deaths had fallen to 138.

The two leading causes of police-officer deaths have been gunshot wounds and traffic accidents. But the use of such broad categories masks the variety of dangers confronting officers and the unusual impact that their deaths can have on a community. Take the history of just one city, Seattle. In 1881, a gunman murdered David Sires, making him the frontier city's first officer killed in the line of duty. A local newspaper labeled the shooter a "worthless loafer and desperado," and said of Sires: "His murder has roused a feeling of deep indignation in Seattle, where he was a popular man and officer, and unless his slayer meets his justice at the hands of the law, the people may take the law into their own hands." In 1910, an officer guarding prisoners on work detail was killed when an inmate struck him with a pickax. In 1911, on Independence Day, police officer Henry L. Harris was directing pedestrian traffic in Pioneer Square, where two thousand people had gathered to celebrate, when a man approached from behind and fired a bullet into the back of the officer's head. The gunman was never caught. His motive remains a mystery.

Over the years at least a half-dozen Seattle police officers suffered fatal injuries while on motorcycles, hitting a pole or an automobile or a guardrail or a delivery truck or even a streetcar. In 1924, officer Amos Comer responded to a report of a man at the Business Men's club threatening to "shoot the first guy who bothers me." When Comer found the man and searched him, the man made good on his threat, producing a revolver and shooting Comer twice. Two Seattle officers died when their own guns accidentally fired, one at the police department's headquarters. In 1955, officer James Brizendine, searching for a prowler, shone his flashlight into a house. A man inside, jittery, mistook Brizendine for the prowler and responded with a shotgun blast. In 1968, John Bartlett was in the middle of a traffic stop when a passing truck's mirror hit him, throwing the officer ten feet. In 1974, two officers in a police helicopter died when their chopper collided with a Cessna 150. In 1984, officer Nick Davis was shot and killed while struggling with a man who bolted from the International House of Pancakes without paying his $4.55 tab.

In Seattle and across the country, the death of Officer Davis is more the norm than the death of Officer Harris, the Seattle cop who was killed while directing traffic. Dozens of police officers get shot and killed each year in the United States. But the shootings typically occur during an arrest or chase, or some other spur-of-the-moment circumstance. Rarely do officers get hunted down and executed simply for the uniforms they wear. The exceptions stand out because they are just that—exceptions.

The death of Dave Mobilio was an exception. On November 19, 2002, in the predawn hours, Andy Mickel, then twenty-three, spotted Mobilio, a police officer, at a gas station in the small town of Red Bluff, California. Mobilio was married with a nineteen-month-old son. He was working for another officer too sick to fill his shift. Mickel approached Mobilio—and executed him, shooting him twice in the back, once in the head. On the pavement next to Mobilio's body, Mickel left a homemade flag that said: "This was a political action. Don't tread on us." Days later Mickel went on the Internet and, using an alias for his last name, wrote: "Hello Everyone, my name's Andy. I killed a Police Officer in Red Bluff, California in a motion to bring attention to, and halt, the police-state tactics that have come to be used throughout our country. Now I'm coming forward, to explain that this killing was also an action against corporate irresponsibility." Raised in Ohio, Mickel had attended Evergreen State College in Olympia, Washington. In the Pacific Northwest he had joined in protests against the World Trade Organization and was once arrested for interfering with a Seattle police officer, supposedly reaching for the officer's gun.

The *Sacramento Bee* wrote: "Mickel did not fit the profile of a cop killer. He wasn't a criminal or drug dealer. He was a college student. He'd been a peace activist. He'd served in the Army. His middle-class parents were college teachers, his brothers were successes, his childhood friends were solid citizens with promising careers." Mickel may not have fit some preconceived notion of what a cop killer's background should look like, but inside his head was a storm of grievances. At trial, when he was convicted and sentenced to death, Mickel sermonized about patriotism and the need to rise up against oppressive government. For Mickel, the natural stand-in for that government was a person carrying a gun and handcuffs.

Grievances that result in violence sometimes take the form of race—and the person feeling persecuted can be white just as easily as black. In April 2009, Richard Poplawski, twenty-two, put on a bulletproof vest and lay in wait for Pittsburgh police officers to respond to a domestic-dispute complaint phoned in by Poplawski's mother. Armed with an AK-47 rifle, a shotgun and a handgun, Poplawski killed three officers at point-blank range, then traded gunfire with other police before being wounded and captured. Poplawski was a high school dropout and a Marine Corps washout who never managed to make it in whatever field he fancied, be it dentistry or computers. In online postings attributed to him, Poplawski criticized what he called "the black attitude," including "head bobbing and the lip smacking and the ebonic bubonic slurring." Weeks before killing the three officers, Poplawski, on an Internet radio show, talked of how he had created a hit list that included a black, a Jew, his ex-girlfriend, her parents and his neighbors' pets. The list also included a Pittsburgh police officer. Poplawski posted messages on white supremacist sites and believed Barack Obama's election as president meant the government would soon take away his guns.

In the United States, police-officer deaths have declined in recent years. This can be attributed in large part to a drop in the number of officers killed in traffic accidents. But even shooting deaths have dipped. The forty recorded in 2008 was the lowest figure in more than fifty years. But the kinds of crime committed by Mickel and Poplawski—the ambush killings of police—can prove so unsettling that they cast statistics to the wind. They destabilize our sense of order. On the radio, in the newspapers, in coffeehouse conversation, one sentiment prevails: To attack the police is to assault a community. "There's an increasingly desperate population out there," says Eugene O'Donnell, a former New York City police officer who now teaches at the John Jay College of Criminal Justice. "Other than in rare cases for ideological reasons, we really haven't seen people taking on the cops head-to-head. Something is amiss. It should be cause for grave concern."

And in the fall of 2009, the Puget Sound had not one, but two men intent on hunting down and killing police officers.

On October 31, 2009, an old Datsun 210 hatchback drove past a couple of police officers engaged in a traffic stop near the intersection of Martin Luther King Jr. Way and East Jefferson Street in Seattle. It was Halloween night, at 9:46 p.m. The Datsun's driver proceeded to the next intersection, turned, and pulled into a small park. There, he backed into a raised grassy area and killed the car's headlights, now pointed in the direction from which he'd come. To a nearby woman walking her dog, it appeared that the driver was watching the two police officers.

The week before had not gone as Christopher Monfort had planned. The police took the bait, they drove into the maintenance yard, they were about to park next to Monfort's booby-trapped vehicles, but then a city worker drew them away, saying he'd seen a suspicious man in the yard. When the bombs went off, no one was close enough to be injured. So now, Monfort switched tactics. If he couldn't get the police to come to him, he would go to the police.

There was no drama to the traffic stop Monfort gazed upon. A police report later described it with one word: "uneventful." The senior officer was Timothy Brenton, a nine-year veteran of the Seattle Police Department who now worked as a field-training officer, helping rookies apply their classroom training to the streets. Brenton was married and had an eleven-year-old daughter and an eight-year-old son. His father had been a Seattle cop. So had an uncle. Other officers held Brenton in high regard. He shrugged off praise and was quick to joke.

This was Brenton's second night of training Britt Sweeney, a thirty-three-year-old officer just two months out of the police academy. Sweeney had moved to Seattle from New England and had previously worked as a personal trainer. Her first shift with Brenton, the night before, had generated more excitement than this one. They'd responded to an accident and found a U.S. Army veteran passed out behind the wheel, next to an open can of Four Loko malt liquor. When he came to, the driver told medics "Leave me the fuck alone" and punched his car's windshield. When Brenton read the man his rights, the driver yelled "Fuck you!" Taken to a police holding cell, the driver threw up and then lay down in his vomit.

Monfort didn't know either officer. All he knew was that they were cops.

Christopher Monfort was now forty-one years old, but unlike Maurice Clemmons, he'd left so scant a trail—so little paper, so few friends—that police later likened him to a wraith. He grew up in Hartford City, a small town in northeastern Indiana. His mother was white, his father black; his parents never married and his father left town. When Monfort was eleven or so, he filled out an application for an after-school activity. When the form asked for race, Monfort took a pencil and checked African American. Then he flipped the pencil around, erased the mark and checked white. It was ever so with Monfort, a boy who didn't fit who became a man who didn't fit. When he was still shy of his teenage years, Monfort moved from Indiana, from a town so white the 1980 census recorded not a single African American, to Bethel, Alaska, a town in lake-dotted tundra that is home to the Yup'ik Eskimos. From Alaska he moved to Denver, Colorado, to a place he might have fit, but if he did, his high school yearbook doesn't show it. No clubs, no honors, no sports. While other students picked pithy quotes to accompany their senior portraits, Monfort left his space blank. In the yearbook he's pictured with a wispy mustache, a pinky ring, and a necklace with a crystal pendant dangling over a black and blue sweater.

After high school Monfort moved to California, worked as a waiter and talked of becoming a cop, but it was only talk. In 1999 he moved to Seattle, a guy in his early thirties who cut the profile of someone ten years younger, searching for a career, an educational path, an identity. He worked as a security guard. He worked as a short-haul truck driver. He toyed with the guitar. He dabbled with art, most of it abstract, all of it awful, canvases and the occasional mannequin splashed with paint, primary colors accompanied by Monfort's bold statement that his artistic expression was unbound by any rules.

In 2002 he enrolled at Highline Community College, a commuter school south of Seattle. He was thirty-four years old, surrounded by students ten years his junior. He picked a program, Administration of Justice, that pointed to a career in law enforcement. Garry Wegner, a criminal justice instructor, saw in Monfort a mature student just discovering his potential. "He was one of those people you thought would make a difference, a positive, constructive difference. He always seemed to be a natural leader, and people would gravitate toward him." Other people saw the opposite. "He was a square bear," says Kolesta Moore, the school's student-government president who later became a successful R&B singer under the stage name Choklate. "He was someone with a lot of social communication setbacks. He was a loner like no other. I never saw him in jovial sits, in a casual social environment with other people. He was always alone. Always alone." Monfort's intensity unnerved other students, along with the occasional faculty member. Visiting one teacher in his office, Monfort became so loud and heated that another instructor called campus security. Monfort later blamed this outburst on too much coffee.

In the fall of 2003 Monfort ran for Highline's Student Senate, a surprise given how little he interacted with other students. This wasn't an election for president or Congress, but Monfort acted like it was. While other candidates talked about cafeteria food and campus lighting, Monfort pledged to end the war in Iraq. To bring the soldiers home. To restore the nation's civil liberties. He railed against the Bush administration for cheating and lying to students: "Too many of us walk around with our head in the clouds. Our freedom is under attack." Other candidates papered the campus with fliers. Monfort remained standoffish, just a name on the ballot. The results amounted to a stunner: Monfort won in a landslide. But a review of the numbers raised immediate suspicion. The turnout was twice what was anticipated. More telling, the college's IT staff discovered bizarre strings of votes cast at particular computers, each vote separated from the next by mere seconds. The student ID numbers attached to these rapid-fire ballots were sequential, as though someone had been sitting at a terminal, guessing at IDs. One Highline administrator envisioned a line of people twenty deep in which every person happened to be lined up by Social Security number. Monfort denied rigging the election: "I think that the fraudulent votes favored me because I'm the one with the strong platform, and I really want to bring the people from Iraq home. People feel so strongly about what I'm trying to do that they would resort to unethical means to make sure I get in." The college couldn't pin the fraud on Monfort but did toss the results. Monfort ultimately landed a Senate seat anyway (with only fifty-six votes, in a re-election with anemic turnout), which he promptly used to alienate other students. When they talked, he sighed. "He made younger girls cry," Moore says. "If he could make you upset, it was really satisfying to him."

Monfort earned his two-year degree from Highline in 2004, but nothing changed. He worked as a security guard. He worked as a short-haul truck driver. He ranted about the Patriot Act, he ranted about the National Security Agency's wire-tapping program, and when he bought a guitar and amp and joined others from the trucking firm for an after-hours jam session, he kept on ranting to the point the others told him to knock it off, that it was time to shut up and play.

In 2006 Monfort enrolled at the University of Washington, where he majored in Law, Societies & Justice, a boutique program favored by left-leaning, politically active students. He bore into criminal justice—in particular, jury nullification, a way for citizens to push back against the system's racial disparities. But his skepticism of government was as apparent as ever. His research carried this project title: *The Power of Citizenship your Government doesn't want you to know about. How to change the inequity of the Criminal Justice System immediately, through Active Citizen Nullification of Laws, as a Juror.*

Monfort sought to "illuminate and further" the scholarship of Paul Butler, a law professor at George Washington University in Washington, D.C. Butler had become a leading expert on jury nullification, a practice in which jurors disregard a judge's instructions and render a verdict they consider just, no matter what the law says. "The jury votes its conscience" is how Butler puts it. Butler argued that it was appropriate—desirable, even—for African-American jurors to take into account the defendant's race. If the defendant was black—and the crime nonviolent, say, drug possession—then jurors should consider acquitting regardless of the evidence to send a message about skewed priorities, racial inequities, and the need to put the brakes on the nation's runaway prison population. In a 1995 article in the *Yale Law Journal*, Butler wrote: "My goal is the subversion of American criminal justice, at least as it now exists. Through jury nullification, I want to dismantle the master's house with the master's tools."

An African American, Butler grew up on Chicago's South Side, raised by his single mother. He excelled academically—Yale undergrad, Harvard Law—and joined the U.S. Justice Department. But while working in Washington, D.C., he was charged with criminal assault. He moved from the prosecutor's table to the defendant's. The jury (10 blacks, two whites—and race matters, Butler will be the first to tell you) acquitted Butler, who had the evidence on his side but didn't kid himself that the evidence alone mattered. In his book, *Let's Get Free: A Hip-Hop Theory of Justice*, Butler writes: "My story is different from those of most of the approximately 14 million Americans who get arrested every year. I had the best defense attorney in the city, because I could afford her." Re-evaluating the role he'd been playing in the legal system, Butler quit the Justice Department and became, in his words, "a recovering prosecutor."

Butler writes in his book: "The biggest threat to freedom in the United States comes not from some foreign or terrorist threat but rather from our dysfunctional criminal justice system. It is out of control. We define too many acts as crimes, punish too many people far longer than their crimes warrant, and therefore have too much incarceration." He calls the result "Incarceration Nation," offering a flurry of numbers familiar to criminologists:

> The United States has 5 percent of the world's population and 25 percent of its prisoners. ... A young black man has a 32 percent chance of going to prison. A young white man has a 6 percent chance. ... For the same crimes, American prisoners receive sentences twice as long as English prisoners, three times as long as Canadian prisoners, four times as long as Dutch prisoners, five to ten times as long as French prisoners, and five times as long as Swedish prisoners. Yet these countries' rates of violent crime are lower than ours, and their rates of property crime are comparable.

Butler condemns the ways in which courts have allowed police powers to expand. Police can lie to you. Police can search your car without telling you of your right to say no. In lots of places police can stop you if you're black and happen to be in a white neighborhood. He writes: "Reclaiming justice sometimes requires speaking truth to power, including to the men and women in blue. The police are usually our friends—but not always. Sometimes they make requests of law-abiding citizens that are unreasonable. … Sometimes the most patriotic act is to not help the police." Butler also argues that the country's exploding prison population fuels disrespect for the law. "Freedom has a special resonance for African Americans. Slavery limited their liberty; it was a way of controlling blacks. Now prison serves the same function. It causes many African Americans to harbor strong feelings of resentment against the government. Indeed, 'hate' would not be too strong a word to describe the feeling in some urban communities toward the criminal justice system and the police—the most visible agents of the state."

Qualifiers accompany Butler's support of jury nullification. He's no anarchist. He recognizes the need for public safety. He wants violent criminals arrested and imprisoned. His chief complaint stems from the nation's war on drugs, which, he says, has decimated the African-American community without making the public safer. The core of Butler's proposal—that jurors take it upon themselves to reset society's priorities—resonated with Monfort. But whether Monfort appreciated the qualifiers is hard to say. He wrote an abstract of his research on jury nullification that betrayed a lack of maturity, all excited exaggeration, inelegant writing, and big silly words: "I believe that once citizens are enlightened as to the extent of their individual power. These enlightened citizens cannot help but spread their knowledge to others, effectuating positive change at an exponential rate. Much like the elation and excitement of the young eaglet, that realizes it can fly for the first time."

In his jury-nullification project, Monfort cited UW professor Katherine Beckett as his mentor. Beckett, a sociologist, conducted a complex analysis of the Seattle Police Department's drug-enforcement practices. The department's focus on crack cocaine meant blacks were far more likely to be arrested than whites, even though most of Seattle's drug traffic involved whites, Beckett concluded. In Seattle, powder cocaine and Ecstasy were used more than crack cocaine; but nearly three quarters of those arrested in targeted drug sweeps were busted for crack. And three quarters of the suspects in the crack cases were black. Beckett's analysis included comparisons to other midsized U.S. cities and found that Seattle had one of the highest disparities between the drug-arrest rates of whites and blacks. Her students were "shocked" by the study's results, Beckett says.

Monfort impressed instructors at the UW with the depth of his research. But there was no getting around the fact that he was different. He was still *apart* more than *of,* someone who seemed stuck on preparing his path rather than walking it. In March 2008, when he was six months shy of forty, Monfort earned his bachelor's degree. For so long he had toyed with the idea of law school, or graduate school, or maybe getting a doctorate and becoming a history professor. Instead, he kept driving trucks.

He also continued to wrestle with his identity. He volunteered as a teacher at the King County Juvenile Detention Center's in-house school. The kids—mostly teenagers, held in custody pending trial on criminal charges—listened as Monfort lectured about American history, especially slavery. "He spoke magically, beautifully," Monfort's supervisor says. He spoke about racial disparities in the criminal justice system, and how the black males in class were more likely to wind up in the penitentiary than college. And he gave them a thorough grounding in constitutional rights. You have the right to remain silent. If questioned by police, you can ask for a parent to be there. You have the right to a lawyer. He believed the kids would listen to him because he looked so young, even though he was pushing middle age. In Roxy Hill, his supervisor at the detention-center school, Monfort found something of a confidante. Hill, a white woman in her fifties, had biracial children. Monfort identified with them, talking of how he had struggled with being half black, half white. He once told Hill that he didn't know which side to be on. She told him: You don't have to choose. You're Chris. You don't have to pick a side. When Hill watched Monfort teach, she'd see the same struggle play out. "It seemed he was so extreme on the black side, but it seemed to me that he felt white." One time, someone at the center commented on Monfort's hair, how it was a little on the red side. The next time Hill saw Monfort, his head was shaved. All that hair was gone.

In February 2009, a news story broke that caught Monfort's eye. Prosecutors released video evidence in their case against Paul Schene, a King County sheriff's deputy charged with assault. Local TV stations aired the footage. Then the video went viral on the Internet, drawing viewers from all over. Here's what the video showed:

Schene and a second deputy, a trainee, escort a fifteen-year-old girl into a jail holding cell. Asked to remove her shoes, the girl slips off her left sneaker and kicks it at the deputies. Schene charges into the cell. He kicks the girl, throws her against the wall, grabs her hair and slams her to the floor. With the girl prone, her face to the ground, Schene winds up and lands two blows with his right fist. The trainee, Travis Brunner, does nothing. He doesn't hit the girl. Nor does he protect her. Holding the girl's hair, Schene jerks her to her feet and removes her from the cell.

The teenager, Malika Calhoun, an African American, went on CBS's *The Early Show*, where she was interviewed by Julie Chen.

"Tell me about the beating. How hard was it?"

"It was horrible, like my head hit the wall when he first came in and kicked me. And then my head hit the wall in the back. And then he kept—threw me to the ground, was pulling my hair constantly. And it was just horrible."

"Were you screaming for him to stop?"

"Yes. I said, 'I'm not resisting. I'm not resisting.'"

For Monfort, this incident and all its attendant coverage became a source of obsession. That teenage girl was the very kind of kid he'd spent hours counseling. The beating exemplified a kind of police abuse he believed to be all too common. Schene was charged with misdemeanor assault, but when two consecutive juries hung—11-1 to convict, then 11-1 to acquit—prosecutors dropped the charge.

By the fall of 2009, Monfort had been fired from his job as a truck driver. He'd drifted away from his volunteer work at the juvenile detention center. Now, on Halloween night, he sat in his car, eyeballing the two Seattle police officers, weighing his next move.

At 10:06 p.m., Brenton and Sweeney left the intersection near Martin Luther King Jr. Way. With Brenton in the passenger seat, Sweeney drove the patrol car six blocks away and parked on a narrow residential street, allowing the two officers to discuss any lessons to be gleaned from the traffic stop.

Soon after, Monfort pulled up next to the patrol car and stopped, side by side, so close that Sweeney could have reached out and touched the Datsun. Sweeney knew right away that something was up, something was wrong. She sensed it. She ducked and yelled for Brenton to do the same, but everything happened so fast, she saw the muzzle flash, she heard the night explode, she felt the top of her head sting, and she knew her partner was hit, the bullets kept flying through her window, one after the other, so many shots that a man at a nearby Halloween party assumed fireworks were going off.

Finished shooting, Monfort elected not to put his car in drive and punch the gas. Leaving that way would have exposed his car and license plate to the patrol car's camera, which faces forward, mimicking the driver's vision. Monfort backed up and turned around, giving Sweeney, grazed by the gunfire, precious seconds to recover. She radioed for help—"Shots fired, north on Yesler!"—and fired at the Datsun as it drove away. Then she returned to the radio: "Help me. Shots are fired! … My partner's dead! … Help me. … I need medical."

One of Sweeney's bullets hit Monfort's car, but Monfort escaped, leaving a scene that placed the Pacific Northwest's largest city on edge. Seattle police couldn't remember another time when an officer had been ambushed like that. Brenton had been assassinated, pure and simple, and whoever had killed him had also meant to kill Sweeney, and whoever the killer was, he might be planning to assassinate more officers yet.

Days passed without Monfort emerging as a suspect. But leads came in, the police were able to identify the killer's car as an old Datsun 210, and on the day of Brenton's memorial service, six days after he was killed, a lead came in that made all the difference, a call from a property manager in Tukwila, south of Seattle, about a tenant who had been acting strange and who happened to have an old Datsun 210 recently covered with a tarp. While police from Canada and California, Oregon, Idaho and Washington fell into line and drove through Seattle's streets, filing past hundreds of people standing along the procession route, while taps were played and a twenty-one-gun salute was fired inside Seattle's KeyArena, police closed in on the man who had caused all this suffering and the community's sense of loss.

A trio of homicide detectives arrived at Monfort's apartment complex and saw him come down some stairs and walk into the parking lot. When the police identified themselves, Monfort pulled a gun and pointed it at one detective's head. He pulled the trigger. The gun clicked but didn't fire. Monfort had loaded the gun but neglected to chamber a round. He dashed for his apartment door. The detectives opened fire, hitting him in the face and abdomen, with one bullet lodging in his spine. Monfort fell, alive but paralyzed.

Inside Monfort's apartment police discovered three rifles, a pistol-grip shotgun and several bombs fashioned from propane bottles, duct tape and nails. Seeing all those weapons, police realized it could have been so much worse.

While Christopher Monfort was planting bombs and firing bullets, Maurice Clemmons' support system kept fraying. Boo Man was out—and now, so was Nicole. In mid-November, a week after Monfort was shot and captured, Clemmons talked to Nicole on the phone. Four months earlier he had told his wife: "I just want you to know, I love you and really respect you." But there was no talk of love now. There was no talk of respect. Their relationship had started turning south a couple of weeks earlier when Nicole visited the jail and Clemmons told her that the Scriptures say a woman must obey a man at all times. Well, what about my opinion? Nicole asked, to which her husband replied: "You don't got no opinion, it's my opinion, when we become married, we become one flesh, and so it's what *I* say." To compound matters, Clemmons had rebuffed Nicole's request for power of attorney, a designation she wanted so she could get a handle on their finances.

When they talked on the phone on November 12, Nicole had reached her limit. "Screw you," she said. "I don't even know you anymore."

Boo Man, ever eager, had been willing to do just about anything Clemmons asked, convinced, as he was, that God was behind it all. Nicole, ever competent, had been willing to take care of Clemmons' bail and their bills and the contractors and his prophecies and whatever Clemmons needed doing in his quest to emerge as the second coming of Donald Trump. Now, both were gone.

But Clemmons still had Rickey, his half brother. He still had Keith, another half brother. He had Eddie. And he had one or two friends like Little Rod, a guy Clemmons had helped before, back when Little Rod had gotten out of prison. These were the people Clemmons reached out to now.

Because he received forty days off for good behavior, Clemmons' 120-day sentence for the parole violations expired in November. But that was just the first obstacle he had to clear. The second was coming up with the money needed to post his $190,000 bail on all the pending felony charges.

Seattle Bonding Company, the outfit that posted Clemmons' $190,000 bail back in July, persuaded a judge in mid-November to be taken off the financial hook, saying Clemmons failed to honor the payment plan that had been negotiated. That meant Clemmons was back to square one—and that he was out the $6,000 he'd already paid to the company (he had paid $5,200 plus two $400 payments), a fact that steamed Clemmons to no end. Referring to Lucille Fisher, the company's eighty-year-old owner, Clemmons told his brother Rickey: "When I get out, that bitch gonna pay me my money or I'm gonna whup her motherfucking ass. I don't give a damn how old she is. You hear me?"

Clemmons called Fisher from jail and tried to get her to go back on the bond.

"It ain't gonna be no problem for me to make money," he told her. "It's ways that I can do things without talking about it on the phone."

"I don't want to talk about it," Fisher told Clemmons. "But see, the other time you didn't pay me like you promised me."

Clemmons gave his word that he'd take care of his court matters and make good on what he owed her. Fisher told him: "I spoke with some friends of yours—who, I don't need to say. And I'm aware—that was one reason I moved the other time—I'm aware that you know, you have ways, and you can make money. I know that." But Clemmons and Fisher never managed to reach an agreement, forcing Clemmons to look elsewhere for another bond company.

Clemmons squeezed his friends and family for help, determined to raise the money that could spring him. Rickey, in a statement that smacked of braggadocio, told Clemmons he was doing all he could. "We been running the streets all night, trying to put this money together, duck dodging, hiding from the police, fighting, shootouts, all kinds of shit like that."

In the end, Clemmons scrounged up $8,000 by tapping Eddie, Keith and Little Rod. He assured Rickey and other friends and family that once he was out of jail, he'd get the money flowing again, and when he talked this way, he no longer talked of doing godly things. All that talk from summer was over. "When I hit these streets, everything gonna turn around. Let me get out and handle my business. ... Boss of bosses, that what you gonna see. ... My game elevate, it don't stagnate. ... I'm gonna be on it like a crackhead. ... Once I'm out, you know what I'm saying, I got a nice lick that a brother gonna hit. It'll put me right back in the saddle. It'll put me past the saddle."

"We gonna be untouchable. Untouchable," Clemmons told Rickey.

"I know you got something in your head," Rickey said. "You got some good ideas up in there."

"Worst thing they could of done was give me time to think," Clemmons said.

Determined to find a company, any company, that would post his bail, Clemmons had Eddie and Doug Davis march through the yellow pages, calling companies in alphabetical order. Allwest Bail Bonds: *You need 10K.* Arnold's Bail Bonds: *Disconnected.* ASAP Bail Bonds: *Can't do it.* On and on it went. CJ Johnson Bail Bonds: *Oh my god, dude. You got a big bail. Oh my god.* Liberty Bail Bonds? *No go.* The same for Signature Bail Bonds. The companies told Clemmons he needed more cash than he had, or they challenged his collateral, saying he didn't have as many properties as he claimed or as much equity.

On November 18, Clemmons was about out of patience. "Call somebody else," he told Eddie. "Ain't nobody else?"

"Uh, they got Jail Sucks Bail Bonds."

"Who?"

"Jail Sucks."

"Yeah, try that."

So Eddie called Jail Sucks, a bail-bond company in Chehalis, a town of seven thousand people halfway between Seattle and Portland. As Clemmons listened in as part of a three-way call, a woman named Tiffany answered the phone.

"How much money do you guys have?" she asked.

"I can come up with $8,000," Clemmons told her.

In a few weeks he could get them another $2,000, Clemmons said. That would still leave him short—the total charge was $19,000, or 10 percent of his $190,000 bail—but Clemmons said he could pay the rest in installments.

After checking with the owner, Tiffany told Clemmons: It's a deal.

Jail Sucks attached two conditions. One, Clemmons had to put up a house as collateral. Two, he had to agree to wear a GPS bracelet on his ankle, allowing Jail Sucks to track his whereabouts should he get any idea of fleeing the state. Clemmons accepted both terms.

But soon after, Clemmons began to entertain doubts. The company's name was so sophomoric, *Jail Sucks*, he wondered if the outfit was for real. He wondered if he was being played, if he was being set up for the old okey-doke. Call the Better Business Bureau, Clemmons told Eddie. Run the company's name. So Eddie did. But the Better Business Bureau had nothing on the company. That didn't mean Jail Sucks was a scam. It just meant the bureau had no records on it. Be extra careful, Clemmons told Eddie and Rickey. Go with the Jail Sucks people to the window to post the bond. Make sure you get a receipt. And don't let them leave your sight until you see me walking out of the jail.

While Clemmons worried about being in the dark about Jail Sucks, it was really Jail Sucks that was in the dark about Clemmons. Jail Sucks had been in business for two years; in that time, the biggest bond the company had ever agreed to post was this one, for $190,000. The company's owner, John Wickert, a former reserve police officer, felt secure in taking so big a risk on Clemmons. That's because Jail Sucks had used a commercial backgrounding service to run Clemmons' criminal history, and that search had turned up empty. Jail Sucks, like Aladdin, had failed to find even one of Clemmons' nine prior felony convictions.

The day he was set to be freed, Clemmons called his Washington lawyer, Daniel Murphy, from the jail. Clemmons told Murphy that he'd found a new bail bondsman, that he was tired of waiting for Lucille Fisher and the Seattle Bonding Company to come through. Murphy said he had a theory about Fisher's balking. He believed Nicole had called Fisher and told her that Clemmons planned to run if released.

"That's Nicole doing some underhanded shit," Clemmons said.

Murphy's theory proved to be on the nose. Clemmons' wife had indeed called Fisher. Nicole had told the bondswoman: "If he's getting out, I got to get my family out of here." The fear in Nicole's voice had helped convince Fisher to cut ties with Clemmons. Fisher even regretted helping Clemmons out the first time, back in July. "I'm ashamed I ever wrote his bail," she says. "That one was a disaster, not because of the financial part, but for having a part in ever putting his feet on the ground."

Murphy, talking to Clemmons on the phone, reminded him that upon being released from jail, he had to report to his community corrections officer. "Once you get out, don't forget, within twenty-four hours. You have to report to your new CCO officer, or they'll hang your ass."

"Yeah, I know," Clemmons said. "I got it."

Clemmons needn't have worried about Jail Sucks. The company was legitimate. He made bail on November 23 and, after sunset, left the Pierce County Jail. It was the third time in six months that Clemmons had bonded out. It would also be his last.

10

THE COFFEE SHOP

THE THANKSGIVING TURKEY HAD BEEN CARVED, the Stove Top stuffing chowed, the first pieces of Costco pie devoured. But Greg Richards wasn't done. He snuck away from the table—once, twice, three times—and disappeared into the kitchen, where the remainder of the pie, apple and pumpkin, awaited. Whoosh, went the whipped cream. Whoo whoo, came a cheer from the kitchen. It was Richards' I'm-eating-pie cheer, a hoot his family knew well. Richards' fifteen-year-old daughter, Jami-Mae, cracked up in the kitchen. His wife and sister-in-law chuckled from the table.

Greg Richards worked as a police officer in Lakewood, just outside Tacoma. He'd been with the department for only five years, not enough seniority to get holidays off. But this year he had snagged not only Thanksgiving, he was in line to get Christmas off, too.

His nickname was "Perma-grin," a testament to his sunny-side-up approach to life. He was forty-two but goofy as ever. He danced in front of the TV. Mayonnaise made him throw up. He'd get lost driving but never admit it. With the kids, he was the soft touch, the parent who'd eventually say yes, so long as you kept asking. His favorite song changed a lot, but these days it was "Shine," by Collective Soul. *Love is in the water—love is in the air / Show me where to look—tell me, will love be there?* He liked things neat. He kept his closet straight. He vacuumed his patrol car. He enjoyed his job and the rituals that went with it. He'd get coffee in the morning—maybe Starbucks, maybe Forza, maybe someplace else—and since his shift started so early, he could hardly go without it.

Each day, when Greg left for work, his wife, Kelly, said to him: "You come home to us." Greg was family first, cop second, but Kelly knew that if the moment came, Greg would do what he had to do, that he would never let his fellow officers down. But how often do officers even draw their guns? Some go a career without firing a shot.

They had met eighteen years earlier, when Kelly was twenty-one. Greg had a mullet—business in the front, party in the back—and played the drums in a band. One night, they traded glances in a bar. "He was too good to be true, almost," Kelly says. "I thought, 'What the heck, I am going to get him.'"

The youngest of four kids, Richards had grown up in Southern California. After graduating from high school in Hacienda Heights, he joined the Army, earning good-conduct and humanitarian-service medals and a commendation for marksmanship while stationed at Tacoma's Fort Lewis. He left the military after four years but stayed in the Pacific Northwest. He settled into the lumber industry, working as a timber grader. Twelve years later, he applied to be a state trooper but failed to get in. Richards wondered if he was meant to be a cop. But he tried again, applying to the Kent Police Department, and this time the answer was yes. He started there in 2001. Much as he enjoyed being a police officer—"He loved going to work every single day," Kelly says—he did not relish telling work stories. "He learned he had to stop talking about his job," his sister, Gayle Goeller, says. "It made everyone afraid."

Greg and Kelly had three kids: Austin, sixteen; Jami-Mae, fifteen; and Gavin, ten. Cop life can be hard on families, but Richards did not fit the cop stereotype. He was too much of a goofball—"a weirdo," to Jami-Mae, and she said the word with love. Greg continued to play the drums, now in a band, Locked Down, with other police officers. "He was a rocker at heart," Kelly says. "That was his wild side." He loved dessert and thought nothing of running out late at night to buy a pie. He tried to let stress roll off him. "It is what it is," he would tell his children. Just before Thanksgiving he had taken his family on a long drive, hunting for a car for Austin. During the trip, he told Jami-Mae what kind of man she should marry. He told Austin what kind of man he should be. The needlepoint scroll in the family's kitchen said: "Having a place to go: home. Having someone to love: a family. Having both: a blessing."

Greg and Kelly had moved often in their eighteen-year marriage, but they'd finally settled in Graham, a semirural town in the Cascade foothills. In the fall of 2009, they were still fixing up their new home. With Kelly a stay-at-home mom and Greg a patrol officer, the couple couldn't afford ornamental stonework. So they gathered rocks from vacant lots, hauling them around in a wheelbarrow until their hands blistered, to get the landscaping effects they wanted. Richards was also putting in a cement parking pad for his police cruiser. And he was building a gazebo. That gazebo was his pride and joy. Friends and family laughed, seeing him. He'd just stand out there in the backyard, a cop with his gazebo, happy.

One of the home's draws was proximity to family: Kelly's sister, Melanie, lived a few blocks away, while one of Greg's sisters was in Puyallup. In the early afternoon of Thanksgiving, Greg and Kelly and their three kids had walked over to Melanie's house, carrying a dish of sweet potatoes and a rum cake. Kelly's whole family was there—mom, dad, sisters, the kids. They ate on paper plates. No fuss, not this year. When it came time for the Thanksgiving dinner ritual—what are you thankful for?—Greg burst in.

"I'm going first! I'm going first!" He paused. Everyone knew what would come next. "My family."

"Oh, he took mine," Kelly said.

After dinner, as the tryptophan in the turkey went to work, Greg pulled out the movie *Up* and asked everyone to gather around. "Sit down, I want to watch this with you guys," he said. The family settled in on the couch. A four-minute scene, early in the movie, is a wordless homage to love: a couple's courtship, their shared struggle with the crushing disappointment of infertility, the intimate arc of their decades-long marriage, and, finally, their golden years, still in love. Then the wife dies, and the grieving husband prepares for his final chapter—a long-delayed exotic trip, in a house held aloft by balloons. The widower moves on while still cherishing his wife's memory.

In the waning hours of Thanksgiving, Melanie mentioned to Greg that he had never held his niece, Maddie Lynn. The eight-month-old baby had survived open-heart surgery, and until that day, Greg had been afraid to hold her. Greg reached for her, and the baby fixated on her uncle as he cradled her in his arms. "She was just mesmerized with him," Melanie says. With the baby in his arms, Richards smiled.

Maurice Clemmons also spent Thanksgiving with family. But his holiday was nothing like Richards' Thanksgiving. Forget giving thanks. Forget celebrating the company of family and friends. Clemmons busied his mind with darker thoughts.

Clemmons joined Doug Davis and an old friend from Arkansas, Darcus Allen, and drove through the suburban sprawl around Tacoma and into the industrial warehouse district of South King County. For Clemmons, it had come to this. Nicole had kicked Clemmons out of his own house. She'd taken his clothes and moved them to another of his properties, leaving no doubt where they stood as a couple when he had bailed out of jail. So he wasn't spending the holiday with his wife. He wasn't spending it with his stepchildren. He was spending it with two men he'd referred to as "retarded" or "space monkey."

Clemmons and Allen had done time together in Arkansas, back when Allen had been sentenced to twenty-five years for his role in a 1990 liquor store robbery that left two people dead. The parole board had approved his release in 2005, but, like Clemmons, Allen struggled to go straight. In the spring of 2009, Little Rock police named him a suspect in a Bank of America robbery and issued a warrant for his arrest. But Allen got lucky. That warrant was not entered into the National Crime Information Center database, which alerts other police departments to outstanding warrants. So when Allen moved to Washington and was stopped by Pierce County sheriff's deputies for a traffic infraction, the deputies had no clue of the warrant. Instead of arresting Allen, they cited him for failing to have a driver's license and for lying to police. Allen skipped a subsequent court hearing. That meant he had not one, but two warrants out for his arrest.

In Washington, Allen had done some work for Clemmons' landscaping business. Over the summer he had called Clemmons at the Pierce County Jail and broken down on the phone, crying so hard he blubbered. He talked of being lonely and lost, with hardly a friend to speak of in Washington. "I miss you, man. ... I really miss you. ... I love you, man." Clemmons told Allen: "Stay strong. ... Go out and beat the streets and try to make something happen." But then Clemmons turned around and told Nicole: "When I get out, Dorcus gonna have to find his own way, take care of his own business. I'm going solo." But Clemmons never followed through. Allen stayed on as part of Clemmons' inner circle, a circle that seemed to be growing ever smaller.

After crossing into King County on Thanksgiving Day, the three men stopped at a rundown yellow duplex in the town of Pacific. This was the home of Clemmons' Aunt Letrecia. Clemmons claimed at times to own the place, but like so many of his claims, it wasn't true. Inside the home were his aunt and her thirty-two-year-old daughter, Cicely.

Clemmons, finally out on bail, had no intention of playing by the rules. Although his lawyer had reminded him to check in with the Corrections Department within twenty-four hours of being freed, Clemmons had blown off that requirement. What's more, he had done so without consequence. In a remarkable twist, Clemmons had disappeared off the department's radar. The agency that had put so much effort into keeping Clemmons in jail didn't even know that he had gotten out. Clemmons' community corrections officer, John Hinson, later said he checked the jail register on November 23, saw that Clemmons was still behind bars, and didn't check again for the rest of the week. Had the department known that Clemmons had made bail and failed to report, the agency could have issued a warrant and dispatched the fugitive team to go get him, just as the team had done in August.

So this was the Thanksgiving gathering at Aunt Letrecia's duplex: Doug Davis, a felon; Clemmons, a man evading Corrections Department supervision; and Allen, a twice-wanted fugitive.

During dinner, Clemmons announced the results of all the stewing and planning that had filled his time in jail. He showed the others a gun and said he planned to kill. He would kill children at a school. He would open fire in an intersection. And he would kill cops.

Cicely told him to stop talking about it. The others sat quiet.

"Watch the news," Clemmons said.

Clemmons said he had even started putting his plan into action. He told the Thanksgiving gathering that he had cut off the GPS bracelet attached by Jail Sucks, intent on drawing police and the Corrections Department to his door in Pierce County. He would be just like Richard Poplawski in Pittsburgh. When police arrived, Clemmons would open fire. "Knock, knock, knock, boom!" he said at the holiday dinner.

As it turned out, Jail Sucks either didn't know the bracelet had been removed or took no action if it did know. Clemmons seemed to be doing all he could to attract notice—blowing off the Corrections Department, destroying the bail bondsman's monitoring device—only to be met with … nothing. If the police wouldn't come to him, he would go to the police.

Clemmons awoke early on Sunday, November 29. He was living at his house on 132nd Street South in Parkland, with his brother Rickey and Eddie and Doug Davis. The night before, he had grabbed the keys from Rickey for the white pickup truck used for the Sea-Wash business. Without waking the others, Clemmons fired up the truck and left at around 7:30 a.m. to pick up Darcus Allen, who was living in Clemmons' rental house on Asotin Street. Clemmons found Allen on a futon in the garage, where he'd fallen asleep while playing video games.

The streets drew little traffic that early on a Sunday, except for the personnel for the massive McChord Air Force Base less than a mile away. McChord and the adjoining Army base, Fort Lewis, have been the area's economic core since development squeezed out hop and tulip farms in the fertile lowlands between the Nisqually and Puyallup rivers in the 1970s. The sprawl joined what were once distinct towns—Steilacoom and Lakewood to the west, Puyallup to the east, Spanaway to the south, and Tacoma to the north. Strip malls abutted fast-food restaurants, tanning salons bordered gun shops, big-box stores mixed with used-car lots, all of it broken up by the few remaining patches of the Douglas fir and cedar trees that once made Tacoma's Frederick Weyerhaeuser one of the country's wealthiest timber barons. Clemmons' home turf of Parkland is less a town than a slice of sprawl on McChord's eastern edge.

As Clemmons and Allen drove south along the chain-link fence at McChord's eastern boundary, they saw Lakewood police cars parked at Forza, an upscale coffee shop in a strip mall that also housed a teriyaki restaurant, a nail salon and a cigar store. After Clemmons and Allen continued south a bit more, Clemmons told Allen to turn around. The truck swung back north, past the coffee shop again. Clemmons got out, and Allen parked at a self-serve carwash a few hundred yards up the road. Allen walked across the street to a gas station and bought a Black & Mild cigar with a twenty-dollar bill. He went back to the truck in one of the carwash bays, and pulled out the spray wand. But he did not turn on the water. Other people saw him standing there, waving this dry wand around, pretending to wash the truck. They figured he must be waiting for something.

At a little after 8 a.m., Tina Griswold was eating a cinnamon roll as she waited for her morning latte at Forza. She wasn't slotted to work on this Sunday, but to make extra money for Christmas shopping, she had volunteered to fill in for a fellow Lakewood officer who had celebrated his birthday the night before. Her shift was scheduled to start in a few minutes, and she had paperwork to catch up on. Griswold, the daughter of a law-enforcement officer, was now on her fourteenth year as a cop. Despite standing four feet eleven and weighing one hundred pounds, she exceeded the fitness standards for male officers; she could pound out thirty or more push-ups, no problem. Co-workers joked that the quickest way to end a bar fight was to throw Griswold in the middle of it.

The Lakewood Police Department was just five years old, and many of its hundred-plus officers had transferred in from other jurisdictions. Incorporated in 1996, Lakewood had grown from a bedroom community along Tacoma's south border into a city of its own. By the 2000 census, fifty-eight thousand people called it home. Western State Hospital, the region's psychiatric hospital since 1871, occupied several hundred acres of stately brick buildings on Lakewood's western edge.

Sitting next to Griswold, working on a laptop, was Sergeant Mark Renninger, eating an apple fritter with black coffee. The Pennsylvania native and former Army Ranger was one of the state's top SWAT team members and instructors—a born leader, an expert marksman, a "cop's cop." Across the table was officer Ronald Owens, who was drinking orange juice and also working on a laptop. A former state trooper, Owens was a second-generation cop whose professionalism and gentlemanly demeanor had won him commendations. Greg Richards, a fourth officer, was approaching the front counter, wallet in hand, ready to place his order.

They were regulars at Forza. So were lots of other cops. The coffee shop sits at an intersection that divides four police jurisdictions: Parkland, Lakewood, the Pierce County Sheriff's Office and the Washington State Patrol. It is a natural meeting spot when cops need to trade information—wanted-suspect fliers, car-theft reports, tips—but do not want to be too far from their patrol areas. Forza, Italian for "strength," was even launched by an ex-cop. The place's black leather couches, faux-fresco paint, and black-and-white photographs of 1930s auto races lend an air of sophistication. The twenty-foot ceiling exposes ventilation ducts, and when the hand-operated espresso machine whooshes, the sound fills the space. The espresso counter is at the rear, so customers walk the length of the shop before ordering.

On this early Sunday morning, there were just two other customers in addition to the four police officers. Daniel Jordan and his wife, Lola, relaxed on black leather armchairs in a corner next to the front door. Daniel checked e-mail on his phone while Lola scanned the newspaper for Christmas sale ads. They planned to go shopping later.

Behind the counter were two baristas—Michelle Chaboya at the drive-up window in the rear of the store, and Sara Kispert, who was working on Griswold's latte. Both women were twenty years old. Richards had just reached the counter when the chime on the coffee shop's front door rang.

Maurice Clemmons didn't enter right away. Instead, he poked his head in and looked around. Sara said hi to Clemmons and asked how he was doing. Clemmons didn't answer. To Sara, Clemmons' demeanor seemed off somehow. "He didn't seem to be there to order coffee," she says. Clemmons wore a puffy black jacket over a hooded sweatshirt and carried a newspaper. He walked past Jordan and his wife. But instead of approaching the counter, Clemmons walked straight toward the table where the three officers sat, two of them tapping at their keyboards. Richards, meanwhile, stood near the cash register, underneath a menu listing Forza's specialty drinks (the "Holy Spumoni"—pistachio, cherry and chocolate syrups, whipped cream) and next to a pastry display behind glass.

What happened next is not entirely clear. Police have spent hundreds of hours trying to reconstruct the scene, analyzing the evidence, conducting interviews, running tests in the crime lab. This is the best guess of investigators:

Clemmons stopped next to the officers' table, halfway between the front door and the back of the café. Sara saw Clemmons pull out a gun. He'd been hiding the pistol, either in his sweatshirt pocket or underneath the newspaper. It was a 9 millimeter, stolen during a burglary in Seattle years before.

Without a word, Clemmons raised the gun and began shooting. The gunfire eclipsed the sound of the espresso machine, a shocking roar bouncing off the walls. Sara told Michelle, "We've got to get out of here," and the baristas bolted through a green door at the back of the shop. Richards spun around, dropping his wallet on the floor.

Clemmons' first shot hit Griswold from maybe a couple of feet away, a bullet to the back of the head that killed her instantly. His second shot hit Renninger in the temple, a fatal wound.

Daniel, the customer who'd been checking e-mail, jumped at the sound of the gunfire and looked up as Renninger was gunned down. Believing they were next, the couple went for the front door, but it wasn't as easy as that—Lola had scoliosis, a spinal deformity that can limit movement. Daniel grabbed his wife and pulled, desperate to get her out. Together, they stumbled out the door, leaving behind their newspaper and her purse. Outside, Lola fell to the sidewalk. She regained her feet and the couple fled for their car.

With two officers down, Clemmons turned to shoot Owens. But the 9 millimeter jammed. Instead of ejecting, the last casing had become stuck in the chamber. Clemmons tossed the 9 millimeter aside and pulled out another handgun—a .38-caliber Smith & Wesson that he'd tucked away. Owens sprang from the table and lit across the four feet between him and Clemmons. Tall and lanky, Owens grappled with Clemmons, 240 pounds of muscle.

Richards, at the counter, started running toward Clemmons and Owens, who were clinched in hand-to-hand combat, knocking over tables and chairs. Clemmons continued to fire, over and over, spraying bullets through the café. One of the rounds hit Owens in the neck. He collapsed in the middle of the coffee shop.

The battle became one between Richards and Clemmons, and it was fierce, with Richards disarming Clemmons, knocking the .38 away, and drawing his own weapon, a .40-caliber Glock. Together, the men pitched toward the entrance of the coffee shop, slamming into the front door's frame. Clemmons grabbed for Richards, ripping off his holster belt. The two men wrestled over the Glock, fighting for control, and during the scramble the gun fired twice. One bullet hit Clemmons in the back, near his right armpit, a shot that would have felled many men. The other bullet hit Richards.

The officer hit the floor. He died on the sidewalk, his head just inside the door.

By now, Daniel and Lola sat, in shock, in their car. They had driven a short way up the street and stopped, to call police. Clemmons, bleeding, staggered past them, now holding Richards' Glock. Most likely, he did not see the couple. He continued on.

The baristas, after fleeing out the back, had hopped into a car and sped around to the front. They wanted to go south but, seeing a red light, instead turned right, heading north. Driving past the coffee shop, Sara saw Clemmons and Richards struggling on the sidewalk. The baristas raced a quarter-mile north to an AM/PM gas station across the street from the carwash. As they dashed into the mini-mart, they ran into four men who were gassing up their dirt bikes. Sara borrowed one man's cellphone and tried to call 911, but was so rattled she couldn't punch the numbers. One of the men made the call for her.

At the gas station, while police were being called, Michelle looked up and saw a terrifying sight. A man was walking toward them—and it was the shooter, Michelle was sure of it. Clemmons came up the sidewalk, a hundred yards away, then eighty, then sixty. He glanced over his shoulder. He quickened his step as sirens began to fill the air. Clemmons kept coming, now fifty yards away, heading straight toward them. "Sara, we need to go inside," Michelle said. "This isn't safe." Just as it seemed inevitable that Clemmons would see them, he stopped short of the AM/PM. He veered off the sidewalk and headed into the carwash, toward Darcus Allen and the pickup truck. As Clemmons climbed into the passenger side of the truck, Allen saw blood on Clemmons' hands and a gun sticking out of his pocket. As the baristas watched, the truck sped away.

A short time later, Rickey Hinton saw Clemmons walk through the rolling gate of his home on 132nd Street. The truck had been ditched at a grocery store a half-mile away.

I've been shot by police, Clemmons told his brother.

Clemmons woke up Doug and Eddie Davis. Rickey threw them the keys to a white Pontiac and said to get Clemmons out of there. Then Rickey handed his twelve-year-old grandson his cellphone. Delete everything having to do with Maurice, he said.

Clemmons lay across the Pontiac's back seat, and the three took off.

Shot, bleeding, and author of a crime that would leave nine children without a mother or father, Clemmons sounded satisfied.

I took care of my business, he said.

May 9, 2009, mug shot of Clemmons after his arrest for the rampage.

July 1, 2009, after he returned from New York and was arrested again.

Clemmons with Bishop E. Bernard Jordan in New York City on June 13, 2009. "God called me," Clemmons told Jordan. Jordan believed Clemmons was mentally ill.

August 20, 2009, after he was picked up for violating his parole.

September 25, 2009, during a jail trans-fer, when he was vowing revenge.

Lucille Fisher bailed Clemmons out once but refused a second time, after being warned that he planned to run. "I'm ashamed I ever wrote his bail. That one was a disaster, not because of the financial part, but for having a part in ever putting his feet on the ground."

Jail Sucks Bail Bonds, the last to bail Clemmons out. Located in Chehalis, Washington, Jail Sucks posted a $190,000 bond when Clemmons came up with $8,000 plus collateral and promised to wear a GPS bracelet. Clemmons cut off the bracelet after his release.

The Forza coffee shop in Parkland, where Clemmons walked in and shot four officers on Sunday morning, November 29, 2009.

Officer Tina Griswold   Officer Ronald Owens

Sergeant Mark Renninger   Officer Greg Richards

A SWAT team mobilized for the manhunt after the November 29 shootings.
More than six hundred people were involved in chasing a thousand tips.

Firefighters salute while bodies are transported to the Pierce County
Medical Examiner's Office. An impromptu memorial at the Lakewood
police headquarters overflowed with flowers and cards.

Early November 30 during the manhunt, police
and SWAT teams fired flash grenades and tear gas
into Chrisceda Clemmons' home in Seattle.
Chrisceda Clemmons, left, had told police that her
nephew was coming to her house.

Seattle police question and search a man during the manhunt November 30.

The scene in Seattle after Clemmons was gunned down December 1. The car with its hood up had been reported stolen, prompting officer Benjamin Kelly to stop.

Benjamin Kelly, the Seattle officer who shot Clemmons four times, killing him.

Greg Richards' wife, Kelly, center, holding hands with daughter Jami-Mae in court.

Seattle officer Daina Boggs looks at Greg Richards' .40-caliber
Glock, which she recovered from Clemmons' body.

Sara Kispert, a Forza barista, testifies in the LaTanya Clemmons trial about what she saw inside the coffee shop.

Governor Chris Gregoire with the four caskets in the Tacoma Dome on December 8, 2009. The memorial drew 20,000 officers from across the United States and Canada.

11

WE NEED A STORY

THE FIRST 911 CALL came in at 8:16 a.m. Within four minutes, police arrived at the coffee shop. They found the .38 in a sun-splashed corner of the café, near the front. The 9 millimeter was found halfway across the coffee shop. By 8:32 a.m., it was confirmed: All four officers were dead. All four were from the Lakewood Police Department. But questions came faster than answers. The wounds inflicted by Clemmons were such that police couldn't identify the fallen officers with any kind of certainty. The dead were unrecognizable. So police dispatch began the grimmest of roll calls, dialing the cellphones for each Lakewood officer on duty that Sunday morning. At 8:42 a.m., a call to Mark Renninger's phone elicited only a ring, a ring that sounded inside the Forza coffee shop. The phone went unanswered. Tina Griswold didn't answer her phone. Nor did Ronald Owens, nor Greg Richards.

Before local TV stations broke in with word of the massacre, the news went viral on the cellphones and BlackBerry devices of law-enforcement officers across the region. While dispatch called officers, officers' spouses called dispatch, desperate for reassurance. At 9:11 a.m., Greg Richards' wife, Kelly, called and said she'd been unable to reach her husband; she asked for someone to call her back. Not long after, Kim Renninger called and asked for the same regarding her husband.

Kelly Richards knew her husband was a regular at Forza. When she'd heard the news of the shootings, she'd rounded up their family and headed for the police station, fearing the worst. On the way there, she received a call from police, telling her to go back home. Officers were on the way to meet her. Kim Renninger also feared her husband was among the four. When officers showed up at her door with the awful news, she thought maybe the shootings were the work of a violent street gang. Maybe the shooters had sought her husband out. Maybe they would now hunt his family. Police, unsure what they were dealing with, took no chances. They posted officers outside Renninger's home. Police also stood watch over the other officers' families.

Early on, investigators caught a bad break. Forza was wired for video surveillance, but the coffee shop had not yet installed the cameras. That meant there was
no clear image of the shooter. The cameras' absence also compounded the challenge of reconstructing the crime. But while they struck out with video of the
shootings, investigators discovered they had exceptional eyewitnesses. The baristas provided an accurate description of the get-away truck—make, model, color,
pin striping, even a close estimate of the year. Those details paid off. At 9:12 a.m.,
a Pierce County sheriff's deputy spotted the truck in a grocery store parking lot on
Parkland's Pacific Avenue. The truck, its engine still warm, yielded two invaluable
clues. The first concerned the gunman's condition. Some kind of fluid, fresh and
red, stained the passenger's side armrest. A crime-scene technician confirmed it
was blood. Had the gunman been wounded in the shootout? The odds of that were
looking up. The second clue concerned the gunman's identity. The truck was registered to Sea-Wash—the landscaping business owned by Maurice Clemmons, the
same Maurice Clemmons who had assaulted two sheriff's deputies in May, the
same Maurice Clemmons who was facing a charge of child rape.

When a sheriff's sergeant—the supervisor of the two deputies who had been
beaten by Clemmons—heard of Clemmons' possible involvement, he warned
away an officer who had gone immediately to Clemmons' house and was writing
down license plates. Back off, the sergeant said. Be careful. Don't go in by yourself. It's too dangerous.

Rick Adamson pulled into the Forza parking lot at 9:17 a.m., an hour after the
shootings. But the scene was still charged with chaos and fear. Patrol cars were
scattered about, parked every which way. Officers with assault rifles ran about,
with no discernible pattern to their comings and goings. Richards' body lay on the
sidewalk, covered by a blue tarp. Inside the coffee shop, chairs and tables lay on
their sides. Bullet holes pocked the walls. Shell casings littered the floor. Police
found Clemmons' two guns in different parts of the café. But Richards' service
weapon was gone, presumably now in the hands of the gunman who had shot up
the place.

Adamson, chief of operations for the Pierce County Sheriff's Office, was no
stranger to the hazards of law enforcement. In thirty years of military and police
service, he'd held a range of positions: special agent with the U.S. Air Force Office
of Special Investigations; captain of the sheriff's Criminal Investigations Division;
homicide detective; supervisor of the Gang Intelligence Unit; commander of the
SWAT team. He knew more than a dozen people killed in the line of duty. They
included his training officer in the military and sheriff's deputy John Bananola,
who was gunned down in 1995 by a suspected drug dealer. Adamson's office was
on John Bananola Way East in Puyallup, named in honor of the deputy. In 1999,
Adamson was in a patrol car when a fleeing suspect opened fire. The bullet

pierced Adamson's windshield and hit a radio microphone that Adamson was holding to his face. Luck had turned a potentially fatal shot to the head into a wound to Adamson's hand. During his career, Adamson had seen a lot of violence and had killed three people. But in all his years he had never seen anything of this magnitude.

At Forza, Adamson consulted with the on-scene captain and assumed control as incident commander, directing a sprawling investigation in which each passing minute carried the threat of additional bloodshed. This gunman had obviously targeted and assassinated cops. Who knew what he planned next? Police cut the lock on an empty storefront in the same strip mall as Forza; there, the Sheriff's Office established an ad hoc command center. The Red Cross unfolded tables and set out sandwiches, Gatorade and gallons of hot coffee.

When word of the shootings first went out, law-enforcement officers from all over the Puget Sound area abandoned their weekend plans and headed to Parkland, offering to help. State troopers arrived. Fish and wildlife agents arrived. So did corrections officers and federal agents from the Drug Enforcement Administration. But Adamson needed more than a phalanx of officers in body armor. He suspected this crime might be an act of terrorism, or possibly a coordinated strike by one of Tacoma's violent gangs. So he reached out and dialed the number for the FBI's regional Joint Terrorism Task Force, a decision that paid immediate dividends. The task force's resources—criminal intelligence, electronic surveillance and massive manpower—were placed at Adamson's disposal. Federal agencies, including the FBI, DEA and ATF, searched case files for Clemmons' name and began sending information back to the command center. Sources cultivated by the FBI during an ongoing investigation into one Tacoma gang told detectives about a safe house used by Clemmons and his friends.

Local police agencies followed suit. SWAT teams from five jurisdictions volunteered. Nick Weber, the fugitive-task-force officer who had arrested Clemmons in August, showed up at the command center with a thick file on Clemmons' family and associates, including some home addresses and phone numbers. He would stay for the next twenty hours, driving himself to exhaustion. The Seattle Police Department sent a command team to the scene. So did the Washington State Patrol and the King County Sheriff's Office. For the first hours those teams stayed to the side, at the ready should Adamson request help tracking down leads. The State Patrol scrambled a plane and scanned the I-90 corridor in Eastern Washington for any sign of the gunman. Lawyers with the U.S. Attorney's Office and the state attorney general worked on warrants. At least six hundred people and sixteen law-enforcement agencies joined in the manhunt, the largest fugitive search in state history. At times, the response became too much. One SWAT team, armed in full, showed up at the command center and began eating sandwiches and getting in the way of others. The team was shooed away.

A pair of detectives turned immediately to all of the recorded telephone calls Clemmons had placed from the Pierce County Jail. Between July 2 and November 23—*November 23*, just six days ago, just six days before these four police officers were shot and killed—Clemmons had made more than three hundred calls. The jail staff hadn't listened to them. The prosecutors arguing Clemmons' bail hadn't listened to them. The two psychologists evaluating Clemmons' mental capacity hadn't listened to them. Now, two detectives listened—and the threats they heard, chilled. "I'm gonna shoot him dead in his face ... The strategy is gonna go, kill as many of them devils as I can, until I can't kill no more."

Investigators inserted a mug of Clemmons into a photo array and showed the line-up to the two baristas. One was too shaken up to make an identification. But the second, seeing the picture of Clemmons, said she was fairly sure he was the gunman. On a scale of 1 to 10, she put her confidence level at 7. At this point—given the Sea-Wash truck, given the blood in the truck, given Clemmons' criminal history, given the barista's tentative identification—Adamson felt confident calling Clemmons the prime suspect.

Just after 10 a.m., the head of the state Department of Corrections received a telephone call during breakfast. Maurice Clemmons is the guy police are looking for, he was told.

The hunt was on. And, for the Corrections Department, so was the heat.

It didn't take long for investigators to determine that Maurice Clemmons was an Arkansas parolee under the supervision of the Washington State Department of Corrections. Clemmons had a department number, six digits long, attached to his name. For corrections officials in Washington, this meant a potential return to all the questions their agency had faced back in 2006, when two Seattle police officers and a King County sheriff's deputy had been killed in three separate incidents by felons under the department's supervision. At the time, Governor Gregoire had demanded changes to minimize the chances of any repeat. And now, this.

At 10:28 a.m., two hours and fifteen minutes after the shootings at Forza, the head of the Corrections Department, Eldon Vail, sent an e-mail to a spokesman for the agency: "Primary suspect is Maurice Clemmons 866697. Anna, Scott and I are headed in. This will get national attention." Anna was Anmarie Aylward, head of the department's division charged with overseeing Clemmons and other felons on community supervision. Scott was Scott Blonien, the department's legal adviser.

Vail's prediction received quick confirmation. On Sunday, the shootings of the four police officers became the lead story around the country. The Corrections Department's leaders knew the agency would soon be fielding all kinds of questions—about the two warrants for Clemmons that had been issued by Arkansas, about the interstate compact, about Clemmons' eight pending felony charges and how he had been released from jail three times in the past six months. On Sunday Vail wrote the head of the agency's communications department, saying he wanted: a "complete and accurate criminal history" for Clemmons; "a more detailed time line to include when he was in jail, out of jail, on supervision, off supervision"; "an accurate and thorough account of our conversation with Arkansas regarding this case"; a statement to the media; and a statement to the department's staff.

But Vail knew that rounding up information wasn't enough. The state and local agencies also needed to control that information. They needed to make sure that one agency wasn't saying one thing while another agency was saying the opposite. Vail directed Blonien to reach out to the head prosecutor for Pierce County: "Try and get a conversation with Mark Lindquist as soon as possible. Try and get us on the same sheet of music about why Clemmons was out of jail. It is important that we understand how and why he was released." For all these public agencies being inundated with questions—the Lakewood Police Department, the Pierce County Sheriff's Office, the state Attorney General's Office, the Governor's Office, the state's social services agency, the Corrections Department—the keys were simple. Coordinate. Funnel the information. Don't stray off message. When the state's attorney general, Rob McKenna, went on radio and TV, he was told: "Stick to the script."

The script. For the Corrections Department, there was one. The agency came up with a list of anticipated questions and suggested answers. Seeking advice on media strategy, the head of the agency's communications department shared this script with Robert Calkins, a public information officer at the Washington State Patrol. Calkins wrote back: "These are all very good, but I would recommend you develop a set of talking points to guide your discussion rather than just a Q&A to answer questions. If you just answer questions the reporter can go any old place. If you have a focus to your intended comments you'd be surprised how frequently the resulting story ends up equally focused. It really works!"

While hundreds of law-enforcement officers searched for Clemmons, dozens of state and local officials searched for answers about Clemmons' past. They contacted Arkansas and asked for the full file of Clemmons' prison record there. They braced for all the questions they knew would be coming. The Corrections Department realized that for three years it had tagged Clemmons a low-risk offender, subject to minimum reporting requirements. (His official designation had been "RMD," or Risk Management D.) Given Clemmons' record in Arkansas—nine felony convictions, dozens of prison disciplinary counts, his parole violation when first released—that designation was a head-scratcher. "I'm gonna need an understanding of why he was RMD for awhile," Vail wrote to Aylward, who, in turn, passed the question down, writing to another employee: "We need a story." The department and other public agencies contemplated ways to focus the media's attention, to point out paths that they hoped the newspapers, TV shows and radio stations would take.

By late Sunday morning, three hours after the shootings, helicopters from local television stations circled over the coffee shop and the command center, creating so much noise that officers had trouble making cellphone calls. As media Web sites provided early accounts of the massacre—albeit with no name for the shooter, at least not yet—the first of about a thousand tips flew in to a special hot-line staffed by detectives. Most proved worthless. Still, sifting the good from the bad took time. And while Clemmons had emerged almost from the get-go as Suspect No. 1, investigators couldn't rule out other possibilities.

One man called 911 from a pay phone, claiming to be the shooter. A SWAT team swarmed to the phone's location, only to find the receiver hanging, the caller gone. A woman called 911 and said her friend, a warehouse worker named Martin Quintero-Lewis, had told her on the phone that he was the shooter. He'd told his mother the same thing, saying he'd "flipped out" after coming across the Lakewood officers. Quintero-Lewis claimed to be hiding in the woods near a storage locker, about a mile north of Forza. Ed Troyer, a detective and spokesman for the Pierce County Sheriff's Office, held a media briefing near those woods while holding an assault rifle. You're not safe here, he told reporters. He ordered a SWAT team to surround the media pack. Detectives and dozens of patrol officers wasted nearly four hours chasing down the lead only to discover that Quintero-Lewis had been playing a prank. (Quintero-Lewis later compared his false confession to a prank on the MTV show *Jackass*, and said: "It was an inside joke, like a black joke or Jewish joke you tell that is not supposed to leave your circle of friends.") Yet another tipster claimed the shooter had shown up at St. Joseph Medical Center in Tacoma, seeking treatment. After reviewing surveillance tapes, detectives ruled that lead out as well.

To catch Clemmons, police leaned on the manhunt's most obvious asset: the massive mobilization of force at the command's beck and call. Investigators suspected Clemmons would try to hide out, giving him time to heal, giving him time to arrange transportation to Arkansas. Medical experts theorized that Clemmons was still bleeding, with his chances of infection rising. He might even die before he could be found. But with four officers already dead, Adamson suspected more violence lay ahead. "We knew he was not going to just drop his gun and give up," he says. "It was going to be a gun battle." Using Weber's Corrections Department file, police reports and intelligence from various agencies, investigators compiled a dossier of potential hideouts for Clemmons, many linked to his family and friends. The command center dispatched teams of undercover officers to scout each home. If the officers saw no sign of Clemmons, they would stand pat, waiting to see if Clemmons would show up. In some instances police secured search warrants and busted in, hoping for clues to Clemmons' whereabouts.

On 131st Street in Parkland, on a cul-de-sac lined with ramblers, a team of police and Corrections Department officers camped outside Clemmons' home. It was late morning, early afternoon. The officers were armed and suited up in body armor. But they weren't going to approach the house. It was too dangerous. Instead, they elected to wait for a SWAT team to show up with a warrant. While these officers waited, others began sealing off the street's only entrance and exit, to create a quarantine zone. With so much anxiety in the air, so much tension and firepower, the officers could hardly believe what they saw next. An SUV pulled up to the house. A man with a graying beard and notebook got out. The guy walked up to Clemmons' house and knocked. The officers outside the house exchanged looks. A reporter? How did he know Clemmons was involved? How did he get through the roadblock? And what was he doing knocking on that door? The man must have balls of steel, they thought. Or maybe he was crazy.

The man was Mike Carter, a veteran reporter with the *Seattle Times*. He'd arrived just as the perimeter was being sealed. Going through the cul-de-sac entrance, he'd slowed down and waved. Although Clemmons' name hadn't been made public yet, the newspaper had picked it up. Another *Times* reporter, sick at home, had learned the suspect's identity from a source and phoned it in to the city desk. The city desk dispatched Carter, who had been at the crime scene, to Clemmons' house. For Carter, this was nothing new. A former Associated Press reporter, he had covered some of the country's biggest breaking news stories, from Unabomber Ted Kaczynski to D.C. Sniper John Allen Muhammad to Ahmed Ressam, a terrorist who planned to bomb Los Angeles International Airport. At Clemmons' home, Carter saw all the cops. But he elected to go up and knock anyway. "There were so many people with guns around, I was probably the safest person in the world," he says. No one answered the door. So Carter went from neighbor to neighbor, picking up details about what they saw in May, back when Clemmons had thrown all those rocks and assaulted those two sheriff's deputies. Carter figured that once inside the perimeter, don't leave. Police won't let you back in.

As the hours ticked away Sunday, all kinds of people were pulling together the threads of Clemmons' life. Detectives. Bureaucrats. Reporters. An FBI informant tipped police that Clemmons was likely with Eddie Davis, one of the two cousins sent up from Arkansas so that Clemmons could set them straight. ("I've been trying to change them," Clemmons had told the Corrections Department.) Eddie became a target of the manhunt. So did other relatives and friends with ties to Clemmons. One person who was not part of the dragnet was Clemmons' wife, Nicole. A few hours after the shooting, Nicole and her nineteen-year-old son were taken to a sheriff's precinct for questioning. Nicole proved exceptionally cooperative, investigators said later. She provided cellphone numbers for Clemmons and described his spider web of contacts and places where he might go. She told investigators that the last time she saw Clemmons was Thanksgiving. She'd gone to his new place—the home where he'd resettled after Nicole kicked him out—with a plate of food.

Just before 1 p.m. Sunday, the Corrections Department issued an arrest warrant for Clemmons. The warrant didn't accuse Clemmons of killing the four officers. It accused him of failing to report to the department within twenty-four hours of getting out of jail. The same warrant could have been issued five days earlier—if only the department had flagged Clemmons' failure to meet the requirements of his supervision, if only the department had seized the opportunity it had yearned for to put Clemmons back behind bars.

By late Sunday afternoon, the Sheriff's Office had yet to name Clemmons publicly as the investigation's chief suspect. The *Seattle Times*, with more than a dozen reporters working the story, had gathered enough information to write a portrait of Clemmons—with details about his pending felony charges in Washington, with details about his criminal history in Arkansas. Around 5 p.m., a highly placed source confirmed Clemmons' status as the suspect. The newspaper broke the story on the Web and provided updates through the evening, with details that resounded in Arkansas and in Washington, D.C., the nation's political nerve center. The stories described how Mike Huckabee—the Arkansas governor turned presidential candidate—had granted clemency to Maurice Clemmons nine years before. They also quoted Larry Jegley, the prosecuting attorney in Little Rock and one of Huckabee's harshest critics on clemency issues. "This is the day I've been dreading for a long time," Jegley said.

For Huckabee, the ramifications were clear. If he wanted to understand the fallout, all he had to do was turn on his TV (Chris Matthews on *Hardball*: "Is Mike Huckabee now Huckawas?") or check out the political blogs (Michelle Malkin: "Huckabee's Willie Horton").

Since finishing as GOP runner-up in the 2008 presidential race, Huckabee had continued to maintain a high profile. He now hosted his own TV show on Fox. He had a book out—*A Simple Christmas*, his seventh—that was a *New York Times* bestseller. And his political prospects remained bright. In early November a *USA Today*/Gallup Poll showed Huckabee as the Republican front-runner for the 2012 presidential election. A couple of months before that he'd won the Values Voter Straw Poll, reflecting his appeal to social conservatives.

This very morning—two hours before Maurice Clemmons opened fire in that coffee shop—Huckabee had been interviewed on *Fox News Sunday*. Speaking from Arkansas, Huckabee described the chances of his running again in 2012: "It's less likely than more likely, just because I would have to see that the Republicans would be willing to unite behind me. The last time out, my biggest challenge was with the establishment Republicans who just never showed their support." Of course, three years from an election, most potential candidates remain uncommitted. Mitt Romney. Sarah Palin. Tim Pawlenty. They were all uncommitted. What Huckabee and every other potential candidate wanted to avoid was having that do-I-or-don't-I decision made for them, through some ill-chosen words or a horrible turn of events.

For Huckabee, the shootings of four police officers threatened to be just such a turn, exemplifying the political risks attached to almost any showing of mercy. In times like this, in the face of attacks both potential and real, a politician cannot afford to sit back and let the story be crafted by others. The Swiftboating of John Kerry showed the dangers of that. A politician needs to respond—and quickly. On Sunday evening, Huckabee's press team released a statement that acknowledged the shooter might be a repeat offender from Arkansas, and went on to say:

> The murder of any individual is a profound tragedy, but the murder of a police officer is the worst of all murders in that it is an assault on every citizen and the laws we live within.
>
> Should he be found to be responsible for this horrible tragedy, it will be the result of a series of failures in the criminal justice system in both Arkansas and Washington state. He was recommended for and received a commutation of his original sentence from 1990. This commutation made him parole eligible and he was then paroled by the parole board once they determined he met the conditions at that time. He was arrested later for parole violation and taken back to prison to serve his full term, but prosecutors dropped the charges that would have held him. It appears that he has continued to have a string of criminal and psychotic behavior but was not kept incarcerated by either state.

The statement closed by calling the officers "brave and heroic." Boiled down, Huckabee's release hit these points: Don't minimize the tragedy. Honor the officers. Deflect blame. He managed to strike back at Larry Jegley (*prosecutors dropped the charges*). He implicated the "system" in not one state, but two. And he described Clemmons' history without acknowledging his own role in it (*received a commutation*—the equivalent of "Mistakes were made"). For Huckabee, the statement released Sunday was but a start. In days to come, he would keep to his strategy, only sharpening the edges.

Honor the officers. Deflect the blame.

Just before 8 p.m., nearly twelve hours into the manhunt, members of the Corrections Department's fugitive task force pulled into Renton, a city south of Seattle where Boeing once built the B-29 Superfortress and now churned out 737s. By now, darkness had fallen. The temperature was close to freezing. The task-force members didn't know their exact destination, but they knew the command center had good reason to send them here.

With the help of the federal agencies enlisted by Adamson, police had been tracking cellphones linked to Clemmons. Nicole's help was proving invaluable; she'd supplied police with some of these cellphone numbers. The police were availing themselves of a cutting-edge technological tool—one with extraordinary capabilities for locating a fugitive, but one that simultaneously raised alarms about invasions of privacy.

Whether in use or not, cellphones constantly send out "pings" to check for nearby cell towers. Every seven seconds or so, these pings result in the phone's location being registered by the cellular network. In urban areas—and Renton would count, with a population exceeding eighty thousand—knowing the nearest tower can narrow the location of the phone's holder to within two hundred feet. Triangulating from the nearest three towers can narrow the location even more. Or, better yet, trackers can use a cellphone's GPS system, allowing networks to close the range to about fifty feet. Under a rule passed by the Federal Communications Commission to assist in tracing 911 calls, wireless providers must provide law enforcement with latitude and longitude of pings. Law enforcement's use of the technique has exploded; one cellular provider reported that a secure Web portal for cellphone pings was accessed 8 million times in a year. Civil liberties groups have described the threats to privacy that can accompany such tracking abilities. Imagine: A person's movements might disclose an extramarital affair; or political and religious affiliations; or long struggles with illness. While police used this technology to hunt Clemmons in Washington, federal judges in Pennsylvania were being asked to determine what limits, if any, should attach to the technology's use. But in the fall of 2009, there was no doubting the tool's value to police. "We were twenty minutes to two hours behind Clemmons all day," Adamson said later.

With a working range for Clemmons' whereabouts—but not an exact location—the fugitive team focused on several blocks near Renton High School. Officers began stopping cars coming and going from the area. Each stop was a gamble. Clemmons could be anywhere, ready for the shootout that Adamson dreaded. Between stops, the task-force members sat in their cars, on edge, eating cinnamon bears. One member, Evan Brady, had no doubt of the dangers. "It was freaky sitting in the pitch black, wondering if he was going to sneak up behind you," Brady says. "You always felt a step behind."

This step proved no different. The officers in Renton didn't see Clemmons Sunday night. But later they learned that one of his relatives lived nearby. Maybe he'd popped through there. They could never say for sure.

Maurice Clemmons had never been particularly adept at evading detection. That was true when he brought that gun to high school, at the age of 17. That was true when he got caught with the $10,000 in cash in the Walmart bag, at the age of twenty-nine.

So with six hundred officers now dogging his steps, Clemmons' odds of escaping the manhunt seemed slim. But Clemmons had a few things going for him. He had a head start, for one. It wasn't an enormous head start—the shootings occurred at 8:15 a.m., and his truck was found an hour later—but it was enough to get him out of Parkland. Clemmons also had family and friends, along with a forceful way of bending people to his will. He'd fallen out with Nicole. He'd fallen out with Boo Man. But he still had a girlfriend or two he could turn to. He still had friends and family from Arkansas.

After opening fire in the coffee shop—and after getting the keys to a white Pontiac from his brother Rickey—Clemmons went with Doug and Eddie Davis to the same home where he'd spent part of Thanksgiving. He showed up in Pacific and banged on the door of the duplex where his Aunt Letrecia lived. Needing first aid, clothes, money and transportation, Clemmons forced the people he knew into a decision. I killed four cops, he told them. Are you with me or against me? Right or wrong? He told some family members that he needed to rest and heal—so that he could go out and kill more. Faced with a choice, some family and friends opted to help Clemmons, the consequences be damned. "It ain't right, but family's more important," his Aunt Letrecia said later.

Clemmons also had one other advantage: His wound wasn't as bad as the cops thought. The bullet fired by Richards had hit Clemmons in the upper right back. But it never entered his chest cavity. It missed his vital organs. The bullet bounced around his rib cage before coming to rest beneath the skin just below his right nipple. While on the run Clemmons packed the wound with nearly a foot of gauze, to stop the bleeding. To manage the pain he popped OxyContin pills—or at least that was the theory police embraced later.

Sometime Sunday, after he left Letrecia's house, Clemmons wound up at a shopping mall in Auburn, south of Seattle. He called Quiana Williams, his longtime girlfriend. The two even had a child together—the baby that Nicole had found out about back in May. Williams drove to Auburn and picked Clemmons up, and they went back to Williams' house in South Seattle. Williams bought gauze, peroxide and bandages, and washed Clemmons' bloody clothes.

Around 7:30 p.m., as the Corrections Department task force was heading toward Renton, Clemmons called his Aunt Chrisceda, or "Ceda" for short. He wanted to know if she'd be willing to help.

Ceda, eight years older than Clemmons, used to babysit him in Arkansas. As adults, they stayed close after both moved to Washington state. To Ceda, Clemmons was no monster. He was someone who had become mentally ill, starting in May. "He has helped our family enormously," she says. "He was a kind, gentle being. That's who he was to me. He can be intense and gruff, but I have never seen any aggression personally." Ceda and her husband, Michael Shantz, had a steel drum band, Bakra Bata, that toured from Canada to Brazil. Earlier Sunday, the band had played at the opening of a new light-rail station in Seattle. The couple lived with their kids in a nice home in Seattle's Leschi neighborhood, on the shores of Lake Washington. Shantz, who is white, says of his wife's family: "They grew up in a siege mentality of 'us against them.' The main contact with the white world is police. … The family wouldn't be here if they didn't help each other."

Clemmons had been to Ceda's house before and thought it might be a good place to lay low. And he trusted his Aunt Ceda. On the phone, he admitted to killing the four officers. He said he was still armed and needed a place to heal. "Tired of them bitches," he said of the police. At the same time, Ceda heard resignation in Clemmons' voice. "He told me he was basically ready. He wanted to die." As with the rest of his family, Clemmons was now forcing Ceda and Shantz to make a decision. He wanted them to rent a car so he could drive to Arkansas. With me or against me?

Panic swelled in Ceda and Shantz as Clemmons called again—and again, and again. Ceda and her husband talked with LaTanya by phone about Clemmons' request for a rental car. Shantz mulled over asking a doctor he knew to treat Clemmons. Clemmons called again. He was getting closer. It was time for a decision. "You cannot come to the house," Shantz told him. To Shantz, the decision came down to minimizing the damage ahead. "Our first concern was for our family. Our next concern was for loss of life. He told Ceda that he wasn't going to go down, that he was going to kill more people. Our concern was, how many more people are going to die and what's our best move?" But Clemmons wasn't dissuaded. He remained determined to come. So as Clemmons got nearer to Ceda's house, Ceda and Shantz arranged for their kids to go elsewhere. Then the couple drove to a nearby police station.

Police investigators already knew about Ceda's connection to Clemmons—she was in Nick Weber's file. And now here she was, telling them where and when Clemmons would appear. A solid tip. Police pounced.

At 8:15 p.m., as SWAT teams were mobilizing, undercover detectives parked near Ceda's house. Within minutes, they saw a white Plymouth Breeze pull up and a heavyset black man, in a puffy black jacket and a dark brown hat, jump out. He climbed the stairs to the front porch. The detectives drove past the house and were turning their car around when they saw the Plymouth speed away. The detectives, believing Clemmons had gotten back in the car, gave chase while radioing in for other officers to keep an eye on the house. When police stopped the Plymouth about a mile from Ceda's house, they found not Clemmons but his girlfriend, Quiana Williams, behind the wheel.

I just dropped off Maurice, she told the officers.

Despite her years with Clemmons, Williams now seemed scared of him and started crying. "Who is going to protect me?" she asked the officers.

As detectives questioned Williams, SWAT teams arrived and surrounded Ceda's house. Within minutes, the news spread among cops, then the news media: Clemmons was hiding in a house in Seattle's Leschi neighborhood. Investigators received confirmation by listening to a phone call between Rickey Hinton, who was being questioned at a police station, and Clemmons' sister LaTanya. Maurice is holed up in a house in Seattle, LaTanya told Rickey.

A helicopter scanned the dense woods behind the house with an infrared camera but saw no motion. The SWAT teams began an all-night barrage of "flash-bang" grenades and lights. Police launched more than seventy rounds of tear gas into the house, breaking windows and saturating the walls with fumes. Some canisters bounced into a neighbor's home, filling it with gas. Fumes wafted through the neighborhood, stinging the eyes of onlookers and nearby homeowners. Police evacuated the residents of the closest homes, taking them to a lakefront steakhouse a few blocks away.

As dawn broke the next morning, SWAT teams entered and swept the house, tossing furniture and the couple's collection of African artwork. They found bloodied gauze, a handgun on a woodpile behind the house, and a shotgun on the seat of a car parked in the driveway.

But Clemmons was nowhere to be found.

For the Washington State Department of Corrections, the questions were coming from every which direction. Reporters from *USA Today* and CNN and *ABC World News* and the Associated Press. But it wasn't just reporters who were requesting records and asking about Clemmons' past. State lawmakers and their staffs wanted information, too. Legislators in Olympia were already contemplating changes to the state's laws or even its constitution, ways to protect police and to keep dangerous felons like Clemmons from securing their release. For the Corrections Department, questions also bubbled up from within. One department employee sent an e-mail suggesting the agency's officers should start using hand-held metal detectors on offenders when they reported in person. "If Clemmons had decided to commit these crimes at a DOC field office there would be far more victims since we are essentially unprepared for these situations," she wrote.

On Monday, the day after the shootings, the agency's communications department distributed a "Media Plan" to help deal with the fallout. The plan's "Communication Objective" was: "All audiences understanding that the Department of Corrections supervised Maurice Clemmons as closely as the law permits."

To reporters, the department insisted that the latest Clemmons warrant out of Arkansas—the "technical warrant" issued in the fall—did not provide Washington with the legal authority to hold Clemmons without bail. Although Arkansas disputed Washington's stand, the department treated the issue as clear-cut—pointing out how the warrant hadn't been entered into the National Crime Information Center database, pointing out how Arkansas hadn't checked the box indicating the state planned to come get Clemmons and take him back. So when a lawyer for Washington took a different tack—acknowledging the issue came with shades of gray, that it wasn't merely black and white—the department was not happy.

Not long after the shootings, the *New York Times* published a story with this paragraph:

"Ronda Larson, an assistant state attorney general in Washington involved with interstate offender supervision, said that the Arkansas warrant could probably have prevented Mr. Clemmons from being released on bail, but that the rules in such situations, including who must enter the information into certain databases, 'have a lot of ambiguities in them, and this is one of the places where they need improvement, obviously.'"

Ambiguities. Reading that, Eldon Vail, the head of the Corrections Department, dashed off an e-mail to Brian Moran, chief deputy to the state attorney general. Vail provided a link to the *New York Times* story and wrote four words: "This was not helpful." Ten minutes later, Moran responded. "Agreed. … Sometimes lawyers get caught up in super-technical issues and lose sight of how it will sound when reported." Moran wrote that he believed the "entire issue distills down" to the fact that Arkansas didn't enter the warrant into NCIC. "Very, very simple. We will follow up with Ronda. Please accept my apologies."

But if Washington was so convinced that it was in the right—and that Arkansas was in the wrong—another question emerged. Why didn't Washington file a complaint with ICAOS, the system that oversees the interstate compact? Two states had interpreted the compact's rules in ways that contradicted. Why not determine which state was right? One reporter who pushed this point was Austin Jenkins, a correspondent for the Northwest News Network, a collaboration of public radio stations. He wrote to Glenn Kuper, a spokesman for the governor: "Glenn, I guess my question stands—what about going to the Interstate Commission either by filing a formal complaint or asking for a dispute resolution—something the commission tells me they will do upon request? Is there any downside unless Washington risks losing?" Kuper responded that Washington preferred to "work collaboratively right now" with Arkansas. But Jenkins refused to go away. "But if there is ambiguity in the rules ... doesn't that need to be clarified for all states to prevent future tragedies?"

Kuper punted the question to Vail at the Corrections Department, writing: "Not sure how you want to respond to this." Vail wrote back that the department was not "ruling out the formal process. But first, we are focused on the memorial service." But the memorial service would come and go, and still, the department would not file a complaint. Jenkins' question remained a good one. "Is there any downside unless Washington risks losing?" But Washington never provided him with a good answer.

Clemmons' disappearing act at Ceda's house frustrated police and unnerved the region. Come Monday morning, police suspected Clemmons was still in Seattle. They continued chasing tips, one after the other. For a metropolitan area, Seattle has a low rate of violent crime, registering a couple of dozen homicides in a typical year; so the image of SWAT teams zipping through city neighborhoods, with officers clinging to the side rails of police vans, proved especially jarring. Anxiety took hold. Officers searched a building at the University of Washington after a witness reported seeing someone resembling Clemmons getting off a nearby bus. Dozens of officers spent the day bushwhacking through Cowen Park, a leafy, eight-acre ravine in North Seattle, after someone reported seeing a blood trail leading into the woods. A report of bloody gauze found in Seattle's Chinatown International District prompted police to stop a black man at gunpoint, resulting in an iconic photograph that encapsulated the region's unease.

All the tips proved fruitless. And all the while, as police went here, then there, as the manhunt's second day proved as futile as the first, Clemmons was fast asleep—and just a few blocks from where police had thought they had him surrounded the night before.

When the Seattle police detectives had chased Quiana Williams' Plymouth Breeze the night before, Clemmons saw something that spooked him. He probably bolted into the wooded greenbelt behind his Aunt Ceda's home, scrambling through the unlit forest. Around midnight, Richard Frederick, a forty-three-year-old crack addict with a history of drug-related crimes, spotted Clemmons about a half-mile from Ceda's house. Clemmons said his name was "Mo." He asked for a cigarette. Frederick had never seen Clemmons before, but when Clemmons offered $50 for a ride to Tacoma, Frederick leapt at the chance for quick cash.

The two men went to Frederick's house, where Clemmons lifted his shirt to reveal a bloody bandage. I need a T-shirt, peroxide and a cellphone, Clemmons told Frederick. Frederick asked no questions. The home is a well-known crack house, hidden from the street by a thick hedge—the type of place where one does not ask for a life's story. Frederick left to go hunt up a car. When he returned— after having no luck finding one—Frederick saw Clemmons asleep in an alcove, unaware that a small army of police was laying siege to Ceda's house just blocks away. Clemmons was still asleep when Frederick left early Monday. When Frederick returned home Monday evening, Clemmons was just waking up. They talked again about finding him a ride to Tacoma. Then Frederick left.

On Monday, as Clemmons slept, the circle of family and friends he could turn to contracted. Eddie Davis was arrested. Doug Davis was arrested. Rickey Hinton was arrested. Found with the help of cellphone pinging, all three were booked into jail on suspicion of rendering criminal assistance to Clemmons. Investigators also found and interviewed Clemmons' friend Reggie Robinson, the self-proclaimed minister. Robinson gave up Darcus Allen, divulging the hotel where he could be found. Police also questioned other people who knew Clemmons, making it less likely they would stick their neck out should Clemmons ask for help.

Frederick came back Monday night and poked his head into the alcove. Clemmons was gone. He was back on the streets of Seattle, increasingly isolated but still armed.

That same night—as Clemmons continued to evade police—Mike Huckabee went on *The O'Reilly Factor*, the popular talk show hosted by Bill O'Reilly. The program appears on Fox, the same network for which Huckabee worked, hosting his own show on weekends.

O'Reilly opened with a nod to Huckabee's courage. After all, Huckabee had agreed to come on O'Reilly's show and answer his questions.

"Thanks for being a stand-up guy, governor. A lot of people want an explanation. This is a bad hombre, and you let him out. Why?"

"Well, Bill, first of all, I think the tragedy of this—if I could have known nine years ago this guy was capable of something of this magnitude, obviously, I would never have granted a commutation. It's sickening. The two people in this country that I value the most are soldiers and police officers, because they're the only thing standing between our freedom and total anarchy."

Honor the officers.

From there, Huckabee proceeded to rewrite the case's history. He said Clemmons had been sentenced to 108 years "for two crimes when he was sixteen." (Clemmons' 108-year sentence had actually been built upon eight felony convictions involving five separate incidents.) When O'Reilly asked about Clemmons' abysmal prison record, Huckabee said: "We didn't have any information from the prosecutors. We sent notices, which is the practice in Arkansas, to five different people: the attorney general, secretary of state, the prosecutor, the judge, and law enforcement. The only official that we have record of getting notification from is the judge who agreed with the recommendation of the parole board." (By referring to "the practice," Huckabee confused what he was supposed to do with what he did. When he was governor of Arkansas, the state's failure to provide appropriate notice was a key factor in his eventual mea culpa concerning his handling of clemency applications. What's more, the commutation file in the Clemmons case includes no record of the prosecutor's office being notified.)

"Well, it's not your fault, governor," O'Reilly said.

The host went on: "I don't think anybody watching thinks it's your fault. But the judges in Washington state? Come on. I mean this guy moves from your state, Arkansas, to Washington state, and then he racks up eight felony charges. Eight felonies, including the rape of a twelve-year-old."

"That's inexcusable, Bill."

"And these clowns, these judges, give him a $15,000 walk, which he makes through a bail bondsman. … I mean, this is insane. … There's no excuse on earth for that, governor. Would you agree?"

"I would totally agree, Bill. And one of the things that's sad is that, after this guy was commuted, that just made him parole-eligible. Then he qualified for parole and was paroled. But he violated his parole in Arkansas, was put back in prison. Now, here's the real tragedy. The prosecutors failed to file the paperwork in a timely way, and so they had to drop the charges. That's what released him the second time."

Deflect the blame.

The O'Reilly appearance typified Huckabee's reaction to the shootings. In print and on the airwaves, Huckabee blended defiance and regret. He told CNN: "If you think a 108-year sentence is an appropriate sentence for a sixteen-year-old for the crimes he committed, then you should run for governor of Arkansas. You're looking at this nine years later and trying to make something as if that, you know, I could look into the future. I wish I could have. Good Lord, I wish I had that power." Huckabee went on Joe Scarborough's radio program and said: "It really does show how sick our society has become that people are more concerned about a campaign three years from now than those grieving families in Washington. It is disgusting, but people use anything as a political weapon." Huckabee continued to remark on the absence of any objection from Larry Jegley's office. (In fact, if Jegley's staff had been notified of the clemency request, it's a virtual lock they would have objected. The office's policy was to oppose clemency in all cases involving violent offenders.)

But no matter what Huckabee said to explain or defend, some pundits and political experts saw no way for him to overcome the damage done.

"His career in politics is done," Mark McKinnon, former media adviser to President George W. Bush, said on MSNBC. "Stick a fork in him."

And this was from someone who admired Huckabee. "I think he actually has been a great elected official," McKinnon told Chris Matthews. "He's been a great candidate. I think he is good for the Republican Party. He brings a lot of optimism and good policy ideas to the table. I think we'll miss him, but he ain't going to be there, Chris. I can guarantee you."

Criticism of Huckabee was not universal. Newspapers like the *Los Angeles Times* wrote editorials defending Huckabee's decision in the Clemmons case. But if there was any doubt of mercy's standing in the political world—all risk, no reward—three of Huckabee's potential rivals for the 2012 GOP presidential nomination dispelled it.

Sarah Palin, the former governor of Alaska, called Huckabee's commutation of Clemmons a "horrible decision."

Minnesota Governor Tim Pawlenty said: "I don't think I've ever voted for clemency. We've given out pardons for things after everybody has served out their term, but again, usually for more minor offenses. But clemency? Certainly not. Commutation of sentence? Certainly not."

Mitt Romney went on *Larry King Live* and said that in his four years as governor of Massachusetts, he didn't issue a single commutation or pardon. "My conclusion was, if somebody has been convicted by a jury of their peers, and they've been prosecuted, and the police were able to get the evidence necessary to put them behind bars, why in the world would I step in and reverse that sentence?"

Romney's approach defeats the very foundation of clemency. It makes no room for mercy, no room for changing times or changed people. His approach may be safe. But it also lacks for courage.

The *Washington Post*'s Howard Kurtz asked Huckabee if he believed the fallout from the Clemmons commutation would turn his political future to toast. "I don't know. Could be," Huckabee said. "If it is, it is."

Roll call for the graveyard shift in the Seattle Police Department's south precinct started at 7 p.m. It is normally a straightforward affair, fifteen minutes or so. But on this Monday night, the routine became electrified. Clemmons had not been seen since Sunday night. As printouts of police bulletins about Clemmons circulated the room, the patrol officers received a warning. Intelligence reports put Clemmons in Seattle, possibly in South Seattle. He was likely still armed with Richards' gun. He was wounded. Expect him to shoot on sight.

Officer Benjamin Kelly took it all in. The thirty-nine-year-old officer had been hired by the Seattle department five years before, after earning a master's degree in investigative psychology from the University of Liverpool and working as an investigator for the Washington State Gambling Commission. Kelly preferred to work alone. Even on this night, with a cop killer on the loose, Kelly turned down his sergeant's suggestion that officers double up. Kelly, whose patrol sign was "Sam 22," felt that isolation kept him sharp, less distracted.

Just after midnight, as Monday turned into Tuesday, Kelly heard a report about a stolen Acura Integra, silver, license plate 454 XMO. The owner had called in the theft after hearing his car start up and watching it roll away. It was the third stolen car in the neighborhood that night, an unusual number. Kelly decided to cruise the surrounding area to search for the Acura and the other stolen cars. His patrol zone reflected the economic diversity of Seattle as a whole, going from the mansions on the Lake Washington shore to cramped midcentury ramblers on cinderblock foundations. He steered his patrol car through dark side streets shiny with rain.

Around 2:30 a.m., with ninety minutes left in his shift, Kelly turned west onto South Kenyon Street and noticed a man rounding the corner in a dark blue sweatshirt, with the hood pulled up. Kelly drove past the man and continued up the quiet residential street toward the thoroughfare of Martin Luther King Jr. Way. Nearing the end of the street, Kelly saw a car with its hood up and exhaust spewing. He hit the brakes. Car trouble? Or something else? Kelly aimed his floodlight at the driver's seat. No one was there. The car was a silver Acura. Kelly backed up. His headlights lit up the license plate: 454 XMO.

"Sam 22," Kelly said into his radio. "I have managed to locate our earlier stolen, the Acura Integra, 454 Xray Mary Ocean. It's unoccupied at 44 and Kenyon."

As he notified dispatch, Kelly glanced in his rearview and side mirrors. Police are taught "situational awareness"—to keep their sensory perception taut, to know at all times what is around them. In the rearview mirror, Kelly saw the man in the hooded sweatshirt, about fifty feet behind his car. The man stepped off the sidewalk and began walking down the middle of the street.

"Copy," the dispatcher said. "On view recovery at 44 and Kenyon of 454 Xray Mary Ocean."

Kelly glanced up again. The man was getting closer. This guy is not trying to avoid me, Kelly thought. He is coming at me.

The man was at Kelly's rear bumper when Kelly jumped out of his patrol car and turned to face him. The street was empty but for the two men, who both stood in the glow of a streetlight. The hooded man lifted his head. Recognition flooded Kelly with adrenaline. The face, the build, the mole.

Maurice Clemmons was just a few feet from him.

"Let me see your fucking hands, show me your fucking hands, let me see your motherfucking hands!" Kelly shouted as he unclipped his holster and whipped his gun out. A thought flashed: I could be dead in seconds. Clemmons gave a look Kelly later described as "Oh, crap."

Clemmons shoved his hands into the pocket of his sweatshirt, reaching for a gun. He bent over into a half-crouch and sprinted past Kelly and around the front of the patrol car. Wearing sweat pants, a triple white stripe running down the legs, Clemmons appeared to be limping, just a bit. Kelly fired three shots in a burst, then four more, the whole time pivoting, tracking Clemmons as he sprinted through the fog of the Acura's exhaust. Shell casings scattered across the empty street and at Kelly's feet. Clemmons ran across the sidewalk and dived through an eight-foot hedge that fenced off a house to the patrol car's right.

Again, he was gone.

The entire confrontation, from Kelly getting out of his car to firing the last of his seven shots, had taken only three seconds, a manic burst of action with uncertain results. Maybe Clemmons was hit, maybe he wasn't.

Kelly hit the call button on his shoulder-mounted radio. He got a dead signal— a "bonk," in police jargon. Six seconds later, he tried again. Another bonk. Kelly tucked his head into his car and tried the car-mounted radio. It, too, bonked.

The realization was quick and chilling. It was 2:35 a.m. on a deserted street. Kelly had no backup and none on the way, and the most notorious cop killer in the nation had just vanished into the night. Kelly thought, "I'm alone out here on the street, I don't know where he is but he knows where I am."

He reached back into the patrol car, grabbed his shotgun, and aimed over the car's roof. Kelly tried the radio once more. This time, the call went through.

"Sam 22. I have shots fired on the suspect in the homicide down in Lakewood, just approached my vehicle and ran off." Kelly's voice was tight, his breathing heavy.

Dispatch: "Where, where are you sir?"

"I'm out in front of 4430 South Kenyon. He ran northbound through the yard."

"Copy. Suspect ran northbound from 4430 South Kenyon."

It was the call that law enforcement all across the region had been waiting for. Within two seconds, the first Seattle patrol officer radioed that he was on the way. Then another, and another, and another. Patrol cars, lights flashing, screamed through South Seattle. The first backup arrived in thirty seconds. The street turned into a blaze of red and blue.

With so much light now trained on the hedge and the opening through which Clemmons had disappeared, the arriving officers could see what Kelly had not been able to. They saw that Clemmons had collapsed, face down, on the concrete path leading up to the house.

But was he conscious? Would he open fire if officers approached? Officers began clustering behind the Acura, their pistols and shotguns trained on Clemmons' body. They didn't know what, if any, danger to expect from inside the house. They saw the front door open and close several times. Was Clemmons trying to make it into the house? Were these Clemmons' friends or family?

Within five minutes of the first backup's arrival, three officers lined up behind a bulletproof shield. The decision had been made: Drag Clemmons out, then check the house. Guns drawn, the train of officers, crouched behind the shield, reached Clemmons. The lead officer pressed the blast shield down against Clemmons' body. Another officer, Daina Boggs, patted Clemmons down until she felt the butt of a gun sticking out of his right pocket. She knew the feel of the gun: a Glock 22, the type she carried—and that Greg Richards carried. She pulled. The gun stuck. The trigger guard was caught firmly on the zipper—a fortuitous turn that may have saved Kelly's life.

At 2:45 a.m., 10 minutes after Kelly opened fire, Clemmons was dragged across the street to waiting paramedics. It turned out Kelly was remarkably accurate. Clemmons had four fresh bullet wounds—three to the back, one to the thigh. At least two of Kelly's shots were fatal, each hitting a lung. A third ruptured Clemmons' kidney and bowel.

Clemmons died on the way to the hospital.

Less than four hours later, at 6:28 a.m., the chief of staff for Governor Chris Gregoire sent an e-mail to the head of the state's Department of Corrections and to other officials in the Governor's Office: "They got Clemmons. Shot by Seattle Police Officer. Dead at the scene. So, now the questions will come fast and furious."

The chief of staff, Jay Manning, wanted to get a prepared Q&A in front of the governor. He also wanted to know if everyone could huddle later that morning "to put a game plan together." In the end, the Governor's Office singled out Arkansas for blame. Gregoire held a press conference announcing that Washington would no longer accept any new parolees from the other state pending further investigation. "If Arkansas doesn't like it," she said, "sue me."

On Tuesday night, Bill O'Reilly was back on the air, back to flogging the two Pierce County judges, John McCarthy and Thomas Felnagle. O'Reilly had no doubt where the blame lay. He said the two judges "let that cop killer out on low bail. Outrageous."

O'Reilly's program attracted about 3.5 million viewers a night, making it the most-watched news show on cable TV. For this flogging, he brought in help from two legal analysts, Lis Wiehl and Kimberly Guilfoyle. After the show put up pictures of both judges, O'Reilly bristled at one judge's hesitation to comment for fear of compromising any pending cases against the people accused of aiding Clemmons.

"Bull, bull, bull. That's a lie."

O'Reilly kept saying the judges let Clemmons out on $15,000 bail. In fact, each judge set bail at $190,000. (McCarthy went even further, granting a no-bail hold on the original fugitive warrant, which Arkansas subsequently rescinded.) Washington law requires judges to set bail on pending criminal charges. So they set bail. And the number they settled upon was closer to the $300,000 initially requested by prosecutors than the $40,000 urged by Clemmons' lawyer.

O'Reilly kept flipping things around. When Guilfoyle said prosecutors "asked for $200,000," O'Reilly assumed that figure represented the 10 percent typically needed to pay a bondsman. He assumed the prosecutors had asked for ten times $200,000.

"That would have been $2 million bond, $200,000 out," he said.

"Right. Exactly," Wiehl said.

"OK? So the prosecutors thought it was insane. I just want to be clear."

O'Reilly was wrong. Wiehl was wrong. But none of that mattered. O'Reilly had made up his mind.

"It's the judges' fault," he said.

"They failed to protect the public," Guilfoyle said.

"Right," O'Reilly said.

12

HALF-STAFF

THE FIRST PATROL CAR ARRIVED AT 5 A.M., pulling into a massive lot outside McChord Air Force Base, the designated staging area for a memorial procession unlike any in the history of the Pacific Northwest. The air was unusually frigid for Pierce County, part of the temperate zone west of the Cascades. It was three hours before sunrise, four hours before the temperature would reach twenty, five hours before the procession would begin. That first arrival might have seemed ridiculously early, but if anyone thought so they didn't think so for long, not if they watched the police cars and the motorcycles and the fire department vehicles descend on the lot, one after the other, line after line, a dense block of black and blue and red that would stretch for more than a dozen miles when uncoiled.

On December 8, 2009, nine days after the four Lakewood police officers were shot and killed, a thousand members of the Royal Canadian Mounted Police came to the Puget Sound area to pay their respects, unmistakable in their scarlet coats, midnight-blue breeches with yellow strip, and brown riding boots. A hundred police officers came from Boston, 2,500 miles away. About the same number came from New York, and about the same from Chicago. Police came from Florida. They came from Los Angeles. They came from Bozeman, Montana, and Teton County, Wyoming, and Black Butte Ranch, Oregon, and Allegheny County, Pennsylvania; Elk Grove, California; Port Moody, British Columbia; and Coulee Dam, Washington. In all, 1,982 law-enforcement vehicles filled the staging lot, and still they kept coming, forcing organizers to direct overflow to a side street from which the additional cars could attach to the procession's tail.

The procession route covered 10.2 miles, a winding course that started at McChord's north gate, zigzagged north and west to the Lakewood Police Department, then shot east and north to the Tacoma Dome, an arena accustomed to hosting hockey games, bull-riding events and monster-truck rallies, or concerts by Green Day, Springsteen, The Rolling Stones. Officers from more than three hundred seventy agencies participated in the procession, which traveled at speeds of between 5 mph and 10 mph, a slow rolling testament to kinship. More than six hundred officers came from British Columbia, reflecting the ties that span the border, the shared sense of loss, the two countries' flags flying side by side, the Maple Leaf and the Stars and Stripes. The kinship among first responders—police officers and firefighters—could be seen as the procession passed under American flags draped from crossed fire ladders. There was the kinship of uniform. As the caravan of cars left McChord, an Air Force sergeant, in dress blues, remained at attention for more than three hours, a statuesque figure against the bright cold sky. "It was what I felt I needed to do," he said later. And there was the kinship among law-enforcement officers no matter their agency. Neighboring police departments volunteered to patrol Lakewood's streets, freeing Lakewood's 102 officers to participate in the procession and memorial service.

One of the day's most striking examples of kinship could be seen not on the streets but on the sidewalks that lined the procession's channel. The sidewalks became home to thousands of people, standing, determined to say thank you with their presence alone, determined to testify to the kinship of community. In scarves and stocking caps, their breath visible on the air, some people saluted as the procession passed. Some crossed their heart. Some flew flags, small ones gripped in one hand or large ones that were unfolded and required three people to hold. Some people cried. It was a Tuesday, a school day, but some parents pulled their children out of class and brought them along, figuring there were lessons to be learned here, too. Many businesses along the procession route closed so that their employees could attend. Employees at some other places took off on their own. One woman said of her boss: "I didn't ask him. I told him." As they passed in their cars, some police officers locked eyes with people outside and pressed their hands to the window, a way to connect.

The community had wasted little time in rallying around the police. It started with a single red rose, or at least that's how the story came to be told. On the Sunday the four officers were killed, someone went to the Lakewood Police Department and set down a rose, a small gesture that sparked so much more, providing the community an outlet for its grief. The sidewalks outside the police department turned into a community meeting place, and that rose turned into a wall of flowers. Then people added to the flowers, dropping off candles, balloons, flags, stuffed animals. A cash box was set up to raise money for the officers' families. The idea of creating a trust fund for the officers' nine children took hold. Corporations donated. Local businesses donated. A group of inmates serving life sentences at a state prison donated. When Papa John's pizza shops in Washington elected to donate profits from two days' sales to the fund, individual stores set sales records. In Spokane, 225 miles from Tacoma, one Papa John's sold so much pizza that it ran out of dough. The wait at another store stretched to two hours.

Another store had to stop answering its phones in order to keep up. Within three months the fund collected more than $2.1 million. People would have given more, but the organizers stopped taking money, saying the account was fully funded.

One Lakewood police officer recounted a visit from a boy, three or four years old, and his mother. The mom had driven her son forty miles to the Lakewood Police Department. They came on a Sunday and, finding no one at the front counter, had waved down the officer in the parking lot. The officer wrote:

> I walked over to her and saw that the little boy was holding a plastic baggy containing a dollar and some change, and was clutching a well-worn stuffed dinosaur. The woman told me that her son, AJ, had seen the stories on the TV about our 4 slain officers. She said that they had driven to our station all the way from Kingston because her son was so intent on helping the children of these officers. I opened the gate and the boy handed me the plastic baggy containing all the money from his piggybank and a note on which he had written, "AJ … From me to Pleec. I Love You." And then, with tears in his eyes, he handed me his stuffed dinosaur. AJ's mom explained that he wanted to give the children of the slain officers the most precious thing that he owned, and that was his dinosaur, Bruno.
>
> I told AJ that I would take the money that he wanted to donate, but that I thought the best thing he could do for the children of our 4 officers was to keep Bruno safe with him but to keep those kids in his heart when he hugged his dinosaur. He agreed and gratefully took Bruno back from me and held him tightly as if he never wanted to let him go again.

The officer wrote that he and other officers had experienced and witnessed many acts of kindness since the shootings. "We have hugged more friends and strangers than we could have ever imagined and have mended broken ties with people we haven't talked to for years. Yet nothing has touched me deeper, or given me more hope for the future, than AJ and his stuffed dinosaur. I gave AJ one of our department challenge coins, explaining to him that we only gave them out to the bravest and most deserving people we came across. I hope he will realize someday how much more than a dollar and some change he gave to me and to the Lakewood Police Department today."

The need to say thanks could be seen the day of the memorial. Along the procession route, a woman from Olympia raised money for the Lakewood Police Guild by selling bracelets. She'd threaded each one with blue and black beads, for the colors of police, and four silver beads, one for each officer killed. For the memorial itself, UPS donated the cost of printing twenty-five thousand programs that were distributed at the Tacoma Dome.

But that kind of support wasn't universal. An undercurrent could be picked up, although there was no saying how deep it ran. A Seattle punk band designed a T-shirt glorifying Christopher Monfort, the man who killed a Seattle police officer. The National Black Foot Soldier Network designated Maurice Clemmons a "Black History Hero," putting him alongside Nat Turner, W.E.B. Du Bois, Malcolm X. The comments section on newspaper Web sites revealed similar push-back, with commenters like "ballardboinger" decrying "the tyrannical police state fascists who control our city." "The blue shirt gang are the enemies of all free men," ballardboinger wrote.

At the memorial service, police strived to minimize the chances of further violence. More than one hundred officers worked security in and around the Tacoma Dome. There were SWAT teams, bomb squads, intelligence groups, air support. Snipers took positions on rooftops.

In grief, sharing comforts. So many police cars participated in the procession that its head reached the destination before the tail set out. Four hours passed before the final vehicle finished the ten-mile route. Twenty thousand police officers filled the Tacoma Dome. They were joined by such national and state figures as FBI Director Robert Mueller, Washington Governor Chris Gregoire, and Congressman Dave Reichert, a former King County sheriff. Members of the public watched on live television or in satellite locations set up for the event. In grief, tradition comforts. Pipers played and drummers drummed. Amazing Grace and Echo Taps filled the massive space. Symbols comfort, too. Officers placed black strips across their badges. Flags flew at half-staff. A police horse walked the grounds, riderless, empty boots in the stirrups facing backward.

But maybe what matters most are the stories—a chance to put a face on what was lost, to replace the easy shorthand, the Lakewood Four, with the emotional challenge of looking at pictures pulled from family albums and listening to friends and family and colleagues. All four "were executed because they were cops," Lakewood police officer Matt Brown says. "But none of them saw their lives that way." At the memorial service, the four officers were remembered as people in full, with lives that extended beyond police work. "They were good people and they were great cops," Lakewood Police Chief Bret Farrar told the gathering, and lest anyone miss the "people" part, objects were placed around the dome to reflect the officers' passions outside the police station. There was Ronnie Owens' dirt bike, Greg Richards' drum set, and Tina Griswold's boxing gloves along with a favorite pair of high heels. Mark Renninger loved NASCAR, so organizers managed to bring in a car that Bobby Labonte drove at Daytona.

Renninger was thirty-nine years old. He and his wife, Kim, had three children: Ashley, fifteen; Allyson, twelve; and Nicholas, three. He grew up in Bethlehem, Pennsylvania, starred in football at Liberty High, joined the elite Army Rangers, and worked as a police officer in Tukwila, Washington, before moving over to Lakewood's police department and becoming head of an interagency SWAT team. "Every once in a while, Mark would say, 'Do you have a minute, sir?'" Farrar said at the memorial service. "The translation was, 'I want some really expensive SWAT gear and would you hear me out.'"

Mike Villa, Tukwila's assistant police chief, described one of his first calls with Renninger. It was a home burglary. The burglar fled on foot. The police needed to track him, but the canine unit wasn't available. So Villa and Renninger started from where the burglar was last seen. They came to a T. The burglar could have gone right or left. "He would have gone right," Renninger said. So they went right. They went down the street, but only part way, because while they were running Renninger said, "I think he would have left the street here." Renninger looked right. He looked left. He studied the grass, he looked for disturbed vegetation. "He must have gone left," Renninger said. So they turned left—and this time, within seconds, they found the burglar hiding under a porch. Villa told the memorial gathering: "I just remember thinking at the time, 'Who is this guy?' We didn't need a canine. We had the man-tracker."

Villa recounted how Renninger had led the department in felony arrests. How he'd arrested one of America's Most Wanted, a murder suspect from Oklahoma staying at a local hotel. How he'd disarmed a sixteen-year-old threatening to kill himself with a ten-inch knife. How, while arresting a man on a felony warrant at a Tukwila hotel, he had noticed the toilet was running. For twenty minutes that toilet ran, wasting water and eating at Renninger's sense of order. "Mark's other passion in life was home plumbing repair," Villa said. Renninger went into the bathroom and jiggled the toilet handle. But that didn't work. The toilet kept running. So he lifted the lid on the tank—and discovered a plastic bag, with nearly a pound of cocaine, interfering with the flushing mechanism. "That was a great success story," Villa said. "He fixed the toilet and found the dope."

Another time, Renninger responded to a call triggered by someone's residential alarm going off. At the house, Renninger found the door ajar. He yelled inside: Tukwila police! A voice answered: "Hello?" Renninger yelled back: Come out with your hands up! The voice answered: "Come in." Renninger yelled: No! You come out! By this time, other police cars began pulling up, their lights flashing and sirens sounding. Renninger started over: Tukwila police! Come out! The voice from inside said: "Hello?" Now tired of this routine, Renninger consulted with a second officer. He decided to poke his head in, to get a look around the corner, and when he did, he discovered that his suspect was ... a parrot, "a beautiful, talking parrot."

While Villa praised Renninger as a cop—"I would have gone through any door with Mark. And I trusted him on any mission"—he emphasized how Renninger adored his wife and kids, how his demeanor, the tough Pennsylvania SWAT guy, always softened when the subject turned to family. At the memorial service, pictures from Renninger's life flashed on a large screen, and the one that wouldn't let you go is a shot of Renninger with his son, holding hands, their backs to the camera, the boy's head coming to Renninger's waist, the two striking out on some trail.

Tina Griswold was forty years old. She had a grown daughter, Nicole, and an eight-year-old son, Marcus. Before joining the Lakewood Police Department she had served as an officer in two other Washington towns, Shelton and Lacey, where she'd become one of the state's few women to complete SWAT basic training. Her first marriage ended in divorce, but she remarried in 2007, wedding an Army veteran who had served two tours in Iraq. Labels did not attach easily to her. You could call her a tomboy—she rode dirt bikes, engaged in mixed martial arts, belonged to the National Rifle Association—but if you did, you'd also have to account for the joy she took in dressing up and going out, the joy she found in staying home and cooking for family and friends. "What Tina most desired in her life was a close relationship with God, a clear purpose in life, a high degree of integrity, and to be a good mother, wife and friend," Pamela Battersby, a friend of Griswold's, said at the memorial. The photos of Griswold included a close-up with her son, cheek to cheek, smiling big as can be, and back-to-back shots that captured her many facets, with a picture of her in a beautiful black gown—formal, the hem sweeping the floor—followed by a photo of her in a bulletproof vest.

As a collection, the pictures of the four officers became a sort of family album, full of the kinds of pictures that decorate walls in homes all over—the childhood shots of a boy or girl sleeping on top of the family dog, or holding a basketball, or sitting on Santa's lap, the vacation shots at the Grand Canyon or at Disneyland with Mickey and Minnie, graduation pictures, wedding pictures, holiday pictures, a father holding a baby up to the top of the Christmas tree as though she's an angel or star.

For Ronald Owens—or Ronnie, as everyone called him—there's a picture that every father knows, a photo of Owens, asleep, with his baby daughter nestled into his chest. Owens was thirty-seven years old. When he died, his daughter was seven. At the memorial service, Owens' sister, Ronda LeFrancois, spoke about her brother:

He was the baby of our family, but he also was the rock. ... After my dad passed away, Ronnie stepped right up to take the lead in our family. ... He was such a kind and gentle man. ... He had friends wherever we would go. You could never go anywhere with Ronnie without someone knowing who he was. ... He was so dedicated to anything he did. In high school we would watch in horror as Ronnie entertained my friends by break dancing in the kitchen and singing to

Barry Manilow. I would do anything to go back to those days. … Ronnie's greatest joy in life was being a father. He enjoyed spending every free moment he had with Maddie. She is daddy's girl. I know how much he was looking forward to watching her start her first basketball season. I know Ronnie will be watching her every game from heaven.

The last officer to be memorialized was Greg Richards. At forty-two, he was the oldest of the four. But he also had the least seniority. The prospect of speaking in front of twenty thousand people would intimidate just about anyone. And to do it at a time like this? But the three people tapped to speak for Richards approached the podium with poise and calm. And maybe that said more than anything else—about Richards, about his wife, about the job they had done raising their family. The three who approached the podium—with a wall of flags behind them and a crescent bend of four caskets in front—were the couple's three children: Austin, sixteen; Jami-Mae, fifteen; and Gavin, ten. They lined up oldest to youngest, tallest to shortest, with Austin taking the microphone first.

"Our dad was a hero to many, even long before he became a policeman," Austin said. "He didn't talk much about serious matters, but the way he lived his life spoke volumes. He had a smile and laughter that radiated like sunshine, warming everyone around him. It made people want to be near him, to find out his secret to being so happy."

Then it was Jami-Mae's turn. The last time she'd seen her father was the Saturday night before his Sunday shift. They'd made hamburgers together. Early Sunday morning, on the last day of Richards' life, Jami-Mae had heard the coffee grinder going, the sound she always heard just before her dad headed off for work. She'd stayed in bed, one of those things that mean nothing at the time but invite regret later, one of those things that can get played in the mind over and over.

"The truth is, just about everything made him happy," Jami-Mae told the waves of police officers. "His family was always enough, even during struggles. My dad taught us to cherish the simple things in life, like five people and one crazy cat smashed in bed to watch a movie, discovering a new favorite song, taking an outrageously long bath, and eating good food, especially dessert. We took many late-night trips to the store, just for an apple or a banana cream pie, or BCP, as dad would call it. He had a nickname for everything and everyone. He had his own language of nonsense words that we all understood. He didn't need anything fancy. He liked a little house and a paid-off car."

When the family took a vacation a year earlier, Jami-Mae said, her dad chose Arizona because he wanted to visit relatives and eat a good steak and an In-N-Out burger. "He never cared where we lived. The house wasn't important. He moved to wherever suited us at the time, and he always picked up some lifelong friends from every neighborhood. He taught us the importance of having good friends and of being one, especially to his fellow officers. My dad knew how to spot good people and how to value them always."

Austin returned to the microphone.

Our dad never changed. He was born with a kind heart, courage, and the drive to do what's right. My Aunt Gabbie will tell you that he made the rest of them look bad as a kid. He never made any trouble. He just loved to play the drums. My grandma Freda drove him everywhere so he could play. His school band even played for the president. And when my Aunt Gayle had a son, EJ, my dad discovered his love for kids. They were inseparable until my dad joined the Army at eighteen. Luckily, that brought him here to Fort Lewis, so that he could meet Kelly Mitchell, our mom. It wasn't long before they were married. My mom says that to say he is a good husband isn't enough. He is perfect. She never had to question his love and loyalty to her. They were best friends who made every decision together, no matter how small. … His friends said he was a family man first, a cop second. He loved his job mostly because it was a better way to provide for us and the lessons it taught us. It didn't change him, either. He didn't become more hardened or angry, just more thankful. Our little brother says that he didn't even hate the people he had to arrest. I guess he didn't see the point of anger. It was always more important for my dad to laugh, which he did a lot. Our Uncle Gary could always make him laugh until he couldn't breathe. There weren't many things he didn't like; in fact, I can count them on one hand: disorganized drawers, mayonnaise, and baggy pants.

At this, all three of Richards' kids looked at each other—and smiled and laughed. They were joined by people all around the arena. Austin continued: "He said that you should dress and act in a way that shows you respect yourself and others around you. That's why he always took good care of the house, rarely cursed, and kept his Lakewood patrol car spotless. He always said it was a privilege to drive that car and to wear that uniform, and then to get a paycheck for it."

Austin turned the microphone back over to Jami-Mae. "If things ever went wrong, if we made a bad choice or someone hurt us in any way, he would want us to leave it in the past and to forgive," she said. "He knew that it didn't do any good to have regrets, to dwell on the things that couldn't be changed. He always wanted us to fix what we could, and look toward the future, and that's what he wants us to do today. Cherish our loved one's memories, laugh, and enjoy the simple things in life every day. That's the secret."

When Austin and Jami-Mae finished, it was Gavin's turn. He looked so short behind that podium, but he spoke with a grace and courage that amazed the gathering inside the dome as well as the people watching on television. "I know my dad is proud and honored by what he sees here today," Gavin said. "It shows us how strong the bond is between men and women in uniform, and how wide it spreads. And we love you all because you all love him. Thank you."

When Gavin finished speaking, people rose to their feet. A release of emotion swept through the rows of police officers, who filled the dome with applause.

The service ended with two more gestures, two more ways of saying goodbye. The month before, when Timothy Brenton, the Seattle police officer ambushed by Christopher Monfort, was honored by seventy-five hundred people at Seattle's KeyArena, the memorial included the traditional twenty-one-gun salute. But inside the Tacoma Dome, the organizers wanted to avoid the sounds of gunfire. The shootout in the coffee shop was too recent, the danger of association too great. So the memorial for the four Lakewood officers used a twenty-one-bell salute, with twenty-one chimes of a brass bell ringing.

To close, a police-radio call played inside the dome, with the dispatcher calling out each of the officers' service numbers—Renninger's, then Griswold's, Owens' and Richards'—and getting nothing in response. Each time, the dispatcher answered the silence with a final farewell.

"Out of service. Gone but not forgotten."

"Out of service. Gone but not forgotten."

"Out of service. Gone but not forgotten."

"Out of service. Gone but not forgotten."

EPILOGUE

YOU COME HOME TO US

"GONE BUT NOT FORGOTTEN." The part about forgetting—that's always the fear. We worry that as the weeks become months, and months become years, we will forget, and in the forgetting we will lose something we should not let go. The memorial in the Tacoma Dome was not the last. Five months later, in May 2010, five hundred people gathered in the state capital of Olympia to present Medal of Honor awards to the families of the four Lakewood officers, as well as to the families of three other officers in the state killed in the line of duty in 2009. In a quiet spot that invites reflection—overlooking the Puget Sound, offering up the Olympic Mountains—Governor Chris Gregoire called it "the deadliest law enforcement year in more than seventy years." "We will remember and cherish their decision to serve," she said. A pastor who delivered the invocation said: "We are gathered here to honor the best of us, and the best in us."

When the body of Sergeant Mark Renninger was returned to his hometown of Bethlehem, Pennsylvania, more than a thousand people gathered for a funeral procession that lasted most of the day, with a horse-drawn caisson, bagpipers and sprays of red, white and blue flowers.

For Maurice Clemmons' family, the act of remembering was more complicated. They could not mourn him—their brother, or uncle, or cousin—in a way that others could see, because that might be misconstrued as support for who he was or what he stood for. So they mourned in private.

It is not easy to find Clemmons' grave. As you approach Marianna—passing the fields of rice, corn and cotton, the fields ringed by old-growth sycamore and oak—signs say you are entering a "Penitentiary Area" and would be wise to avoid hitchhikers. Inside the town, there are signs of decline, not written but unmistakable. Dozens of homes stand empty. One dilapidated house, owned by a member of the Clemmons family, is now home only to feral cats. Hightower & Sons, the funeral home that handled the arrangements for Clemmons' mother in 1999, is boarded up and filled with trash. A temporary banner above the door suggests someone wanted to turn the funeral home into a shoe outlet. But those plans didn't pan out.

You stop in a diner—there's a "For Sale" sign, faded almost white—and you hear a lunchtime table of older white men complaining about President Obama, and you hear them say "boy" and "nigger." You cringe at this. You see a black woman, drinking coffee, within earshot of this conversation, but she doesn't seem to notice. You talk to a cook about Marianna's past. She recalls the battles over integration. "I had a black boy who was a friend," she says. You ask about the grip of racism—about those men over there using the word "nigger"—and she says: "Well, you've just got to understand the southern Negro. They're arrogant. They have a sense that they're owed. They're not like the ones you have up North."

At the home of Ray Clemmons, Maurice's uncle and childhood friend, Maurice's Aunt Mamie sits outside. The porch has three chairs. Two are broken. The family "still does not know what set Maurice off," she says. The family is reluctant to speak to reporters after news coverage portrayed Maurice in a way the family did not recognize. They have prayed for the families of the four officers, she says. Asked where Clemmons is buried, she says next to his mother.

Pilgrim Cemetery, the region's historically black graveyard, stretches out from State Road 1, miles south of Marianna, on the grounds of the Pilgrim Missionary Baptist Church. Some graves display grand marble monuments, but those are the exception. Many headstones are carved by hand, because that's all the survivors could afford. Some graves have no marker at all, with the only evidence of burial being the sunken ground. Searching for Clemmons' grave, you look for dirt that is freshly dug. And in the northwest corner you find it. Beside the headstone for Dorthy Clemmons—"Our Beloved Mother, In Memory of Your Sons"—there's a two-foot-high mound of dirt.

The ceremony was a quiet one, held after Clemmons' body was released by the Pierce County medical examiner in early December. A bouquet of white roses adorns the foot of the grave, which has only a plastic marker, smudged with dirt, on which these words are written by hand:

Bro. Maurice Clemmons
02-06-1972   12-01-2009
37 years

The marker doesn't say much; it's just a name and numbers. But Clemmons' epitaph resides elsewhere—in those one-hundred-plus hours of telephone calls placed from the Pierce County Jail, and in all those court and prison files that seem to have no end.

For public officials in Washington, the decision became how best to respond to the vast record left by Clemmons and to the damage done. In 2010 the legislature passed a series of laws attributable to those four deaths in the Parkland coffee shop. Lawmakers raised the lump-sum payment for survivors of police officers or firefighters killed in the line of duty from $150,000 to $214,000. They did away with a requirement that officers or firefighters have at least ten years of service before survivors can draw an annual retirement benefit. They guaranteed a free college education to the children of cops or firefighters killed or disabled while on duty. They toughened the penalties for people who help criminal suspects elude capture. They put an end to booking bail—the bond-by-formula practice that allowed Clemmons to get out of jail after assaulting two sheriff's deputies. Governor Gregoire went to the Lakewood Police Department and signed all of these bills into law in the spring of 2010. Another measure was to be put before the state's voters in the fall. It would amend the state's constitution and allow judges to deny bail for some crimes beyond capital offenses. Judges could refuse bail, for example, to suspects facing a possible "third strike" and an automatic life sentence.

Another series of reforms made its way before the Interstate Commission for Adult Offender Supervision, or ICAOS, the group that oversees the transfer of parolees between states. In March 2010, the commission issued a formal opinion that said Washington's refusal to accept any more parolees from Arkansas was unlawful. Washington responded by telling ICAOS to take its formal opinion and stuff it. The state held firm, refusing to take any more parolees from Arkansas unless certain changes were made. Governor Gregoire and Washington corrections officials took their concerns to the ICAOS executive committee, pushing for reforms that would protect receiving states from being saddled with unforeseen dangers. Washington officials insisted that sending states disclose the full criminal histories of parolees and take felons back if they committed a serious violation of parole. ICAOS agreed to put those proposals before its national membership. That vote was to take place at the commission's annual meeting in October 2010.

One of the most profound—and predictable—consequences of the four officers' murders has been the backlash against executive acts of mercy. Seven months passed before Gregoire granted clemency again. In June 2010, she pardoned Jose Dominguez, an immigrant farm worker who had been convicted in the 1980s of a drug charge on evidence dubious at best. Gregoire's general counsel called the pardon "extremely rare." That was understatement. At the time, fourteen other petitioners who had received the unanimous backing of the state's five-member Clemency and Pardons Board awaited word from Gregoire. Adam Kline, a Seattle Democrat who chairs the state Senate Judiciary Committee, chafed at the governor's glacial approach to a fundamental task. "If the safety valve is clemency, and clemency is dependent on the political situation, then what kind of system do we have? Justice has been shut off for a year. What the hell kind of system is that?"

The same month Gregoire pardoned Dominguez, *The New Yorker* published a long profile of Mike Huckabee, the man who had granted clemency to Maurice Clemmons in 2000. Huckabee defended his decision to commute Clemmons' 108-year sentence while declining to say whether he would run for president in the next election. *The New Yorker* called the Clemmons fallout "a perfect weapon for his competitors in a Republican primary." Huckabee told the magazine: "But do we really want people who only make decisions in their political lives that are in their own best interest? Frankly, I'm afraid that we might. The truth is, it could be the kind of thing that would keep me from ever being able to run."

For the Puget Sound area, the events that devastated the community in the fall of 2009 will not reach a formal resolution for years to come. Christopher Monfort, the former University of Washington student, must still stand trial for the murder of Timothy Brenton, the Seattle police officer. At a pre-trial hearing in March 2010, Monfort lashed out against police "who are corrupt," saying society must fight back. Ignoring his defense attorney—"Don't do this," she said—Monfort addressed the media and courtroom spectators: "Freedom is not free. I'm speaking with a lisp right now. The side of my face is paralyzed. I can't walk. I'm dead from the waist down. Freedom is not free. It requires sacrifice. And although all the freedom we have now has been won for us by our Founding Fathers, from time to time we must maintain that. Can anybody here tell me the price of freedom? Anybody? It's death. It's not free." As Monfort spoke, his mother, sitting in the courtroom, buried her face in her hands.

In the spring of 2010, the families of the four officers killed by Clemmons filed claims against Pierce County seeking $182 million in damages. The claims faulted the county for failing to monitor Clemmons' phone calls from jail, the ones in which he threatened to kill police officers when released. The public's reaction to the claims was swift and brutal. Many people saw the claims as betrayal—an act that failed to account for the community's outpouring of support in the slayings' wake. Within twenty-four hours, three of the families, devastated by the public condemnation, withdrew their claims. The families said they were motivated not by money but by a desire to change the system. They wanted only to protect other police officers from harm.

Of the seven people charged with aiding Maurice Clemmons, the first to stand trial was LaTanya Clemmons, his sister. A jury convicted her in June 2010 of two counts of rendering criminal assistance, finding that she took Darcus Allen, the accused getaway driver, to a motel afterward and gave him money for a room. The judge sentenced LaTanya Clemmons to five years, the maximum allowed. Four other members of Clemmons' family still await trial. They include Rickey Hinton,

Clemmons' half brother, and Eddie Davis, Clemmons' cousin. Two of Clemmons' friends also await trial. One is Darcus Allen, who has been charged with four counts of aggravated murder and could face a death sentence.

In Washington and beyond, violence continued to be directed at police officers. In December 2009, the month after the slayings inside Forza, Kent Mundell, a Pierce County sheriff's deputy, was fatally shot while responding to a domestic-violence call. Rick Adamson, the man who supervised the manhunt for Clemmons, was a good friend of Mundell's and led the investigation. One week after Mundell's death, an Anchorage police officer was shot while sitting in his parked cruiser, in an attack that bore a remarkable resemblance to the assassination of Seattle's Timothy Brenton. The Anchorage officer, Jason Allen, suffered several wounds to his arms and torso, but survived. His shooter has not yet been found.

In May 2010, in West Memphis, Arkansas, forty miles from Clemmons' hometown of Marianna, two police officers were shot and killed during a traffic stop of a father-son pair who belonged to an anti-government movement called "sovereign citizens." The father, Jerry Kane, embraced all manner of conspiracy theories; among other things, he believed the U.S. government secretly pledged its citizenry as collateral while borrowing money. Two additional police officers—the Crittenden County sheriff and a deputy—were wounded later the same day in a shootout that left Kane and his sixteen-year-old son dead.

The shootings in Arkansas triggered the same reaction as the shootings in Washington: a renewed appreciation for police and the dangers they face every time they go to work. Greg Richards' wife, Kelly, knew about those dangers. That's why she told him, every day, "You come home to us."

The families of Mark Renninger, Tina Griswold, Ronald Owens and Greg Richards gathered in May in Washington, D.C., as those four names were added to the nation's monument for officers killed in the line of duty. The same week, Lakewood announced that an architect and contractor had offered to design and build a permanent memorial for the four officers. They would do this for free. They wanted to make sure we do not forget.

NOTES

For this book we drew upon an array of public documents, ranging from Maurice Clemmons' massive prison file in Arkansas to e-mail exchanges between state officials in Washington. Video and audio records also proved invaluable—in particular, the recorded telephone calls placed by Maurice Clemmons from the Pierce County Jail. These calls, obtained through a public-records request filed with the Pierce County Sheriff's Office, cover a span of nearly five months, from July 2 to November 23, 2009. Clemmons made at least 340 calls to the following people: Nicole Smith, Rickey Hinton, Eddie Lee Davis, Dawson Carlisle, Stephen Morley, Timothy Bean, Daniel Murphy, and representatives of various bail-bond agencies.

Reporters with the *Seattle Times* interviewed more than 100 people while doing the research that forms this book's foundation. They included: Ray Clemmons, Chrisceda Clemmons, Mark Fraiser, Floyd Lofton, Daniel Kobil, Chris Gregoire, Marion Humphrey, Larry Jegley, Deborah Suttlar, Cory Cox, Max Brantley, Terry Hastings, Dave Regan, Garrett Alwert, Jerry Styers, Teresa Berg, Lauren Wallin, Paul Campbell, Dwain Cline Jr., Mark Lindquist, Rob Hayes, E. Bernard Jordan, John McCarthy, Timothy Bean, G. David Guntharp, Harry Hageman, Dan Satterberg, Mamie Clemmons, Carol Henderson, Michael Shantz, Nick Weber, Rhonda Sharp, Kolesta Moore, Kelly Richards, Jami-Mae Richards, Rick Adamson, Martin Quintero-Lewis, Evan Brady, Dan Fruits, Jonathan Brown, Garry Wegner, Katherine Beckett, Roxy Hill, Bryan Stumpf, John Wickert and Lucille Fisher.

This is not an exhaustive list. We interviewed family members and friends of the four Lakewood police officers who were killed and investigators and officials from more than a dozen local and state agencies, including: Pierce County Sheriff's Office; King County Sheriff's Office; Tacoma Police Department; Seattle Police Department; Washington State Patrol; Washington State Department of Corrections; Arkansas Department of Correction; Arkansas Department of Community Correction; Arkansas Post-Prison Transfer Board; Little Rock Police Department; prosecuting attorney's offices in Pulaski County, Pierce County and King County; and Pierce County Incident Management Team.

In the following notes we list the documents and audio or video records that we relied upon for each chapter. We then shift to the more traditional citation format for published sources other than the *Seattle Times*.
Abbreviations:

DOC: Washington State Department of Corrections
SPD: Seattle Police Department
LRPD: Little Rock Police Department
PCSO: Pierce County Sheriff's Office
PCSC: Pierce County Superior Court

ICAOS: Interstate Compact for Adult Offender Supervision

Prologue: The Trouble I've Seen

The dialogue in this prologue comes from the recorded telephone conversations between Maurice Clemmons and his wife, Nicole Smith.

some guards worked unbelievable OT: Ian Demsky, "Overtime Hours, Costs Explode at Crowded Jail," *Tacoma News Tribune*, November 19, 2007.

cracked molar and exposed root: Ian Demsky, "Report Dings Jail on Health," *Tacoma News Tribune*, February 18, 2008.

Chapter 1: A Place to Escape

In researching this chapter, reporters for the newspaper traveled to Marianna and Little Rock and interviewed Clemmons family members, as well as civic leaders and law enforcement officials. We reviewed court files in the Circuit Court of Pulaski County for details on the string of crimes that Clemmons committed when he was a teenager. These files included CR 89-1624 (the burglary of the trooper's home); 89-1357 (the aggravated robbery of Karen Hodge); 89-679 (the robbery of the seventh-grader); and 89-1656 (carrying a handgun onto school property). We also used the written opinions of the Supreme Court of Arkansas and the Court of Appeals of Arkansas. The Supreme Court's ruling in *Clemmons v. Arkansas*, 303 Ark. 354, 796 S.W.2d 583 (1990), included the dialogue between Clemmons and Hodge during the robbery in the parking lot. The quotes from Maurice Clemmons about his childhood were drawn from the taped telephone calls that he made from jail in 2009.

the smell of smoke hung: Bill Terry, "Marianna—A Town Torn by Race," *Washington Post*, February 14, 1972. For the date of the fire and additional details, see: William M. Adler, *Land of Opportunity: One Family's Quest for the American Dream in the Age of Crack* (New York: Plume, 1996), 208-10.

"Firemen do not rule out arson": Terry, "Marianna—A Town Torn by Race."

A white schoolteacher in Marianna: Terry, "Marianna—A Town Torn by Race."

"The idea was to blow them away": Toya Hill, "Lee County Clinic Defied Tough Times," *Arkansas Democrat-Gazette*, September 19, 1991.

called the place a "powder keg": Terry, "Marianna—A Town Torn by Race."

black students held a sit-in: Terry, "Marianna—A Town Torn by Race."

the home of a white sheriff's deputy: Adler, *Land of Opportunity,* 209.

The same deputy had been targeted: Terry, "Marianna—A Town Torn by Race."

the president of the Marianna School Board: Terry, "Marianna—A Town Torn by Race."

a white policeman in nearby Forrest City: Roy Reed, "Widespread Racial Violence Persists in Eastern Arkansas Farming Area," *New York Times*, October 10, 1971.

Adams so despised the medical clinic: George Shannon, "Citizens Counter Black Boycott," *The Citizen*, December 1971. This article is available in the Special Collections Department of the University of Arkansas Libraries.

If an ominous call came: Adler, *Land of Opportunity*, 209-10.

"A notion is going around": Reed, "Widespread Racial Violence Persists in Eastern Arkansas Farming Area."

The boycott leaders issued twenty-three demands: Adler, *Land of Opportunity*, 202-04.

At least eleven businesses closed: Bill Terry, "Ark. Blacks Halt Year-Old Boycott," *Washington Post*, July 27, 1972.

In 1891, cotton-field workers in Lee County: Adler, *Land of Opportunity*, 166-69.

Billy Joe Chambers and three of his brothers: Adler, *Land of Opportunity*, 6.

An assistant principal caught wind of this: Rob Moritz, "Students Arrested at School; 2 at Hall Charged with Having Pistol," *Arkansas Gazette*, May 27, 1989.

one of the first students in the state: Jacob Quinn Sanders, "Kin in state 'sorry,' didn't see violence coming," *Arkansas Democrat-Gazette*, December 2, 2009.

Chapter 2: Years on the Hoe Squad

This chapter relies heavily on the Arkansas Department of Correction file for Maurice Clemmons (Inmate No. 92616), a voluminous collection of documents that includes his admission summary; prison unit transfers; enemy-alert lists; mental-health evaluation; visitor lists; correspondence with prison administrators; disciplinary records (allegations, witness statements, investigative records and findings); job assignments and work reports; changes in custody-level classification; periods spent in segregation; inmate time computations; records regarding his request for clemency and parole; and his parole-risk assessment form.

Some details of Clemmons' journey through the justice system come from the records of his post-conviction proceedings in Pulaski County Circuit Court (CR 89-1624). These include the transcript of a September 5, 1997, hearing in which testimony was taken from Clemmons and his former public defender, Llewellyn Marczuk. Some of Clemmons' quotes—comparing his punishment to Darcus Allen's, ruminating on his mother's death—come from his recorded telephone conversations in 2009.

We reviewed the funeral program for Dorthy Clemmons' service on May 1, 1999, and visited the Old Statehouse Museum in Little Rock, which included an exhibit on the history of the Arkansas prison system. We quote extensively from U.S. District Court Judge J. Smith Henley's ruling in *Holt v. Sarver*, 309 F. Supp. 362 (1970), and from two Supreme Court of Arkansas opinions: *Clemmons v. State*, 303 Ark. 265, 795 S.W.2d 927 (1990), and *State v. Clemmons*, 334 Ark. 440, 976 S.W.2d 923 (1998).

the *Washington Post* published an exposé: Ted Gup, "Tales of Brutality Inside 'The Max'; Discipline or 'Tuning Up'?" *Washington Post*, October 21, 1984.

"You have broken your mother's heart": Sanders, "Kin in state 'sorry,' didn't see violence coming."

"It's the law": Julian E. Barnes, "It's the Law: Criminals Only Serve Bit of Time," *Arkansas Democrat-Gazette*, October 13, 1996.

"The most medieval": "Arkansas: Down on the Farm," *Newsweek*, February 20, 1967.

"Hell in Arkansas": "Prisons: Hell in Arkansas," *Time*, February 9, 1968.

"probably the most barbaric prison system": Ray King, "Prison Observes its 100-Year History," *Pine Bluff Commercial*, December 15, 2002.

went sideways with both Rockefeller and the state legislature: Tom W. Dillard, "Remembering Arkansas: Brubaker Fictionalized Arkansas' Prison Scandal," *Arkansas Democrat-Gazette*, December 30, 2007.

Johnny Cash performed at Cummins: Andy Davis, "Disrepair Clouds Future of Tucker Prison Chapel," *Arkansas Democrat-Gazette*, September 21, 2009.

"When you sentence a man to life": Glenn Fowler, "Thomas Murton, 62, a Penologist Who Advocated Reforms, Is Dead," *New York Times*, October 19, 1990.

"Many Arkansans are the sort": "Arkansas: Down on the Farm."

last prison in the state to achieve: Melissa Nelson, "Inmates Recall Prison Life Before Reforms at Harsh Cummins Unit," *Associated Press*, December 10, 2001.

international scandal linked to shoddy screening: Guy Lancaster, "Arkansas Prison Blood Scandal," *Encyclopedia of Arkansas History & Culture*, listing updated on September 21, 2009.

federal grand jury indicted six Cummins guards: Linda Satter, "Ex-Guard Admits Shocking Inmate; 'Ringleader' Pleads Guilty to Depriving Prisoner of Constitutional Rights," *Arkansas Democrat-Gazette*, October 6, 2001.

"An Arkansas prisoner nearly died": Jon Gambrell, "Inmate Left in Feces Nearly Dies," *Associated Press*, June 23, 2009.

the hard ground was called buckshot: Gup, "Tales of Brutality Inside 'The Max.'"

Chapter 3: An Act of Grace

Documents: Clemency and parole records from the Arkansas Post-Prison Transfer Board, including work sheets, documents of legal notice, comments supporting or opposing Clemmons' requests for relief, Clemmons' application for clemency, and his brief to Governor Mike Huckabee, asking for compassion. For the history of clemency in Washington, we reviewed more than a dozen files from the state's Clemency and Pardons Board; obtained a spreadsheet of the clemency decisions made by the state's last two governors; and reviewed historical records for administrations going back to the 1930s. The Barry Massey file included his petition, a lengthy transcript of his clemency hearing, a summary of the case by the governor's counsel, and letters responding to Massey's request for mercy. Other documents used in this chapter came from Clemmons' file with the Arkansas Department of Correction.

We were unable to interview Mike Huckabee—his representatives declined our requests—but we talked to Cory Cox, his clemency adviser for two years, and to other people who worked for the former governor. We also reviewed Huckabee's writings on criminal justice. He devotes a chapter of his book *From Hope to Higher Ground: My Vision for Restoring America's Greatness* (New York: Center Street, 2008) to the need to stop "the revenge-based criminal justice system." He touches more briefly on the costs of incarceration in *Do the Right Thing: Inside the Movement That's Bringing Common Sense Back to America* (New York: Sentinel, 2008).

Six state lawmakers were indicted: David Ware, "Arkansas State Capitol Building," *Encyclopedia of Arkansas History & Culture*, listing updated November 20, 2009.

Two hundred prisoners stayed behind: Ware, "Arkansas State Capitol Building."

"Get rid of that and just paint": Seth Blomeley, "Office Makeover Done for Beebe as He Vacations," *Arkansas Democrat-Gazette*, April 26, 2007.

"Being tough on crime": Huckabee, *From Hope to Higher Ground,* 87.

"Was advised by him that he would pardon": Seth Blomeley, "Huckabee's 111 Clemencies Granted Set No Record Among State's Leaders," *Arkansas Democrat-Gazette*, July 25, 2004.

Huckabee called himself a "grace" Christian: March 30, 2007, interview of Huckabee by Mike Barnicle on MSNBC's *Hardball with Chris Matthews*.

"for a good reason, a bad reason": Elizabeth Rapaport, "Straight is the Gate: Capital Clemency in the United States from Gregg to Atkins," *New Mexico Law Review* (33 N.M.L. Rev. 349), Spring 2003.

"a tiny glimmer of hope": Daniel Kobil, remarks during panel presentation of "Sparing Cain: Executive Clemency in Capital Cases: Chance and the Constitution in Capital Clemency Cases," *Capital University Law Review* (28 Cap. U.L. Rev. 567), 2000.

"act of barbarism": Pat Robertson, "Sparing Cain: Executive Clemency in Capital Cases," *Capital University Law Review* (28 Cap. U.L. Rev. 579), 2000.

"It's a miracle!": Terry Ganey, "Carnahan Spares Murderer's Life," *St. Louis Post-Dispatch*, January 29, 1999.

"a sort of living fossil": Kobil, remarks during panel presentation of "Sparing Cain: Executive Clemency in Capital Cases."

"justice would wear a countenance": Alexander Hamilton, *Federalist No. 74*, March 25, 1788.

Pat Brown denied one: Bob Egelko, "Ex-Governor Haunted by Life-And-Death Decisions," *Associated Press*, September 4, 1989.

"The contemporary insistence on combining harsh punishment": Gavriel B. Wolfe, "I Beg Your Pardon: A Call for Renewal of Executive Clemency and Accountability in Massachusetts," *Boston College Third World Law Journal* (27 B.C. Third World L.J. 417), Spring 2007.

"Our resources are misspent": Anne Gearan, "Justice Kennedy Says Federal Prison Terms Should Be Shorter," *Associated Press*, August 9, 2003.

Orval Faubus commuted 533 sentences: Blomeley, "Huckabee's 111 Clemencies Granted Set No Record Among State's Leaders."

thirty-four states commuted twenty or fewer sentences: Rachel E. Barkow, "The Politics of Forgiveness: Reconceptualizing Clemency," *Federal Sentencing Reporter* (21 Fed. Sent. R. 153), February 2009.

"I get a lot of recommendations": Wolfe, "I Beg Your Pardon: A Call for Renewal of Executive Clemency and Accountability in Massachusetts."

The state's governors went more than ten years: Shelley Murphy, "Commutation Plea Carries a Political Risk for Patrick," *Boston Globe*, February 27, 2008.

"I have prayed and sought God's help": Julie Stewart, "Huckabee Won't Return Fretwell to Death Row," *Arkansas Democrat-Gazette*, March 6, 1999.

"I had rather face the anger": Steve Barnes, "Death-Row Inmate Spared After Juror Makes Plea," *New York Times*, February 6, 1999.

"had not one advocate": Seth Blomeley, "Huckabee: Clemency Is Rooted in Justice," *Arkansas Democrat-Gazette*, August 18, 2002.

"If one acts by pure raw political instinct": Michael R. Wickline, "Huckabee: Answerable to God on Clemencies," *Arkansas Democrat-Gazette*, December 6, 2002.

"He speaks emotionally about the legacy": Holly Bailey and Michael Isikoff, "A Pastor's True Calling," *Newsweek*, December 17, 2007.

they granted clemency 507 times: Andrew DeMillo, "Huckabee's Record on Pardons While Governor Questioned by Critics," *Associated Press*, December 10, 2007.

"I'm a conservative, but I'm not mad": Bailey and Isikoff, "A Pastor's True Calling."

published an investigative story in 2004: Seth Blomeley, "Clemency: Whom Does Huckabee Let Out Early and Why?", *Arkansas Democrat-Gazette*, August 1, 2004.

if reporters reported the things: Seth Blomeley, "Governor Says News Media 1-Sided in Covering Clemency to Relative of Staff Member," *Arkansas Democrat-Gazette*, August 2, 2001.

"the flames of controversy": David Barstow, "A Request for Clemency Leads to a Political Issue for Huckabee," *New York Times*, December 22, 2007.

"Fortunately, no one to whom": Huckabee, *From Hope to Higher Ground*, 92.

helped win "many, many" clemencies: Blomeley, "Clemency: Whom Does Huckabee Let Out Early and Why?"

"wonderful Christian man": Seth Blomeley, "Pastor Pressing for Murderer's Clemency; Former Detective Cites Viciousness of '74 Slaying in Opposing Huckabee's Proposal," *Arkansas Democrat-Gazette*, July 13, 2004.

"As far as I'm concerned": Blomeley, "Pastor Pressing for Murderer's Clemency."

evidence of guilt "very questionable": Joe Stumpe, "Huckabee Doubts Based on Evidence Judges Didn't Buy," *Arkansas Democrat-Gazette*, October 2, 1996.

at least two members later said: Michael Rowett, "Memories of Huckabee's Role in DuMond Parole Not in Sync; 2 Ex-Board Members Recall Governor's Pressure," *Arkansas Democrat-Gazette*, July 4, 2001. One of the most extensive investigations of Huckabee's role in the DuMond case was undertaken by reporter Murray Waas for the *Arkansas Times* in 2002. See his article: "Special Handling: How the Huckabee Administration Worked to Free Rapist Wayne DuMond."

"Absolutely," he said: Dave Helling, "Mothers of Murdered Women Blame Huckabee For His Part in Release of Killer," *Kansas City Star*, December 5, 2007.

"It's not our goal to just lock": Traci Shurley, "Work Starts on Site for Parole Violators; Unit Meant to Relieve Prison Overcrowding," *Arkansas Democrat-Gazette*, August 9, 2003.

"If you have Johnnie Cochran": Blomeley, "Clemency: Whom Does Huckabee Let Out Early and Why?"

"The governor read your letter": Kate Zernike, "'00 Clemency May Be Issue for Huckabee," *New York Times*, December 1, 2009.

"As I review the whole hullabaloo": Seth Blomeley, "Huckabee Shifts Gears for 2 Clemency Cases," *Arkansas Democrat-Gazette*, July 28, 2004.

"It's more about what the inmates do": Melissa Nelson, "Some Wonder If Religion Guides Governor's Clemency Choices," *Associated Press*, July 30, 2004.

the governor signed a proclamation: Seth Blomeley, "Huckabee Calls Special Session," *Arkansas Democrat-Gazette*, March 31, 2000.

the capitol building caught fire: Jamie Stengle, "Firefighters Douse Source of Smoke at State Capitol," *Associated Press*, March 31, 2000.

"The loss of even one officer": "Huckabee Honors Fallen Officers," *Associated Press*, May 12, 2000.

Chapter 4: A New Life Up North

Details of the April 2001 robbery in Camden, Arkansas, come from the Ouachita County Circuit Court file (CR 2001-137) and the Camden Police Department's probable cause affidavit. For the March 2001 robbery we relied on LRPD records (Incident No. 2001-36792) and the Pulaski County Circuit Court file (CR 2004-1910), which includes Stephen Morley's motion to dismiss. The description of the investigation of possible drug dealing through the mails comes from search-warrant records filed in U.S. District Court for the Western District of Washington (Case No. 05-498M).

    Other records: The LRPD's information report of the 2004 robbery at the Comfort Inn (Incident No. 04-82537); employment records in the Arkansas Department of Correction file; property records from the office of the Pierce County Assessor-Treasurer; PCSC criminal files on Eddie Lee Davis (including file Nos. 09-1-01703-6, 08-1-00202-2, and 07-8-00809-5) and Joseph Pitts (including file Nos. 09-1-01704-4 and 08-1-00207-3); Nicole Smith's Chapter 7 filing in the United States Bankruptcy Court for the Western District of Washington; disciplinary records regarding Stephen Morley with the Arkansas Judicial Discipline and Disability Commission (Nos. 94-163 and 96-107); and Central Pierce Fire & Rescue records regarding the July 5, 2008, fire at Clemmons' house (Incident No. 2008-0008249).

    We drew on the Washington DOC records on Clemmons (Offender No. 866697); these include e-mails, correspondence, audio-taped hearings and chronological notes written by community corrections officers, detailing telephone calls and meetings with Clemmons.

more than eight hundred inmates, the overflow, were housed: "569 State Inmates to be Released Early," *Arkansas Democrat-Gazette*, August 31, 2004.

"We're a country that says": Interview of Marion Humphrey by CNN's Anderson Cooper, broadcast November 30, 2009, on *Anderson Cooper 360 Degrees*.

endowing a $10,000-a-year scholarship: "Morley Brothers Honor Judge Dad with University of Arkansas at Little Rock Law Scholarship," *US States News*, March 8, 2007.

He denied the charges, calling them "absurd": Tracie Dungan, "NLR Judge Says Charges of Misbehavior 'Absurd,'" *Arkansas Democrat-Gazette*, June 17, 1997.

"We had trouble finding witnesses": Andy Davis, "Parolee Jailed, Released 3 Times Before Slayings," *Arkansas Democrat-Gazette*, December 1, 2009.

Chapter 5: Four Days in May

We used records from the PCSO for the May 9 vandalism and assaults (Incident No. 091290686), as well as the corresponding PCSC file (Cause No. 09-1-02365-6). These documents included the arrest report, supplemental reports, and victim and witness statements. For Deputy Christian's account, we also relied on his tape-recorded testimony at a September 10, 2009, DOC hearing. Other documents: Pierce County Jail records for May 9-10 (Booking No. 2009129033), including incident reports and a special watch check sheet; and PCSO reports on the allegation of child rape (Incident No. 091310111).

The description of the devil jumping into Clemmons comes from Clemmons' recorded telephone calls placed from jail. Those recordings were also the basis for most of Clemmons' other quotes in this chapter.

Chapter 6: Thank you, God

Documents/sources: A videotape of the meeting between Clemmons and Bishop E. Bernard Jordan that Zoe Ministries provided to the *New York Daily News* (the event was being videotaped as a remembrance of Jordan's fiftieth birthday celebration); DOC records; the Zoe Ministries Web site; Clemmons' Twitter account; the PCSO supplemental reports in the case of alleged child rape (Incident No. 091310111); Pierce County Jail records pertaining to Clemmons' July 1, 2009, arrest (Booking No. 2009182043); Daniel Murphy's Web site; a transcript of the July 2, 2009, hearing in PCSC; Arkansas Judicial Discipline and Disability Commission records regarding Stephen Morley (Nos. 94-163 and 96-107); court records in the case of *ICAOS v. Tennessee Board of Probation and Parole* (Civil Action No. 04-526-KSF, U.S. District Court for the Eastern District of Kentucky); an ICAOS breakdown of state-by-state offender numbers titled "Offenders on Compact Supervision as of the close of FY 2009"; April 10, 2007, press release by Peter Barnes of the New Jersey State Parole Board; records from Washington state's Child Protective Services; Pierce County property records; and recorded telephone conversations between Maurice Clemmons and Nicole Smith; Clemmons and Morley; and Clemmons and Dawson Carlisle.

For the history of ICAOS, we drew from "The Interstate Compact on Adult Offender Supervision: Using Old Tools to Solve New Problems," by Michael L. Buenger and Richard L. Masters, *Roger Williams University Law Review*, Fall 2003; and "Penal Institutions: Pardons and Paroles: Provide for Enactment of the Interstate Compact for Adult Offender Supervision," by David Walker, *Georgia State University Law Review*, Fall 2002.

We went to Stephen Morley's office in North Little Rock, where he declined to be interviewed.

Lionel Hampton, Salt-N-Pepa: Andrew Jacobs, "The Minister of Rap," *New York Times*, June 30, 1996.

"stopped going to the racetrack": Jacobs, "The Minister of Rap."

"I believe that it is because of race": Julie Lyons, "Prophet or Heretic? Either Way, He Takes All Major Credit Cards," *DallasObserver.com*, February 16, 2007.

all kinds of liquor retailers: Richard Massey, "Macadoodles Plan Gets Liquor Permit; Alcohol Board OKs Booze-Fuel Pairing," *Arkansas Democrat-Gazette*, July 17, 2009.

elected secretary/treasurer: "Business People," *Arkansas Democrat-Gazette*, May 27, 2001.

he'd earned his nickname eating: Peter Eichenbaum, "Inmate: Victim Provoked Fight;" *Asbury Park Press*, June 15, 2001.

Pennsylvania granted 72 percent of parole petitions: Larry Fish, "Officer's '95 Killing Led to a Tougher Pa. Parole System," *Philadelphia Inquirer*, June 6, 2005.

"We're in a box": Chris Joyner, "Lost in the System," *Chattanooga Times Free Press*, November 14, 2004.

Chapter 7: The Gold Package

Documents/sources: Clemmons' recorded telephone conversations from the jail; Stephen Morley's July 8, 2009, letter to Linda Strong; criminal records for Reginald Wayne Robinson in KCSC and Renton and Des Moines municipal courts; e-mails and other documents produced by the Arkansas Department of Community Correction and the Washington DOC; a transcript of the July 24, 2009, hearing before Judge Felnagle in PCSC; and records kept by the Pierce County Jail.

In a survey conducted by the Tacoma newspaper: Karen Hucks, "Felnagle Has Quite the Legal Fan Base; His Patience, Toughness Lead County Attorneys to Name Him Top Judge," *Tacoma News Tribune*, August 22, 2004.

volunteer work in Poland and Egypt: Hucks, "Felnagle Has Quite the Legal Fan Base."

Chapter 8: I Will Be Carried by Six

Documents/sources: Clemmons' recorded telephone conversations from jail; e-mails and other documents from the Arkansas Department of Community Correction and Washington DOC; audio-taped recordings of DOC hearings for Clemmons on August 31, September 1 and September 10, 2009; the October 19, 2009, Forensic Mental Health Report of Clemmons by Melissa Dannelet and Carl Redick; the SPD's Certification for Determination of Probable Cause in the Christopher Monfort case (Offense No. 09-383210) and the corresponding King County Superior Court file (Cause No. 09-1-07187-6).

Chapter 9: In the Line of Duty

The statistics on officer fatalities come from the National Law Enforcement Officers Memorial Fund, a tremendous resource for information on line-of-duty deaths across the country. The Seattle history comes mostly from a compilation of line-of-duty deaths produced by the SPD; that compilation is available on the city's Web site (Seattle.gov). For the murder of officer Dave Mobilio, we drew upon "A Murder in Red Bluff," a five-part series written by Marjie Lundstrom and Sam Stanton, published by the *Sacramento Bee* on July 31–August 4, 2005. Readers interested in knowing more about Christopher Monfort's history should check out: Jonathan Martin, "Accused Seattle Cop Killer Christopher Monfort: Loner, Obsessed by Ideology," *Seattle Times*, July 24, 2010.

Other records: the SPD's Certification for Determination of Probable Cause (Offense No. 09-383210) in the Monfort case, along with King County Superior Court file 09-1-07187-6; SPD records for October 30, 2009, the night before Timothy Brenton was killed (Case No. 2009-382099); dispatch audio from the night of that shooting; videotape of the Paul Schene incident; and Clemmons' telephone calls from jail.

"Mickel did not fit the profile": Marjie Lundstrom and Sam Stanton, "Wrong Turn: A Middle-Class College Student, Onetime Peace Activist and Army Veteran, Andy Mickel Didn't Fit the Profile of a Cop Killer," *Sacramento Bee*, August 1, 2005.

"the black attitude": Rich Lord and Paula Reed Ward, "Who Is Richard Poplawski? A Portrait of Contrasts Emerges From Those Who Knew Officers' Accused Killer," *Pittsburgh Post-Gazette*, April 12, 2009.

"There's an increasingly desperate population": Colleen Long, "Gun Deaths Tried To Fray the Thin Blue Line in '09," *Associated Press*, December 12, 2009.

"Too many of us walk around": Valerie Gollier, "Candidates Tell All at Forum," *The Thunderword*, October 23, 2003.

"I think that the fraudulent votes favored me": Valerie Gollier, "Third Senator Election to Take Place Today," *The Thunderword*, December 4, 2003.

"My goal is the subversion": Paul Butler, "Racially Based Jury Nullification: Black Power in the Criminal Justice System," *Yale Law Journal* (105 Yale L.J. 677), December 1995.

grew up on Chicago's South Side: Paul Butler, *Let's Get Free: A Hip-Hop Theory of Justice* (New York: The New Press, 2009), 23.

"My story is different from those": Butler, *Let's Get Free*, 16.

"The biggest threat to freedom": Butler, *Let's Get Free*, 26.

"The United States has 5 percent": Butler, *Let's Get Free*, 27.

"Reclaiming justice sometimes requires": Butler, *Let's Get Free*, 81.

"Freedom has a special resonance": Butler, *Let's Get Free*, 37.

Beckett's analysis included comparisons: Katherine Beckett, "Race and Drug Law Enforcement in Seattle," *Report for the American Civil Liberties Union and the Defender Association*, September 2008.

Chapter 10: The Coffee Shop

Documents/sources: Clemmons' telephone calls from jail; DOC records; personnel files for the four Lakewood police officers, showing commendations; and search warrant records filed in PCSC after the shootings inside the coffee shop, including an affidavit detailing the evidence against Clemmons (Cause No. 09-1-51110-3). To reconstruct the events inside the coffee shop, we interviewed investigators or representatives from these agencies: PCSO; DOC; King County Sheriff's Office; Tacoma Police Department; SPD; Washington State Patrol; Pierce County Prosecuting Attorney's Office; Pierce County Incident Management Team; and Pierce County Executive's Office. We also drew upon testimony from the trial of LaTanya Clemmons that concluded in June 2010 in PCSC. The prosecution's witnesses included police officers from different agencies and three of the people who were inside Forza when the shooting started: Michelle Chaboya, Sara Kispert and Daniel Jordan.

Chapter 11: We Need a Story

To piece together the manhunt, we interviewed officials from each of the nine agencies listed in the notes for Chapter 10. We also reviewed a crime-scene schematic and a timeline that investigators put together for the minutes, hours and days surrounding the shootings inside the coffee shop. Other sources: DOC records, including e-mails, internal correspondence and audiotapes of parole hearings; e-mails from members of Governor Chris Gregoire's staff; testimony at the April 2010 inquest held in the shooting death of Clemmons (this included medical testimony and the accounts of police officers Benjamin Kelly and Daina Boggs); and SPD video of the encounter between Kelly and Clemmons, along with dispatch audio.

The description of cellphone tracking comes largely from the briefs and the Opinion and Memorandum Order in the case: "In The Matter of the Application of the United States of

America for an Order Directing a Provider of Electronic Communication Service to Disclose Records to the Government" (U.S. District Court for the Western District of Pennsylvania, Magistrate's No. 07-524M). The Letrecia Nelson quote comes from a Declaration for Determination of Probable Cause filed in PCSC in *State v. Nelson* (Incident No. 09-333-0363).

He had a book out: Mike Huckabee, *A Simple Christmas: Twelve Stories That Celebrate the True Holiday Spirit* (New York: Sentinel, 2009).

***USA Today*/Gallup Poll showed:** Susan Page, "Huckabee Leads Republican Prospects in Poll; They're Not Running Yet, But Most Are Staying in Public Eye," *USA Today*, November 5, 2009.

after the shootings, the *New York Times* published: William Yardley and Liz Robbins, "Suspect Slain in Seattle; 4 Are Held as Flight Aids," *New York Times*, December 2, 2009.

Newspapers like the *Los Angeles Times* wrote editorials: "In Huckabee's Defense," *Los Angeles Times*, December 3, 2009.

"horrible decision": Andy Barr, "Palin: Huck Made 'Horrible Decision,'" *Politico.com*, December 8, 2009.

"I don't think I've ever voted": Andy Barr, "Huck: Political Attacks 'Disgusting,'" *Politico.com*, December 1, 2009.

"I don't know. Could be": Howard Kurtz, "Huckabee, Both Source and Subject of Running Commentary," *Washington Post*, December 21, 2009.

Chapter 12: Half-Staff

The *Seattle Times* had reporters at the memorial service and along the procession route. The detail and quotes in this chapter come largely from their dispatches. Some quotes and color come from the reporting of the memorial service done by Seattle's KING 5 TV, which was kind enough to provide us with a digital copy of its full-day coverage of the procession and service. Those discs allowed us to quote at such length from the testimonials at the memorial service. We also drew from Pierce County Incident Management Team documents about the service's planning.

A group of inmates serving life sentences: Mike Archbold, "Fund for Slain Cops' Kids Tops $2 Million," *Tacoma News Tribune*, February 18, 2010.

individual stores set sales records: "Overwhelming Support for Papa John's Slain Officers Fundraiser," *KREM.com*, December 9, 2009.

One Lakewood police officer recounted: Mike Archbold, "Child Offers Up Toy Dinosaur, Piggy Bank to Lakewood Police," *Tacoma News Tribune*, December 17, 2009.

Epilogue: You Come Home to Us

Reporters with the *Seattle Times* traveled to Marianna in November 2009 and again in June 2010. For the passage on Washington clemencies we reviewed petitions pending before Chris Gregoire and interviewed the governor and Adam Kline. The description of Christopher Monfort in the courtroom comes from a *Seattle Times* reporter who was there.

five hundred people gathered: Rob Carson, "Officers Lauded as 'Best of Us,'" *Tacoma News Tribune*, May 8, 2010.

"the deadliest law enforcement year": Carson, "Officers Lauded as 'Best of Us.'"

"We are gathered here to honor": Carson, "Officers Lauded as 'Best of Us.'"

returned to his hometown of Bethlehem: Pamela Lehman and Michael Duck, "End of Watch – 11/29/09; Thousands Gather to Mourn the Death of Bethlehem Native Mark Renninger," *Allentown Morning Call*, December 12, 2009.

at least ten years of service: Jordan Schrader, "Public-Safety Measures Become Law," *Tacoma News Tribune*, April 1, 2010.

"perfect weapon for his competitors": Ariel Levy, "Prodigal Son: Is the Wayward Republican Mike Huckabee Now His Party's Best Hope?," *The New Yorker*, June 28, 2010.

"But do we really want people": Levy, "Prodigal Son."

the U.S. government secretly pledged: Trevor Aaronson, "Kane Convinced He Had Solved the Mortgage Puzzle," *Memphis Commercial Appeal*, May 30, 2010.

architect and contractor had offered: Brent Champaco, "Lakewood Plans to Create Memorial for its 4 Fallen Officers," *Tacoma News Tribune*, May 14, 2010.

CONTRIBUTORS

The lead writers for *The Other Side of Mercy* were Ken Armstrong and Jonathan Martin, both staff writers at the *Seattle Times*.

Armstrong previously worked at the *Chicago Tribune*, where he co-wrote a series that helped prompt the state's governor to suspend executions and empty Death Row. In 2009, he received the John Chancellor Award from Columbia University for lifetime achievement. He has been a Nieman Fellow at Harvard and the McGraw Professor of Writing at Princeton. In 2010, he and Nick Perry wrote *Scoreboard, Baby: A Story of College Football, Crime and Complicity*.

Martin, a native of Washington, has written extensively about his home state during a fifteen-year reporting career in the Pacific Northwest. His assignments have included following a homeless family for two years, witnessing a town being consumed by the Pacific Ocean, and investigating votes cast by the dead. He has twice won the Casey Medal, the nation's top award for coverage of social issues. He was a Knight-Wallace Fellow in Journalism and Law at the University of Michigan in 2008.

The book's lead editor was James Neff, the investigations editor at the *Seattle Times*. Neff is the author of four books, including *The Wrong Man: The Final Verdict on the Dr. Sam Sheppard Murder Case*.

The Other Side of Mercy was copy edited by Jerry Holloron.

The list of *Seattle Times* reporters who contributed to this book is a long one: Mike Carter, Christine Willmsen, Steve Miletich, Jennifer Sullivan, Sara Jean Green, Maureen O'Hagan, Jim Brunner, Nick Perry, Lynda Mapes, Susan Kelleher, Christine Clarridge, Lynn Thompson, Jack Broom, Sanjay Bhatt, Katherine Long, Nicole Brodeur, Charles Brown, Justin Mayo, Mark Rahner and Bob Young.

The photographers who contributed were Ellen Banner, Alan Berner, Cliff DesPeaux, Greg Gilbert, Ken Lambert, Steve Ringman, Erika Schultz and Mike Siegel. Fred Nelson was photo editor for the book.

The book's art direction and cover design were by Denise Clifton and Mark Evans.

LaVergne, TN USA
22 October 2010
201991LV00001B/148/P

9 781608 447343